Canoeing Adventures in
Northern Illinois

To Michelle
Use this in warm and cold.
Hope you will find new places to
paddle

Bob Tyk
7/25/04

Canoeing Adventures in Northern Illinois

Apple River to Zuma Creek

by Bob Tyler

iUniverse, Inc.
New York Lincoln Shanghai

Canoeing Adventures in Northern Illinois
Apple River to Zuma Creek

iUniverse, Inc.

For information address:
iUniverse, Inc.
2021 Pine Lake Road, Suite 100
Lincoln, NE 68512
www.iuniverse.com

Typesetting by Rita Frese
Editing: Ralph Frese
Design: James Aiello

Illinois DeLorme Atlas & Gazetteer
was used as a guide for most of the trips in this guide.
Used with permission.

Phil Vierling's Illinois County Guide was also
an invaluable guide.
All inquires should be addressed to:
Robert Tyler

ISBN: 0-595-31010-9

Printed in the United States of America

Contents

Aimee Tyler and Dad (Bob)
Drawing by Aimee Tyler (1997)

Things you'll see on the river that you won't see at home.

Acknowledgements

I would like to thank the following people and institutions for their assistance in compiling this guide. I usually canoe alone, but several individuals have endured more than one of these adventures. Going back to my first exploration of the Little Vermilion River ten years ago, Andy Carter shared my first small creek adventure. Andy and I also shared a two week trip on the Rock River 35 years ago as kids with the Y.M.C.A.

Andy introduced me to his dentist, Leo Krusack, who in turn introduced me to the Little Calumet River. Leo shared at least a half a dozen of the explorations recorded in this book. Two more canoeists I should mention are Bill Schmid and Jim Hart. Both shared some of the less desirable, along with some of the better, sections of creeks covered.

Next, I would like to thank the many libraries that I used in researching the history that adds so much depth to this volume. First off, thanks to the Elgin librarian who dug through the genealogical section to locate the story in Tyler Creek. Without her I had no history for that chapter.

The following Illinois libraries were most useful in completing text: Amboy, Chicago, Plano, Profitstown, Wheaton, Glen Ellyn, St. Charles, Rochelle, Rockford, LaSalle. Also, the LaSalle County Historical Society and the Chicago Historical Society. And in Wisconsin, the Beloit Public Library.

Many thanks to those who made sense of my sometimes disjointed sentences and paragraphs. Those who added periods, comas, and divided my often too-long paragraphs into more digestible segments.

Caryn Vanko, who was often the first person to set eyes on a newly completed chapter. The next person to proofread each chapter was Phil Carter. Ralph Frese spent quite a few evenings after work editing, crossing t's and dotting i's. Thanks also to Rita Frese for putting all this in proper order with her typesetting abilities. And Ron and Bonnie Yonkoski for their part.

Thank you all for your constant encouragement.

Most of all: my thanks to my wife and daughter—who seem to cope quite nicely without me and don't complain as long as the bills get paid. Sometimes they even come along and end up enjoying themselves. My wife also got this book back on track after two years of it sitting on the shelf by contacting the right people and staying on top of things through the editing and publishing process. Also to my friend and paddling buddy Tom Linblade for additional encouragement.

I would like to dedicate this book to Nathaniel Pope.
Through his efforts in 1818, sixty-one miles were
added to Northern Illinois. Without his persistence,
most of the streams in this volume would be located in Wisconsin.

Some things you might like to know before you start exploring on your own!

When I started canoeing as an adult, I rented a canoe and took several trips on the Kankakee and Fox Rivers before buying my first canoe. I bought an Old Town Discovery and three days later headed to the Vermilion River with a friend. It was a trip where I learned a lot about tipping, swimming, and tying in things you want to keep.

I paddled a good deal that summer. I paddled the Vermilion River at least every other trip, because I was getting addicted to the adrenaline rush of paddling whitewater. By this time, I had bought a copy of Phil Vierling's book, *Illinois Canoe Trails*. I started canoeing every river mile covered in this publication, which was the first guide book I owned.

Next, I joined the Prairie State Canoeists, the largest canoe club in the Chicago area. I wasn't able to go on very many trips those first couple of years because of my work schedule, but from the newsletters, I began to get an idea of which area rivers were recreationally navigable and interesting. I began to run many of these rivers whenever I could find a partner with a car with which to shuttle.

Then an event took place that forever changed the way and the waters I would canoe in the future. I bought a motorcycle. Not a big motorcycle; in fact, a very small motor scooter. It had to be small because I had to be able to lift it into my van. Now I could go by myself on the river.

My average day on the river, since that point in time, goes something like this. Drive to the put-in to drop off my canoe; throw bag, life jacket, and paddles, which is all I usually take along. Next, I drive my van down river to the takeout. I park the van, then ride the motor scooter back up river to where I left the canoe. Then I paddle down to the van, load my boat on the van, and drive back to pickup my motor scooter. I was then able to go paddling whenever I had some extra time. I no longer needed a partner or a second vehicle to help shuttle and I no longer needed to plan a trip very far in advance. I started to explore around the Kishwaukee and DuPage River systems using road maps to guide me to put-ins and takeouts. Not very much useful information about a river can be gleaned from a road map, but it's all I had to work with.

Not long after I started exploring the Kishwaukee, Phil Vierling's books on the DuPage and Kishwaukee Rivers came out. These publications made trip planning much easier by describing the landings and the mileages between different points on the rivers. It didn't take me long to cover most of the miles mapped in Vierling's books.

Just about the time I was running out of new trips on the Kishwaukee and DuPage River systems, the *Delorme Mapping Company* came out with the *Illinois Atlas and Gazetteer*. Here were detailed maps of the whole state of Illinois. Even the smallest creeks were not only shown on the map, but were named also.

That was about five years ago. The creeks in this volume have been explored during those years. Most of these creeks are—according to Illinois law—considered to be not legally navigable as they call for trespassing through private property. This means that you could be arrested if you're caught paddling down one of these small streams.

I usually paddle on weekdays, either alone or with one other boater. However, even with this low profile, I've been stopped on about one out of every six creeks that I have explored. Stopped doesn't necessarily mean arrested. Most landowners can, after profuse apologies and reasonable politeness, be dissuaded from calling in law enforcement. Promises never to return are often met with a "Well okay, as long as you don't do it again!"

This private property problem is particularly disgraceful since, as this volume illustrates, much of the early history of Northern Illinois is closely related to these small streams. Wouldn't it be nice if the state took control of these creeks and maintained them as historic waterway parks?

Well, that's the paddler's dream for the time being. Efforts are being made (as of this writing) to create a system of Northeastern Illinois paddle trails. This would be a good beginning and a large portion of these trails would be very near to the city of Chicago, where the population needs for outdoor recreation are the greatest. Legalizing the smaller streams would be a much bigger project.

Being arrested for trespassing is only one of the dangers of paddling on small streams. One of the most common hazards are fences. All kinds of fencing. Over the years, I have been amazed at the variety of both materials and designs used in erecting barricades across flowing bodies of water.

Canoeists should realize why these fences are built. Very few of the fences I have encountered were built to impede the downstream progress of paddlers. Most were built to contain livestock within a pasture. Let's always remember that farming is a business. Farmers are practical individuals and generally put up a minimal amount of fencing. Most often, only a single strand of barbed or electric wire is all that one encounters. Be especially aware of electrical insulators visible on fence posts, for encounters with these wires can be shocking! A wooden or plastic paddle can be used to carefully lift such a wire overhead without conducting the current to the occupant of the watercraft.

The more formidable fences in this book are detailed in the chapter on the stream they appeared on. Many of these more elaborate fences were designed to keep trespassers out, and as a canoeist, you are a trespasser in the eyes of the law and the landowners. These large formidable structures serve to remind me to keep an extremely low profile. Strangely enough, the bigger the structure, the lower its chance of surviving high water when large trees are picked up and carried downstream. These trees are indiscriminate about tearing up anything in their way when carried downstream in a flood.

Remember that most fences come in pairs, so if you cross one fence-line, keep your eyes peeled for the ever-present second one. Continually scan for wires, especially when traversing livestock pastures. Many times it is easier to spot the fence posts on the creek bank than to spot a single strand of wire over the water. It has been my experience that many fences are moved from year to year as the farmers rotate the use of their fields. A fence can create problems for even the best canoeists when the fast water or a blind turn precedes it. So be alert; these single strand fences have crossed my bow before being noticed on more than one occasion.

Similar to fencing and even more common are log jams and trees that have fallen across the channel. They are sometimes called "strainers" because the water strains through the obstruction, but canoes and canoeists do not. This creates the potential for upsets that could cause more than damage to the equipment. There is the possibility that if a body is washed into the strainer, the force of the current could carry the body into the branches and trap it there—with fatal results. When approaching a logjam or strainer, the canoeist has to assess how to get around the obstruction. My rule of thumb is **Over, Under, Around, or Through.**

Under and through are pretty much the same thing. But again, a word of warning! Make sure you can maintain absolute control of your boat and that you see a clear and secure passage through the blockage before venturing into it. Always remember: when things start going wrong, and you are pinned sideways, **lean downstream!**

If the obstruction is under or at the surface of the water, then I usually paddle fast and try to slide over the lowest section. These first two methods get me over 75 to 80 percent of all the blockages that I run into.

Sometimes, one can stand on such a blockage and slide the craft over. The very last option is to get out on the bank and carry downstream until you can find a suitable place to reenter the creek.

Not as frequent as fences, but more dangerous, are dams. Now I run as many dams as I portage, but then I run Class IV rapids numerous times each year. I'm not saying that it is all a matter of skill, although it helps. The most important consideration is whether or not you want to risk your boat or your life! Much depends on the water level at the time.

Historical Introduction

In 1673 Marquette and Joliet were exploring the North American Continent looking for an inland passage to the Pacific Ocean. They came down Green Bay on Lake Michigan where they found the mouth of Fox River of Wisconsin. They proceeded up the Fox to a point where it comes within two miles of the Wisconsin River, portaging over at what is now Portage Wisconsin, they then followed the Wisconsin River to its mouth on the Mississippi River. While traveling down the Mississippi they made contact with the western boarder of what is now the state of Illinois. The adventurers and their companions went as far south as the mouth of The Arkansas River before returning back up the Mississippi.

On their return trip the intrepid explorers where told of a better route into the Great Lakes by using the Illinois River and what became known as the Chicago Portage, they decided to try the shortcut, while en route the explorers came upon one of the largest native villages in North America. The village near Starved Rock was a tribal and ceremonial center for the five tribes that made up Illiniwek.

Continuing up the Illinois River they entered Lake Michigan via what would become the Chicago Portage. These are the first accounts of European contact with the native population in Illinois, it made a connection between The Great Lakes and The Mississippi River Valley that still exists today.

The French were not the first humans to arrive in Illinois, Native Americans sites in Illinois have been identified and dated at more than 10,000 years old. Unfortunately these early North Americans left no written accounts of their lives. They built homes and other buildings out of dirt and wood leaving only earthen mounds and their contents as evidence of their existence. The tribes that were in Illinois when the Europeans arrived had no knowledge of who had built the burial mounds, even though in some cases those natives were later proved by D.N.A. to be related. Today through modern archeology we have a better understanding of the earliest occupants of the area than did Europeans who had first contact with them.

The French controlled Illinois between 1670 and 1763, the later date marking the end of the French and Indian War at which time the area came under British control. Likewise during the Revolutionary War, George Rodgers Clark and his extraordinary band of Kentucky long knives defeated and captured the British General Hamilton. This event brought the territory under American control in 1779. The American control was confirmed in a treaty with the British, signed in Paris, in 1783.

The land gained from Britain became known as The Northwest Territory by a 1787 act of the United States Congress. This was again divided into territories which were later to become the states of Ohio, Michigan, Indiana, Illinois, Wisconsin, and a portion of Minnesota, all of which boarder the Great Lakes.

To become states these territories were required to meet population requirements. Illinois did not become a state until 1818. In that same year the white population in northern Illinois was restricted to Fort Dearborn (Chicago) built to protect the Chicago portage and the Galena area where lead mining was just getting started. The unpredictability of the Northern Illinois tribes who had been aligned with the British during both the War of 1812 and the Revolutionary War kept American settlement at bay. Settlers flowed up from the south and only slowly did whites move north.

Twenty five years after becoming a state very little land was left unoccupied. The Blackhawk War in 1832 and subsequent removal of all Indian tribes west of the Mississippi River was the single act that brought the flood of American settlement to the Illinois Territory. Most of the history covered in this volume deals with this period of early settlement from 1818 to 1842. County histories written in the late 1800's were valuable resources and supplied much of the information that I have related. This book draws together the two great passions of my adult life, history and canoeing I hope the reader will enjoy reading it as much as I have enjoyed researching and writing about it.

Where are the maps?

First and foremost I don't draw maps, second and just as important is getting to and from the river. Most guidebooks show maps of the rivers themselves, but a second map is then needed to get there. Most canoeists I travel with already use the DeLorme Illinois Atlas & Gazetteer, so the thought struck me that referencing the DeLorme Atlas could solve this book's lack of maps and add information that would be useful to others. The DeLorme also lists campground locations, hunting and fishing hot spots, species of fish found in different creeks and rivers, boat ramp locations, historic sites, museums and more.

In other words the Atlas and Gazetter is a worthwhile travel and canoeing asset that is well worth the added expense. It also lists some of the canoe trails downstate not covered in this volume. **Note:** at the end of each chapter in this guide, reference is made to the page and map coordinates where the creek or river is located in the DeLorme Atlas.

Rivers by size and how often they are canoeable.

Always have enough water

Mississippi River-Major United States waterways with navigational dams
Illinois River-along with heavy recreational and commercial boat traffic
Rock River-Big river with cottages often lining the banks
Chicago River-main branch passes through downtown Chicago, heavy boat traffic
Pecatonica River-meandering river with long miles between accesses
Kishwaukee River-small country stream a favorite with local canoe clubs
DesPlains River-lined by roads but enveloped by Forest Preserves, pleasant
Fox River-a large river regularly broken up by islands, designated canoe trail
Elkhorn Creek-natural tributary of the Rock River, a personal favorite
Little Calumet River-urbanized,channalized, log jammed not recommended
Leaf River-for years someone cleared the log jams on this gem but no longer

Runable for several months each year

Kishwaukee River South Branch-small,pleasant, popular with the locals
Sugar River-nice section through a floodplain forest
North Branch Chicago River-designated canoe trail through forest preserves
Kilbuck Creek-many pleasant miles unbroken by roads
Kytes Creek-country creek with a nice mixture of scenery
Nippersink Creek-country stream running through farms, forest, and towns
AuxSable River-Runs through Illinois-Michigan canal heritage corridor
Big Rock Creek-small with many riffles, a personal favorite
Big Bureau Creek-good paddling from the source to the mouth
West Branch DuPage River-popular suburban river with good variety
Indian Creek-nice creek, big trespassing issues
Galena River-nice paddle in northern Illinois
Plum River-remote river, tributary of the Mississippi, some log jams

Salt Creek-urban creek with only one good section
Turtle Creek-flows mostly in Wisconsin, but best section is in Illinois
Green River-unpleasant river, channelized, more like a canal than a river
Blackberry Creek-nice creek, log jams, landowner fences
Little Indian Creek-surprisingly natural, Private property issues
East Branch Dupage River-urban, small, logjamed, not recommended

Creeks needing heavy rainfall

Big Rock Creek West Branch-small with occasional log jams, pleasant
Big Rock Creek East Branch-small very log jammed not a pleasant paddle
Little Rock Creek-surprisingly few log jams untill last miles enjoyable paddle
Thorn Creek-urban creek runs through forest preserves near expressways
Popular Creek-many blockages by trees and low bridges, but an interesting trip
Little Vermilion River-upper river scenic flat water, down river scenic whitewater a favorite trip each and every year
Covel Creek-another one of my favorite small creeks, good variety
Yellow Creek-the only good paddle is the 8 miles upstream of Freeport
Zuma Creek-channelized and in close proximity to interstates not good
Apple River-upper river is water sensitive and has big trespassing issues
below Hanover the lower Apple runs into the Upper Mississippi Wildlife Refuge
Carrol Creek-possibly the most beautiful creek in Illinois, trespassing issues
Coon Creek-small, log jammed but an interesting paddle for the adventurous
Sinsinawa Creek-small, trespassing issues, pleasant paddle
Franklin Creek-ready pretty canyon with lots of log jams
North Branch of the Kishwaukee River-small and fast and needs a five inches rain

Bob's Summary of Rivers

Best streams for family canoeing

Aux Sable Creek	Big Rock Creek	Bureau Creek	Des Plaines
Du Page (West & Main)	Elk Horn Creek	Fox	Galena
Green	Killbuck Creek	Kishwaukee	Kytes Creek
Little Calumet	Nippersink Creek	Pecatonica	Rock
Salt Creek	Turtle Creek	Little Vermilion (Middle section)	

Best streams for those looking for whitewater

Covel Creek	Ferson Creek	Hickory Creek (Lower)
Pecumsagan Creek	Tomahawk Creek	Little Vermilion River (Lower section)
Vermilion		

Best streams for the adventurous with the skills to match

(i.e., smaller with more deadfalls; possible trespassing)

Blackberry Creek	Carrol Creek	Coon Creek	Covel Creek
Ferson Creek	Kishwaukee North and South		Little Rock Creek
Leaf River	North Branch of the Kishwaukee River		Popular Creek
Somonack Creek	Tomahawk Creek	Tyler Creek	West Branch Big Rock Creek
Yellow Creek	Zuma Creek		

Best streams for wishing to be arrested for trespassing

Apple	Indian Creek	Little Indian Creek	Pecumsaugan Creek
Piscasaw Creek			

Streams best left alone (*too many log jams*)

Bailey Creek
East Big Rock
North Branch of Nippersink Creek
Pecumsaugan Creek
Spring Creek
Stillmans Creek
Any creek that gets you into an argument
with a landowner.

About the Author

Aimee and Bob

Born on the last day of the year 1951, Bob didn't start canoeing until 1959, when he was eight years old and attending a Y.M.C.A. camp. In 1964 a week-long trip down the Rock River in Wisconsin furthered his earlier learning experience. A few years later, a Boy Scout Merit Badge in canoeing was awarded to Bob for his mastery of the basic skills. For the next twenty-one years, these skills would go unused while he tried other hobbies. These included spelunking, skydiving, mountain climbing, and scuba diving. While not canoeing, Bob occupies his extra time as the sound engineer at Chicago's historic Palace Theater. Prior to the Palace, Bob was the engineer at the Chicago, Schubert, and Auditorium Theaters. Before arriving in the Chicago theater scene, Bob traveled with the First National Touring companies of the following shows: *Cats, Evita, Dreamgirls, Dancin', Pippin,* and *A Chorus Line.* Bob's grandfather was the head electrician at several of the downtown Chicago theaters, and his father was founder of Grand Stage Lighting. This was a great legacy for Bob's career in the theater, but was of no help whatsoever in canoeing.

Besides the theater and canoeing, Bob is a devoted husband and father—when he is at home!

Tyler Family trip on the West branch on the DuPage.

Apple River

Although the Apple River may be canoeable further upstream, hostile land owners made me head downstream to Apple River Canyon State Park, where there are signs that say NO BOATING. There are, however, two parking lots that are close to the water and supply excellent access (provided one ignores the rule about no boating). It has been my experience that asking will most likely lead to denial; therefore, driving to the parking lot at the state park and launching as quickly as possible lessens the chance that the rangers will have to talk to you about the rules. Apple River Canyon State Park is also listed on the map as Millville, after the 1836 mill built at this location by three brothers—Thomas, Rollin, and Jackson Burbridge; this was the second mill to be built on the Apple River.

As the name of this state park implies, for the next six miles the Apple River runs through a canyon. Right from the start, you'll know that this trip is going to be special as the beauty of the State Park is indicative of what lies ahead downstream. The Apple River runs swiftly for most of this length over frequent shoals and small rapids; none of these are hazardous, but some of the shoals wash into rock walls that call for precise boat control. The slower pools allow time to take in the splendid scenery. The first road crossed on this section of the Apple River is Townsend Road. Just upstream of Townsend Road, the valley widens out enough for pasture land to share the valley. Rock bluffs are still plentiful, but not as frequent as they are upstream.

The takeout on Scout Camp Road is steep and unimproved; however, the Illinois Department of Natural Resources has recently purchased the adjoining farm and may at some time in the future develop the site further. As of this writing, parking is on the narrow shoulder along the lightly traveled Scout Camp Road. Although six miles is a rather short trip, the next two bridges downstream have access problems. The first one is a rustic old iron bridge with decent parking, but very steep overgrown banks make it an unacceptable access point. The next bridge on South Apple River Road is fenced off, in plain sight of the nearest farm house, and requires permission to be used. The next possible access is at the junction of South Apple River, South Becker, and Goose Hollow Roads. This access point has a short, mowed, level path to the water: a rare occurrence on the Apple River. The downside to this site is a "no trespassing" sign; I'm not sure if the sign refers to the bridge or the adjoining property. The closest house to the bridge has a canoe trailer in the front yard, but both times I used this access no one was home to grant permission to use the path.

The seven-mile trip between Scout Camp Road and the Goose Hollow Road has a steady current and less rock wall than upstream. Farmlands occupy the widening valley and barb wire fences enclosing pastures are encountered at several locations (remember, fences usually come in pairs). The best thing about this trip is the variety of streamside scenery. From high sand and clay banks full of swallow nests, to farm fields and beautiful rock bluffs. Each turn in the river seems to bring on a different view.

From the Goose Hollow Road Bridge, the town of Elizabeth can be seen off on the hillside. Elizabeth was founded by lead miners pushing out from the Galena River diggings and was originally called Apple River Fort in the 1820s. Settlers from mines and farms as far away as Hanover gathered at Apple River Fort in 1832 when the Black Hawk War broke out.

The men, fearing the fort would be besieged, went out to hunt in a large group to lay in a stock of food. Blackhawk and about two hundred Indians used this opportunity to attack the still formidable though undermanned fort. A woman by the name of Elizabeth Armstrong inspired the women and older children to help on the firing line, loading muskets until reinforcements arrived. Their brave actions saved the fort, and it was in her honor that the town of Elizabeth was named. The only man in the fort, George Herclerode, was killed in the battle. A replica of the original Apple River Fort opened in the fall of 1998.

The Apple River skirts the town of Elizabeth, never coming closer than about a mile. Neither Georgetown nor Elizabeth road makes a good access: it is steep and overgrown at the former and fenced off at the latter. U.S. Route 20 has no parking, a long carry to the water, and steep, muddy banks. West Lone Street, just off of U. S. 20, has good parking and is close to the river but has very steep banks.

The best launch site is a nearby corrugated culvert. Launching here is hard because of the steep banks, but landing here would be even harder.

No roads cross the Apple River between U.S. 20 and the town of Hanover, ten miles downstream. This section of the Apple has mostly high muddy banks with only occasional rock bluffs, much like the Pecatonica River. The current is moderate, riffles are rare, and trees never block the entire channel. Much of this trip is through farmland, but the banks are too high to allow much of a view. The Apple River slows as the dam in the town of Hanover draws near. The takeout is above the dam, and parking is a long way off unless permission is secured from one of the commercial plants facing the river. One must also get permission to use the dam as a put-in.

The town of Hanover was settled in 1828 and was originally named Wapello after the Sauk Indian Chief whose village was at one time located here at the falls of the Apple River. Yes, the first dam on the Apple River was built on what was once known as the Apple River Falls.

The water below the dam runs fast for quite a distance, and one can only imagine the rapid that must have existed here at one time.

The Apple River flattens out to the Mississippi River Valley a few miles below the mild but long rapid south of the Hanover dam. The last of the rock walls is also found just downstream of Hanover. About halfway through this trip, large hills and ridges that skirt the Mississippi flood plain provide a majestic view along the banks of the Apple River. The first road crossed on this section is oddly named Crazy Hollow Road. From this point on, Illinois Route 84 is close enough to the river to be heard, but not seen, at least during the summer months. The next road downstream is West Witton Road, providing a good access point ten miles below Hanover. The next access is four more miles down the road that leads into the Savanna River Army Depot.

The United States Army built the depot at this location to augment its facilities at the Rock Island Arsenal. During World War II the United States planned a mission to retaliate for the bombing of Pearl Harbor by bringing the war to the shores of Japan. Known as the Doolittle Raid, the plan was to bomb Tokyo on April 18th, 1942, with sixteen B-25s carrying special lightweight incendiary bombs developed here at the depot (for the Hollywood version of the Doolittle Raid, check out the movie *30 Seconds Over Tokyo*).

The Apple River meanders for four more miles through the Upper Mississippi Wildlife Refuge before it empties its waters into those of the "Father of Waters," the Mississippi.

The current is slow to nonexistent and an almost "day glow" green slime covers the water's surface at various points. Deer, muskrat, beaver, ducks, geese, and blue heron, along with the occasional eagle, are commonly encountered along this scenic stretch of the Apple River.

A mile above the mouth of the river, one passes a low railroad bridge, low enough to require ducking down and perhaps a portage at higher water. A small house rests on the left bank where the Apple and Mississippi Rivers merge; it is the only building on this last section of the Apple River. After paddling in little or no current, the contrast is great when one turns out on to the swift Mississippi River.

The first takeout option on the Illinois side of the Mississippi River is provided by Mississippi River Palisades State Park where camping is also available. Access is across Illinois Route 84, via the park entrance, which boasts three paved boat ramps, restrooms, picnic tables, and plenty of parking. Locating the access is a bit tricky as it is off of the main channel of the Mississippi River in a back bay. The best way to find the bay is to keep an eye out for the long set of bluffs that are the predominate feature of this state park and keeping as far to river left as possible. Only two more miles downstream from the U.S. Route 52 Bridge over the Mississippi, the city of Savanna operates a "no fee", three-lane, paved boat ramp at Marquette Park.

The Apple River offers an interesting variance of scenery from its canyons through its towns and out on to the Mississippi River's ancient valley. The Apple River has a character all its own and would certainly get more paddler attention if its access points were easier.

Illinois Atlas; Page 16 A-1; 15 A-3; 15 B-2; 15 C-2

Matt & John Hall join the Tylers for an early evening on the Apple.

Aux Sable Creek

Baker Park would be a good put-in as it features a parking lot and a level path to the creek. The park also has picnic shelters and tables.

My first recollections of Aux Sable Creek are from exploring the Illinois Michigan Canal. I remember the aqueduct that carried the canal over the creek and a small rapid below. Well, it looked like a rapid at a time before I paddled rapids. Anyway, that was the impression that I had. Scouting at Holt Road and Illinois Route 52 still left me with the impression that the Aux Sable Creek was a mix of light riffle sections, alternating with flatter, slower runs.

The name Aux Sable means Sandy Creek. Nearly the whole length of the creek is wide and shallow with a sluggish current, even at flood stage. It takes a flood stage to bring this creek up to a runnable level. I found that in most places it wasn't more than a foot or two deep. Early settlers claimed that it was "a more pretentious stream that time has tamed."

The highest upstream I dared to put-in was Van Dyke Road, which crosses both the East Branch and the Middle Branch of Aux Sable Creek. The East Branch looked dangerously log-jammed and narrow. Therefore, I chose the bridge over the Middle Branch for a put-in. After the first half-mile the Middle Branch is joined by the West Branch and the water flow increases. However, for the few miles after the McKanna Road Bridge, the creek remains narrow and intimate. Soon the East Branch enters on the left, doubling the flow and the width of the creek.

This area where the branches come together was known as the Aux Sable Timber Indian village. This village of Nay Au Say on the Aux Sable and the village of Main Poche on Big Rock Creek appear to have been the two main Indian villages to take part in the Fort Dearborn Massacre.

Another mile or so downstream will bring you to Route 52 and Baker Park, located on the left side of the creek. Baker Park would be a good put-in as it features a parking lot and a level path to the creek. The park also has picnic shelters and tables. There is another park directly south of the Illinois Route 52 Bridge, but it's not as extensive as Baker Park across the road.

The problem with putting in at Route 52 is that there are several "No Trespassing" signs a short distance downstream. The signs are accompanied by fences that are designed to keep out the potential trespassing canoeist. This is particularly unfortunate, because the next section is the nicest canoeing section on the creek. Three very nice Grade I-II rapids are found between Route 52 and Holt Road, *plus a four-foot-high dam that has a nasty hydraulic behind it.* I was able to paddle over to a high place in the center of the dam to portage. Other than these interruptions, the only thing that prohibits us from pleasurable canoeing here are the aforementioned fences. If it were not for the potential landowner problems, this eight mile trip would be a good introduction to running creeks. Holt Road is a tolerable access point. However, parking is only fair and poison ivy is abundant creek side.

Holt Road is the put-in for the lower section. Below Holt Road, the farm fields and fences fade after passing Interstate 80, and house trailers and rip rap become common sights. The creek's current remains sluggish, even at flood stage. After the I-80 Bridge, the interstate parallels the creek for about three and a half miles. The road is not often seen, but can clearly be heard for more than an hour. At the same time, you will paddle past many less than pretentious residences on the right bank.

A small runnable dam is located a short distance upstream of U.S. Route 6. Nothing much changes below the Route 6 Bridge, except that instead of Interstate 80 paralleling the creek, now a busy two-lane road follows alongside. Dellos Road can rarely be seen, but the traffic noise and housing, mostly mobile homes, are common.

As Aux Sable Creek approaches the Illinois Michigan Canal, some interesting ripples break up the slow water predominating so far. The riffles are visible from the two road bridges and the aqueduct over the canal. This left me with the impression that this lower section might have a faster current than the upper miles. Lots of more slow, flat water lies ahead.

Take a few minutes and walk up the bank to have a look at the Illinois Michigan Canal. This aqueduct is one of four built by the I&M Canal builders to bridge the larger streams that the canal crosses. The other three aqueducts were built over the Fox River, Pecumsaugan Creek, and the Little Vermilion River. Only two of these aqueducts still carry water: the Aux Sable and the Little Vermilion. A canal lock and the lockkeeper's house are located here. This would make a good lunch spot or takeout. It would be possible to continue on the I&M Canal from here to canoe east to Channahan or west to Morris.

An alternative to transferring to the I&M Canal is to continue down the Aux Sable to the Illinois River. Then paddle down the Illinois River about six miles to Morris and the Route 47 Bridge where there are paved boat ramps at William G. Stratton State Park. The remaining few miles below the I&M Canal on the Aux Sable are flat, as are the six miles on the Illinois River. There are neither houses nor roads to mar the view.

Wildlife is more abundant on this last portion of Aux Sable Creek than anywhere on the upper portions.

It is here that the local Potawatomi Indians had a "maple sugar camp." Today there remain a large number of maple trees in the wooded areas near the mouth. A Potawatomi Chief who frequented the area in the spring and fall, tapping maples, went by the name *Sugar* and was well-known by many of the early settlers.

If I had to pick one word to describe this creek, it would be "blah." Running this creek is not worth it.

Illinois Atlas: Page 28, D-1. Page 36, A-1

Long View of the dam on the Aux Sable.

Grade I–II rapids and a dam.

Bailey Creek

*If you are not going to run the falls, how will you and your boat
get back in the water? After pouring over the ledge, Baily Creek
—30 feet below—is surrounded by canyon walls.*

Bailey's Creek is a short tributary of the Vermilion River in LaSalle County. I have included Bailey's in this guide more as a warning than to cite a canoeable stretch of moving water. In high water conditions, you can put in as high up as the town of Tonica. A better place to begin would be at LaSalle County Road 2101, also called Tonica Road.

The creek at Tonica Road runs through a lightly forested pasture. The creek meanders back and forth most of the way down to LaSalle County 2300. After five miles of paddling, all hell breaks loose. Keep your eyes peeled for a small dirt road that fords the creek. Just below the ford is a thirty-foot-high waterfall, immediately in your path. It looks runnable; however, it is easy to get out and scout the fall. Check for a plunge pool before attempting a run…*there is none.*

This waterfall, as well as the one near the mouth, was at one time proposed to be part of the state park system. Starved Rock State Park was proposed at the same time. The Bailey Creek site somehow got turned down. The lower waterfall was de-watered by rerouting the stream to aid the quarrying that's obviously gone on all around you at this point.

If you are not going to run the falls, then the problem is how you and your boat will get back in the water. After pouring over the ledge, Bailey Creek is 30 feet below, surrounded by canyon walls. Boaters must either use ropes to lower boats and descend the sheer walls or make a long unmarked portage.

This marks the top of the difficult (if not impossible) section. Well, not impossible, because I made it. This turned out to be the most difficult and dangerous trip described in this volume.

These are the kind of problems that even an expert paddler cannot completely overcome. The dangers arise from a narrow steep creek bed where the banks rise ten feet or more the rest of the way to the mouth of the Vermilion. Combine this with the high steep shale banks that give way underfoot, where even vegetation cannot grow, and having nothing to grab on to makes for a very hazardous situation.

Keep these things in mind as I describe the last mile of Bailey Creek. After the 30-foot fall, there is a logjam at the end of the pool.

At run-able levels, this creates a small drop and a hole. Following this, Bailey's runs fast and fairly steep. It's fun, but pay attention as a quarry bridge soon comes into view. The creek runs under this through a pair of corrugated metal tubes. The tubes are usually blocked halfway up with debris. But this doesn't matter, because when at optimum water levels, there isn't enough clearance anyway. So, a portage around the bridge is required. Remember those steep banks, for you'll be forced to deal with them at this point. It's also best to scout the final two rapids while you are out of your boat. Creek left is the best place to get out and scout.

The last two rapids are great fun. The first rapid has changed a great deal over the last five years. Five years ago, the rapid consisted of a four-foot ledge that was run left of center. The shale ledge has broken apart and is best run toward the left or right bank at present.

It is the final rapid that is really unique. I like to call it "Pickup," after its outstanding feature. Someone, six or seven years ago, dumped a full-sized truck down the bank into Bailey Creek. There is a rock constriction at this locale, further complicating the route. Perfect boat control is required to make the turn that keeps you from paddling through the windshield. Sharp protruding pieces of the truck also add to the element of danger.

The Vermilion River is directly ahead of you and four more miles downstream on the Vermilion will bring you to first access, Oglesby Road.

Bailey Creek is named, like Bailey's Grove, for Lewis Bailey, one of the first settlers in LaSalle County. Bailey came to Bailey's Grove in 1825. Like most of the first settlers, he chose the south side of the Illinois River, as the timber and the creeks were more abundant. This had been a favorite resort of the local Indians, who were Bailey's only neighbors when he moved here. Bailey's Grove grew to become the town of Tonica. Lewis Bailey's son, Augustus, was claimed to be the first child born in LaSalle County, in actual fact, the Baileys went to Peoria for the child's birth.

Lewis Bailey admired the local Native Americans. In fact, he claimed that they were friendlier, more honest, and more trustworthy than the whites he knew. Ironically, one of the early boarders at the Bailey cabin was a bachelor named William Petigrew. Petigrew later married a widow with two children. They moved to the Davis settlement on Indian Creek where they were subsequently killed in the Indian Creek massacre (see *Indian Creek chapter*).

By the time the Black Hawk War came around, more than a dozen families had settled near Bailey's Grove. There is no mention of Indian trouble near the Bailey settlement, very likely because of the good relationship between Lewis Bailey and the Indians. The Bailey family was typical of the pioneer spirit that it took to be the first to settle an area. In 1840 they were among the first to take the Oregon Trail to settle in the newly formed Oregon Territory.

In conclusion, Bailey's Creek looked great on the *U.S.G.S. topographical maps. There are beautiful spots on the creek and the fast narrow sections are fun. But the difficult portages and dangerous conditions on the lower section make this a trip that might be better to pass up. If this still sounds like a piece of water you might like to run, then I would advise you to hike the mile up from the Vermilion River and judge for yourself.

Illinois Atlas, Page 34 C-2
* United States Geographical survey maps.
Note: In the spring of 1997 the pickup truck that made up the final rapid was washed into the Vermilion River.

The clay walls add interest to the scenery.

Author surfing a quarter-mile above the confluence of Bailey's Creek on the Vermilion.

Big Bureau Creek

In September of the year 1681, Captain Henry Tonti and a company of French soldiers were driven by the Indians from the area of Starved Rock. They had made their escape at night by canoe and stopped about 20 miles downriver at the mouth of a large creek to repair one of their canoes. The only creek that fits their description is Bureau Creek.

Seventy-five years or so after the French made canoe repairs at the mouth of Bureau Creek, a French Creole named Pierre de Beuro began trading for furs with the Indians. The trading post he opened was a part of the American Fur Company's operation in the Illinois River Valley. Pierre de Beuro prospered for a number of years, but was found murdered on the Peoria trail. It was thought that he was most likely killed by a rival trader. His Potawatomi wife took their trade goods back to her village at the mouth of the Fox River for their use. The county—as well as a town in the county and this creek—are all named for their first permanent settler, Pierre de Beuro.

Bureau Creek is the nicest family trip I can think of. It has everything going for it: riffles, wildlife, interesting history, a diversity of scenery, and the potential for canoe camping. Bureau Creek has more than 40 canoeable miles, all of them pleasant. To top this off, one of Illinois' last remaining covered bridges, the famous Red Bridge, north of Princeton, crosses Bureau Creek. What more could anyone ask for? Well, my only problem is figuring out when it has enough water to canoe on it, since it isn't very close to my home.

The farthest upstream that I've put in was by County Road 2200. The best way to find this road is to head north on Illinois Route 26 from Interstate 80 and look for a power transformer. Turn east on this road for a couple of miles until you come to the bridge over Bureau Creek. The trip from here to the Red Covered Bridge is eight and a half miles of great canoeing.

The trip begins on a very small narrow creek that is teeming with wildlife. The only watershed that has the same abundance and diversity of wildlife is the Little Vermilion River. Bureau Creek doesn't have rock outcropping like many of the LaSalle County streams, but it does have high brown clay bluffs—sometimes reaching heights of fifty feet or more.

At the put-in, Bureau Creek is small enough to have an occasional logjam. A fence or two might also be found across Bureau Creek. Lots of riffles bless the upper twenty miles. Waves big enough to bounce the canoe exist at many places in high water, but they're not so big as to put water in the boat

One of my favorite things on any creek is long stretches uninterrupted by roads, bridges, houses, or any other signs of civilization. Bureau Creek has six uninterrupted miles in this first 8-1/2 mile section.

For a takeout, you have a choice between two. At Illinois Route 26 is City County Park, the end of a 7-1/2 mile trip, but I like using the Red Covered Bridge instead. This adds a mile, but it is a very pleasant mile. City County Park was once the camping ground of Chief Shabbona who spent much of his time in this vicinity.

Downstream of the Red Covered Bridge, high banks and foliage help hide the agricultural fields that lie just outside of the creek's corridor. The creek remains remote and wild until Backbone Road approaches. Backbone Road also is a good takeout site. Pastures with their fences are common from above Backbone road to past Interstate 80. The current remains swift with riffles occurring regularly.

After passing under the Interstate 80 Bridge, it is a couple of miles to the iron bridge that carries Railroad Avenue across Bureau Creek. Princeton is out of sight just east of the creek. But you'll not realize it while paddling toward U.S. Route 6.

Route 6 has a great landing in the form of a gravel road next to the bridge that lets you drive right down to the water's edge. There is room to park several cars alongside of this lane. Route 6 is the main east/west street in Princeton and the bridge is only about a mile west of town.

Princeton was the home of Owen Lovejoy, abolitionist, minister, five-term congressman, and conductor on the Underground Railroad. Owen Lovejoy's brother was Elijah Parrish Lovejoy. Elijah was producing an abolitionist newspaper in Alton, Illinois, in 1836, near St. Louis. An angry mob attacked the newspaper, throwing the plates and presses into the Mississippi River. Elijah Lovejoy was killed in this attack. Owen Lovejoy escaped and left Alton to study to become a minister. This incident in Alton was one of the things that led to the Civil War.

In 1838 Owen Lovejoy moved to Princeton to become the Congregational minister to the Hampshire Colony. By 1843 he had been indicted for harboring slaves but was acquitted. Even after being caught once, Owen continued to help slaves escape to Canada. Owen Lovejoy died in 1864 at the age of 53, without having seen the end to the war that would free the slaves. The Lovejoy homestead was a major stop in the early years of the Underground Railroad and is worth a visit if you have the time.

Returning to the creek, Bureau Creek continues to grow larger as it flows down the valley. The scenery continues to be as lovely as it is upstream. There are farm fields in the valley, but they are hidden by high banks and a tree-lined corridor.

Notice the bands of glacial till in the creek bank. Glacial till is the rocky rubble left behind as the glaciers receded. Look for a defined line of small rounded rocks mixed with gravel embedded in the clay banks. This bed of glacial debris is called a ground moraine. There are many places along Bureau Creek where this phenomenon appears. Also, some of the hills in this valley are terminal moraines. A terminal moraine is the ridge that is pushed up in front of an advancing glacier. When the glacier retreats, it leaves a mountainous ridge known as a "terminal moraine."

The next thing that will grab your attention is the Hennepin Canal that was built as a shortcut between the upper Mississippi River and the upper Illinois River. The Hennepin is also named The I & M Canal, like its cousin to the east, but in this case, it means the Illinois River to the Mississippi. To escape the confusion caused by the similarity of names, it was called Hennepin after the town at its eastern entrance. Soon after completing the Hennepin Canal, the Army Corps of Engineers moved on to their next canal building job in Panama. The first encounter you will have with the canal while canoeing on Bureau Creek is where the Hennepin Canal used to cross over Bureau Creek in an aqueduct. The aqueduct is gone and has been replaced by a footbridge. It is worth a walk up the bank to have a look around. Fifty feet downstream of the footbridge is a stream-wide check dam with a two-foot drop. It's not terribly difficult to negotiate, but it looks pretty bad from above. When the canal was being built, Bureau Creek's course was altered through this part of the valley. Below the aqueduct site, the canal stays parallel to Bureau Creek's left bank.

The next two bridges that cross Bureau Creek both offer good access. The first is on County Road 1200 N., north of Tiskilwa. The second is on County Road 1950 E., which can be easily found by following Main Street east out of Tiskilwa to the first road on the left. From this intersection, you can see the modern bridge over Bureau Creek that replaced a quaint iron structure in 1995.

Between these two bridges lies the village of Tiskilwa, known to the early settlers as Indian Town. It was known to the Indians as Wappe. This Indian village was one of the more important of the Potawatomi villages. The history of this village provides great insight into the early years of settlement in northern Illinois.

The Potawatomi migrated here from the Wabash River in Indiana in 1769 under Chief Wappe. The location of Wappe was the reason that Pierre de Beuro decided to found a trading post nearby in 1776. Other Potawatomi villages in the area were located at Lake de Pue, at the mouth of the Fox River, and Black Partridge's village on the Illinois River, below where the town of Henry now stands. Pierre de Beuro married the daughter of the main chief of the village on the Fox River.

The year 1812 found chiefs named Comas, Autuckee, Meommuse and Tiskilwa residing at Wappe. The same year found many of the Indians that took part in the Fort Dearborn massacre hiding out in the area. They built a fort in a marsh using the logs from the abandoned de Beuro trading post and prepared to defend themselves, but no one came. After a few months, the defenders returned to their villages.

But the village of Wappe was the target of a punitive expedition ordered by Governor Edwards and led by a Lieutenant Robinson. The Indians expected the soldiers to ascend Bureau Creek by boat, but they were taken by surprise when Lieutenant Robinson brought up half his force on horseback. The Indians retreated and the soldiers burned their village and fields. Then the soldiers fell back, having accomplished what they intended. For a time, the creek was known as the Robinson River.

The next major event that involved the village of Wappe took place on June 25, 1830. A great council of Potawatomi, Winnebago, and the Sac and Fox gathered to discuss an all-out war on the white settlers. The list of chiefs was impressive: Black Hawk, Senachwine, Shabbona, Waba, Autuckee, and many more. Senachwine was the spokesman for the peaceful faction of the Potawatomi. He gave a masterful speech and persuaded the Potawatomi not to go to war.

Two years later, Black Hawk returned, this time with the Winnebago chief called the Prophet. Again, the Council House on the bluff overlooking Bureau Creek was used for debate. Black Hawk pleaded for the Potawatomi to join the Sac and Fox. The Prophet, along with a sizable contingent of Winnebago, also urged an all-out war on the whites.

Senachwine had died about one year after the 1830 council meeting. Shabbona, the protector of the whites, stood up to speak for peace. Waubonsie, the Potawatomi chief who lived on the Fox River, spoke for the Potawatomi joining the other tribes on the warpath. Again the peace faction won out, thanks to Shabbona's oratory, which was well received because of its sincerity. But it took a three-day council to resolve the question, showing that there were many sides to the issue to resolve. When the war did start, the village at Wappe foresaw the consequences and moved west to be safe.

Not everyone in the village agreed with this peaceful decision. The most notorious dissenter was a half-breed by the name of Mike Girty, known to the settlers as the White Savage. Mike Girty, who was not a chief, had the audacity to rise from the rear of the council and speak out, calling the other Potawatomi chiefs cowards and women who were unworthy of representing the tribe. So Mike Girty became a rallying point for the malcontents that were seeking war.

Mike Girty's father, Simon Girty, was the subject of great controversy during the Revolutionary War in the Pittsburgh and Ohio area. He was captured by Indians at the age of fifteen. Simon much preferred the Indian way of life and so stayed with the Indians the rest of his life. He was a British Indian agent during the Revolutionary War and had no qualms about instigating raids on the western settlements where everyone present was murdered.

Like father, like son—both had the reputation of being scoundrels. Mike Girty tried to live in white society in Ohio, but after a murder, he fled immediately after the incident and was assumed to be the guilty party. Girty ended up living with the Potawatomi on Bureau Creek.

After the council ended, Mike Girty set out to scout as many local cabins as possible. He made note of the number of guns, how the doors and windows were hung, and most important, the number of defenders. Next, Girty's band took to bushwhacking lone travelers on the prairie. These were assumed to be missing persons, but the local settlers knew what had taken place. What happened next was to make Girty's band declare an open war on the settlements.

On May 14, 1832, Major Stillman's 400 volunteers were defeated and scattered by Black Hawk, and Mike Girty started searching for settlers to kill. (*See Stillman Creek.*) Arriving at the first of several cabins which they found abandoned, they took what they wanted and killed any livestock left behind. Shabbona and one of his sons were riding over a five-county area warning the settlers of their danger. The settlers in the Bureau Creek vicinity fled to Hennepin where a small fort had been erected.

Girty moved eastward in the quest for further bloodshed. It is known that Girty and his band were participants in the Indian Creek massacre. Then they moved into Kendall County, where they also found the settlements deserted. My personal favorite story about Girty involves the murder of the Reverend Adam Payne.

Adam Payne was a very well-known missionary among the Potawatomi. The reverend had used Girty as an interpreter at several services that he gave around the great Wappe Village area. It appears that shortly after the Indian Creek Massacre, Mike Girty made a trip to Peoria to trade. At about the same time, Adam Payne was returning to Chicago after a trip to Ohio. He stayed two days in Chicago where he preached several times. He left Chicago and arrived in Plainfield on the DuPage River.

In Plainfield, he found everyone in a state of great excitement over the Indian Creek incident. Fort Beggs was there, but it was thought too small to protect the large number of refugees that had gathered there. So they all resolved to go to Chicago the next day, to the protection of Fort Dearborn. They begged the Reverend Payne to join them. He refused, figuring he had two things going for him. First, a fine horse that was known as the fastest around, and second, an ongoing relationship with the local Indians.

The Indians who killed the Reverend Payne said that they had laid in ambush, waiting for the first traveler to come along. Because of Shabbona's warning, everyone in the five-county area had already fled to safety, so the only person that crossed into their trap was Adam Payne. They fired off a volley that hit both rider and mount. Payne's horse easily outpaced the Indian ponies at first, but the loss of blood eventually caused the Reverend's horse to drop.

Payne stood his ground as the Indians rode up. He held up his Bible and begged for mercy. Two of the pursuers were moved, but the third approached from behind and dispatched the Reverend with his tomahawk. These fun-loving fellows dismembered his body, stuck his head on a pole in their camp, and started to dance and celebrate their debauchery.

At about this time, Mike Girty returned to camp from his trip and jumped right into the festivities. After a time, Girty looked closer at the head over the fire and recognized the bearded Reverend. Mike Girty was beside himself. He broke down and began crying. He took the head down off the pole. He then went out and found the rest of the body and buried it. Girty then burned his most valuable possessions over the grave, trying appease the spirits, both Christian and Indian.

Whether this story is true or not, Mike Girty was responsible for many of the deaths associated with the Black Hawk War. Mike Girty claimed that he eventually joined with Black Hawks band and was taken prisoner at the battle of Bad Axe. He used an alias when taken prisoner, knowing that he would be held responsible for the murders he had committed. Girty then killed a guard while in custody and was put to hard labor until his health failed, at which time he was set free. He died a short time later near Wappe. He was alone, rejected by whites and his adopted tribe alike. His body was found in the spring, partially eaten by wolves.

Below Tiskilwa, the banks of Bureau Creek are high and sandy. The current remains steady if not swift. The high banks hide the Hennepin Canal, which continues to parallel Bureau Creek for about five more miles. A couple of miles downstream from the town of Tiskilwa, you'll cross the Rock Island Railway Bridge where there is an extensive logjam. Shortly before the first Interstate I-180 bridge, Bureau Creek splits around a two-mile long island. The best course is the right channel, for it carries more water, and a logjam blocks the left-hand channel.

The best choice of a takeout is under the second Interstate 180 bridge where Illinois Highway 26 exits the Interstate. Parking is good and Bureau Creek comes right up alongside of the road. It is ten miles from Tiskilwa to the I 180 bridge. After the I 180 intersection, Bureau Creek heads south into Goose Lake and continues into Senachwine Lake. There are public boat ramps at the town of Henry, as well as on Lake Senachwine.

If Bureau Creek were closer to my home, I am sure I would canoe it more often. As it is, I try to make at least one trip on Bureau Creek each year. In the future, I plan to try canoeing higher up. The West Branch also looks canoeable at high water. So I hope to someday explore more of this interesting watershed.

Illinois Atlas: Page 33, A-6; B-6.

"This is the nicest family trip I can think of…wildlife, interesting history, a diversity of scenery, and to top it off, one of Illinois last remaining covered bridges."

Now a footbridge, this is where the aqueduct once crossed the Hennepin Canal.

Blackberry Creek

The Galena Boulevard put-in is truly one of the more unique launching sites to be found anywhere. We used the office building parking lot on the east side of the creek for unloading and parking. Be sure to get permission first.

The west side of the creek is the most interesting, as it is the location of the Blackberry Historical Farm and Village. It is a living history museum with people in period costume making candles, spinning wool, shaping iron at the blacksmith shop, and spinning clay pottery. This is just for starters. There is the Dykstra Carriage Museum, a very large and nicely maintained collection of horse drawn vehicles. Also on the premises are two log cabin replicas, complete with genuine period furnishings. For the kids there are pony rides and a carousel. It could take the better part of a day to see everything.

After putting in at the Galena Boulevard Bridge, there is a series of low footbridges that start a short distance below the put-in. The bridges are part of the Blackberry historical complex that occupies both sides of Blackberry Creek. Before the creek leaves the historic farm site, it winds its way around next to one of the log cabins.

As you leave the park, the banks sport a more natural look with an abundance of wildlife. The only manmade interruptions are found at road crossings, Blackberry Oaks Golf Course, and one small subdivision. Otherwise, it gives the impression of an untouched natural area.

Two roads are crossed in the first few miles. The first is Prairie Road; the second is Jericho Road. Barnes Road runs parallel to the creek's right bank. It can be heard, but can rarely be seen, as it carries very little traffic and doesn't often intrude.

After Jericho Road, there is another mile-long stretch of natural landscape and plentiful wildlife before U.S. Route 30 is reached. Keck Memorial Cemetery, just west of the Route 30 Bridge, would make a good alternate launch site. This cemetery has several markers dating from the 1850s. There is a small residential development a few miles downstream, just before Galena Road is reached.

Do not confuse this road with Galena Boulevard, which was the put-in nine miles upstream. The next road after Galena is Bristol Ridge Road, two more miles downstream. Between these two roads is the Blackberry Oaks Golf Course. As with all golf courses, there is a slew of bridges across the creek, but all will allow passage underneath them. The golf course is open, like a field. Canoeing this section in a strong headwind could be a problem.

The town of Bristol is about a mile northwest of the Bristol Ridge Road bridge and was first settled in a different location. Lyman and Burr Bristol first laid out the village of Bristol in 1834 at the mouth of Blackberry Creek on the Fox River, which included a mill. Later, they also purchased the 1833 cabin of Earl Adams, on the south side of the Fox River. One year later, the brothers sold their holdings on the south side of the Fox River to two cousins, James Cornell and Rulief Duryea. Rulief laid out the town of Yorkville in 1836, naming it after his native state of New York.

For two miles on either side of the Route 47 Bridge, we found eighty percent of the log jams for this trip. There are homes visible in these four miles. The gradient noticeably picks up as one approaches Illinois Route 34. A large number of fresh water mussels can be seen in and along the creek bed. In 1911 the Rehbehn brothers moved their button factory into Yorkville. The factory punched round holes in fresh water mussel shells to form the blanks for mother-of-pearl buttons. The mussel shells were gathered from the Fox River and its local tributaries. This, of course, would have included Blackberry Creek.

Although by the time you've reached Route 34 you are already in the corporate limits of the village of Yorkville, it's not often that you'll be aware of it. After passing Route 34, the waterway again becomes completely natural for most of the remaining distance to the Fox. A city block above the mouth is River Road. Three feet upstream of this bridge is an 18-foot-high dam. This is the site of the 1834 dam spoken of earlier, a mill-site for almost a hundred years.

The portage is steep, and the two-lane River Road carries a good deal of traffic and has shoulder barricades. Be careful, as this is a dangerous crossing, especially on busy summer weekends.

Although 16 miles makes for a long day's trip, it is easily divided into shorter sections. Most of the bridges have good parking and short carries to the water. As with so many smaller streams, it is amazing how remote these creeks can be though within the city limits of many towns.

Illinois Atlas: Page 27, B-7

When you paddle this creek, be sure to stop and visit
Blackberry Historical Farm and Village. This is one of
the cabins you can see from the creek.

East Fork of Little Calumet River

Once again, this small stream and the early history of its area are closely related. This is particularly true downstream of the U.S. 20 bridge where the Indiana Dunes National Lake Shore has preserved two home sites of historic interest, but this is only one small piece of the total package that makes this a unique canoeing experience.

The traditional launch site on Howe Road is excellent, but be sure to leave room for others who also might want to park here, as the area is heavily used by hikers and people fishing (other than canoeists). Up the hill from the put-in is the Bailly Homestead, now maintained as an historic site. It's well worth the time to have a look around. The main house is open on Sundays from 1 p.m. to 4 p.m. A trail from the Bailly Homestead leads to a visitor center, then on to another historic farm from the 1870s.

Joseph Bailly settled here in 1822 and opened a trading post, which eventually consisted of six buildings. Bailly chose this location because two of the main trails in this area crossed here. The Fort Dearborn Trail ran from Chicago to Detroit and crossed the Sauk Trail that ran from Missouri to Rock Island and then on to New England. Because of the large volume of traffic at the time, Joseph Bailly's trading post prospered and grew. The Little Calumet River also served as a waterway to the business. In fact, the portage trail that led from the Little Calumet to Lake Michigan was the trail Bailly had used when originally locating a site to build.

The Baillys were interesting people who were adaptable to the changing times they lived in. Joseph Bailly was of French Canadian descent and his wife, Marie, was part Ottawa Indian. This combination was most common in unions among traders involved in the fur trade. The fur trade was in its declining years by 1822, when Bailly established his enterprise in northern Indiana. In 1822 most of Bailly's business was conducted with the local Potawatomi Indians, whom he treated fairly, as has been attested to by Leopold Pokagon, a tribal leader of Potawatomi. By the 1830s, most of the Indians had moved or had been removed west of the Mississippi and the Bailly's business began to decline. So the Bailly's decided on a change of occupation from fur trading to innkeepers. This required abandoning the homestead and moving about a mile and a half to be closer to the Chicago-Detroit Road, which was receiving increased traffic every year with the tide of immigration. Shortly after completing the inn, Joseph died, but not before seeing the Ottawa and Potawatomi tribes being led by U.S. Calvary down their Trail of Tears.

Joseph and Marie Bailly left no male heir, for their only son had died at the age of 10. Their girls married and took the names of their husbands, so the name Bailly died out in the area. One of the husbands was named Howe, the name of the put-in road, which brings us back to the Little Calumet River.

The first mile or two after the Howe Road put-in goes through a flood plain forest with alternating sand, clay, and dirt banks and bottom. The current is moderate and the scenery natural. No houses are visible from the river, even in winter when the leaves are gone. Logjams and strainers are abundant on this part of the river, as well as above and below. The number of pullovers between the Howe Road put-in and Burns Ditch varies from year to year, according to Leo Krusack, a long-time paddler on this section of the river. "The number of pullovers over the years has been as few as six, and as many as 25."

A little more than halfway through the trip, an interesting railroad trestle appears. The pilings are numerous and are arranged in rows, leaving an opening just wide enough for a canoe to pass through. Be careful of logjams that tend to accumulate against the supports of such trestles.

About a mile below the railway bridge, the banks narrow and a horizon line appears on a bend in the stream bed. **STOP AND SCOUT.** The dam at this location can and has been run, but it is difficult (Class III). The 50 feet below the dam is fast, steep, and requires a quick left turn after dropping over the four-foot drop at the dam. Below the dam, keep your eyes peeled for spawning salmon and lake trout.

The dam stops fish migration further upstream, but below the dam, fish are plentiful. During the salmon run, canoeists are made to feel unwelcome through this part of the river, as well as on other rivers and streams that have un-dammed access to the Great Lakes. During the spring and fall salmon runs, anglers line the banks and wade the waters. When canoeists pass by, they can be blamed for a whole day of bad fishing. So if you canoe the Little Calumet on weekends during the salmon season, expect hostile treatment.

After the dam, the river changes character. The banks are high, steep, and consist of clay and/or dirt. Surprisingly, the deadfall frequency remains about the same as it's been on the last six miles. You'll encounter what we've come to call the "Mother of All Logjams," which is just what it sounds like, the largest blockage on the river. I'm told that it has been there a score of years, and from the looks of it, it will be there a score more. The other thing that's changed is the water velocity. The narrow banks and increased gradient have noticeably sped up the current. Clay shelves in the water increase this effect. I love this part of the river and although more homes are visible here, the fast current and tight turns make up for the occasional residential intrusion.

Soon Salt Creek enters on river left, the river widens, and the current slows. A short distance below Salt Creek, a ditch comes in on river right. This leads to an effluent pool at Bethlehem Steel and is marked "No Trespassing." Past this point, marinas and docks appear on both sides of the river.

The takeout is at an abandoned bridge that is right next to the Indiana Route 249 Bridge. Look for the Izaak Walton League building and park so as not to block other vehicle owners.

Indiana Atlas; Page 19 C-8

Leo Krusack sliding into the Little Calumet after navigating a downfall on a cold wintery day.

Bob Tyler keeping a watchful eye after completing his own portage.

Little Calumet River of Illinois

The Little Calumet River belongs more to Indiana than to Illinois, and another chapter in this volume describes the best section of The Little Calumet in Indiana. To cross the state line via the river, put-in at Riverside Park, which is located between U.S. 41 Calumet Avenue and Columbia Avenue in Hammond, Indiana. Riverside Park runs along the Little Calumet River between these two streets. It's an 8-mile trip down to 159th Street from Riverside Park.

The Little Calumet is enclosed by levies, with steep muddy banks backed by earthen walls; this is the look of the river from put-in to takeout. Roads cross at regular intervals. As you would expect in an area with this density, many of these roads could be used as access points, but none are any better than the Riverside Park. The levies are from 8 to 15 feet in height and hide all but the roofs of the riverside homes. There is a narrow tree-lined corridor that the Little Calumet flows through, but it's only as wide as the levies permit.

The Little Calumet River does tend to have logjams at about the rate of one to the mile, several occurring at the four railroad right-of-ways (two active and two abandoned). Interstate 80/94 is crossed downstream of Calumet Avenue and sound walls along the Interstate help protect the canoeist from some, if not all, of the noise, but the interstate can still be heard for the entire trip. The next bridge below the Interstate is Hohman Avenue, and two blocks further the Illinois/Indiana State Line is crossed.

A log cabin and wooden farm wagon surrounded by a chain link fence can be seen from the river immediately downstream of the Burnham Avenue Bridge. The cabin is home to the Calumet City Historical Society and is located in Veterans Park, which runs along the river for a block or more.

The best section of the Little Calumet River starts downstream of Torrence Avenue, which is recognizable from the river by the 20 screens of current movies showing at two movie theaters—one on each bank of the river. Below the Torrence Avenue Bridge, golf courses are what improve the scenery occupying the right bank much of the time, and the levies decrease in both size and frequency. The other thing that improves are the logjams that disappear after Thorn Creek (*see Thorn Creek*) adds its water, nearly doubling the flow of the Little Calumet.

Downstream of Thorn Creek, 159th Street crosses and the Little Calumet where it starts becoming forested just as Interstate 94 come into view. A good takeout is available at Gouwen Park, which has a walk-in paved boat ramp. Gouwen Park is located just west of the Interstate and just north of 159th Street.

A second 8-mile trip on The Little Calumet can be taken by putting-in at Gouwen Park and taking-out at Calumet Woods Forest Preserve boat ramp. Right from the start, this trip lets you know that the riverbanks are in private hands. Past Gouwen Park, homes grace first one side, then the other, and at times both sides of the river. Besides homes, rail yards are a predominate feature of The Little Calumet; four large railroad yards are passed in the 8 miles. The first is modest in that there are only two sets of tracks crossing over the river. The second yard spans the creek with six pairs of tracks, and two of that yard's control towers can be seen from the river.

Now you might think that the Little Calumet is a river without redeeming quality. Not true. The Little Calumet has a unique quality, urban for sure, but the houses have a wide variety of sizes, shapes, styles, and economic profiles. Besides the homes and railroads, several small factories occasionally adorn the riverbanks. These are not large like those on the area's shipping waterways, but are proportional to the Little Calumet's size. About three miles below the put-in, a World War II tank and a surface-to-air missile are displayed at a roadside park that can be seen from the river, high up on the left bank.

The Little Calumet River finally takes on a more natural look—thanks to Cook County Forest Preserves that pad the river corridor below Halsted Street Illinois Route 1. Thornton Blue Island Road closely follows the river and finally becomes visible above the Ashland Avenue Bridge. Thornton Road follows a portion of Gurdon

Hubbard's 1818 trail. There are whole books written on Hubbard's life, yet his role in Northern Illinois and particularly Chicago's history is often downplayed in history texts.

Hubbard's Trail, which follows the Little Calumet River for a short distance, ran from Chicago to Gurdon Hubbard's trading post on the Little Wabash River in south eastern Illinois and was the first road out of Chicago. Hubbard was a partner in the Illinois Brigade of the American Fur Company, John Jacob Astor's company. Hubbard was in charge of posts not only on the Little Wabash, but also on Bureau Creek, the Kankakee, and the Iroquois River (where his main post was). Hubbard was the most frequent user of the Chicago Portage when he decided that it would be more expedient to cut a trail between his different posts and use horses instead of boats and the Chicago Portage. Hubbard's Trail was another of Gurdon's good ideas, as it was not only faster, but also more reliable when the Portage was muddy or the rivers frozen over. Hubbard was called "Pa-Pa-Ma-Ta-Be" ("Swift Walker") by the Native Americans because he could walk more than 50 miles in a day with a pack and musket. No wonder he thought a trail would be faster!

Continuing downstream from Ashland Avenue's first crossing, Ashland Avenue and Interstate 57 run in a straight line, while the Little Calumet makes a mile-wide ark crossing both roads twice. Two of the aforementioned rail yards are crossed in this mile, but the river stays mostly forested. The takeout at Calumet Woods just below the second crossing to the two aforementioned roads. There is plenty of parking here and a concrete boat ramp into the water,which makes for easy access.

One half mile downstream of the Calumet boat ramp, The Little Calumet River makes an abrupt change. It's still called the Little Calumet, but it's no longer little. The river's course has been dramatically altered, widened, straightened, and deepened, and its flow has been reversed.All this was altered to accommodate the Illinois Deep Waterway System.

What this means to the canoeist is: Below the Calumet Woods boat ramp, expect to encounter barges and pleasure boat traffic on a much larger waterway that still bears the name Little Calumet River. Those willing to continue downstream for 5 miles can takeout at Beaubien Wood Preserve boat ramps located off of 130th Street, but this trip cannot recommended. Downstream, the Grand Calumet River joins the Little Calumet and a lock needs to be dealt with. I personally have no knowledge of the river below the Beaubien Boat Ramp.

In the 21 miles covered in this chapter, the Little Calumet River grows from log-jammed, levied, and small stream into a major navigational waterway. The river has few natural stretches, but nonetheless the Little Calumet has a flavor all its own.

Illinois Atlas; Page 29-D-6 and D-7

Carrol Creek

I first encountered Carroll Creek while looking through the Delorme Illinois Atlas. I noticed the symbol for a canoe launch in the town of Mount Carroll. I found the creek hard to follow on the map, so I called Steve Simpson who canoes and teaches geology at Highland Community College in Freeport. Steve gave me good takeout options, told me the creek had spectacular scenery, and also directed me to bring a flashlight with fresh batteries because there were caves along the creek that were worth exploring. Steve also mentioned that the locals refer to this as Waukarusa Creek. This I found to be partially true. It is called the Waukarusa—an Indian name meaning "winding stream." However, in Mount Carroll it goes by the name of Carroll Creek, and it's also referred to as Staddle Creek above town, so named when an Indian maiden's horse was able to place its hooves on both banks of the the of the creek at the same time.

I put in at Illinois Route 64 east of the town of Mount Carroll and encountered a few log jams, a few fences (one of which was particularly formidable), and a few rock walls before entering town. A better put-in than Route 64 would be Point Rock Park in Mount Carroll (Point Rock is also known as Poet's Rock). Point Rock Park has a large parking lot and an easy, level entrance to Carroll Creek, as long as you put in below the park's low water bridge.

Carroll Creek needs quite a bit of water to be canoeable, but if you can catch it with water, you're in for one of the prettiest creeks that I've run. In fact, had the water not been so muddy, I might have thought myself on an Ozark stream. Carroll Creek is generally fifteen to thirty feet wide, and regularly passes under bluffs between forty and eighty feet in height. Riffles and small but challenging rapids occur frequently; this, along with the narrow width, will hold the attention of even very experienced boaters.

Below Point Rock Park, rock bluffs adorn the banks and continue all the way to the takeout. This section is locally known as the Dells of the Waukarusa. There are several caves along these dells. There is one cave you can't help but notice. Smith's Cave is a natural feature that was enlarged when it was mined after lead was discovered along a vertical crevice in the cave. This cave has been explored by thousands of people over the years, for the Dells was the location of Smith's campground and was the playground of this resort for many years. The Dells was also the location of both the Christian Saw Mill, built in 1838, and the earlier Fulrath's Grist Mill. While paddling the Dells, see if you can identify these bluffs: the Giant's Tea Table, Castle Rock, the Twin Sisters, and the Devil's Backbone.

Wildlife is abundant, and I saw at least six types of ducks, blue heron, an eagle, red-tail hawks, turkeys, beaver, muskrats, and deer on my first trip down Carroll Creek. The trip from Mount Carroll to Jacobstown Road is six miles long; this is a short trip, but it does allow time for cave exploration. The junction of Jacobstown and Scenic Palisades Roads provides good access with roadside parking; the neighbors are friendly, too.

Carroll Creek flows into the Plum River about three miles downstream of the Jacobstown Road, but the next access on the Plum River is a few miles further down at the junction of Illinois Routes 52 & 64 near Savanna. The confluence of the Plum River and the Waukarusa is also another location of the work of prehistoric mound builders called De-Coo-Dah. The mounds found here are different from other Mississippian mounds in that the remains of the dead were cremated before being buried in layers. In most Mississippian mounds, the bodies are laid flat, face up, and surrounded by significant articles from the deceased's life. (*See Plum River*)

The Waukarusa (or Carroll Creek, if you so prefer), receives no higher recommendation than being the best creek in this volume. The only downside is catching it in a runnable state with ample water. The creek does, however, support a year round fish population, so its water supply is constant. The Dells of the Waukarusa are truly spectacular and would be worthy of "state park" status. Camping can be found north of nearby Savanna at Mississippi Palisades State Park.

Illinois Atlas; Page 16 D-1

Some of the many bluffs along Carrol Creek.

Chicago River & Branches

Checagou; an Indian word meaning "odorous swamp." Some say the smell refers to skunk, others say it is onion or garlic, but no matter. The name of the marsh with a small stream running through it into a large lake stuck, and the city named after the river is thriving three hundred years later. The Chicago River was the eastern end of the Chicago Portage, which connected the Eastern Seaboard via the Great Lakes and St. Laurence River with the Illinois and Mississippi Rivers flowing into the Gulf of Mexico. The existence of the portage was well known to the natives, who revealed its location to Marquette and Jolliet on their 1673 voyage of exploration.

The United States Government considered this location important enough to fortify and garrison in 1803. One year later, John Kinzie came here buying the claim that had in the 1780s belonged to Chicago's first citizen, Jean Baptiste. Point Du Sable. John Kinzie was also a trader to both the Native Americans and the garrison at Fort Dearborn. It's ironic that the first non-natives to the area were both traders and that the town that grew here became not only the largest trading center on the Great Lakes, but between our country's two oceans.

The Main Branch of the Chicago River

As far as canoeing the Main Branch of the Chicago River is concerned, I must say that it's very different than most of the other streams in this volume. Let me preface this by saying that this is no place for beginners. The river is walled in, making self-rescue impossible. The walls also refract waves from motorized boats on the river, creating quite numerous waves several feet in height. In peak summer months, tour boats, barges, and pleasure craft make the Chicago River a very busy place for a canoe. As if this were not enough, takeouts are few and many involve parking at expensive downtown parking lots, or going out through the locks and out into Lake Michigan.

The rewards of paddling this section are great since the river passes through the heart of the city. Enough of Chicago's unique architecture lies along the banks of the Chicago River to warrant the Chicago Architecture Foundation running boat tours supplementing their walking tours of downtown. The Main Branch is a little less than 2 miles in length, beginning at the Forks of the Chicago (this area is also known as Wolf Point; named for a tavern once located there). Today, bridges box in the Forks, with the Orleans Street Bridge to the east, the double-decked Lake Street Bridge to the south, and the Kinzie Bridge, to the north, which was made famous during the Great Flood of 1992.

Significant buildings, the history of one of the first settlements of the Northwest Territory, 10 moving bridges, many of Chicago's tour boats, a set of locks,—all in less than 2 miles. There isn't room to include all the particulars, but to say you're canoeing right though the middle of one of the great cities of the world should suffice. Put-ins and takeouts can be achieved at Burnham Harbor East and West boat ramps, or on the North or South Branches of the Chicago River.

South Branch of the Chicago River

The South Branch is only 4 miles long. It begins where Ashland Avenue crosses the river near the junction of the Stevenson and Dan Ryan Expressways (Interstates 55 & 90/94) and ends at the forks in downtown Chicago. Three waterways converge at Ashland Avenue: The Chicago Sanitary and Ship Canal, The South Branch of the Chicago River, and its South Fork, also known as Bubbly Creek. One of the basins used for turning boats and barges is located here, as is a new park. Canal Origins Park commemorates the Chicago terminus of the 1846 Illinois Michigan Canal.

The Illinois Michigan Canal was the main stimulus for Chicago's amazingly rapid growth in the 1840s and 50s. The Canal made Chicago the hub of trade in the Midwest. Before the opening of the Illinois Michigan Canal, Chicago wasn't even one of the great cities in Illinois, let alone one of the great cities in the world. Before the canal was built, a West Fork of the South Branch flowed from the (long ago drained) Mud Lake. The South Branch and its West Fork, Mud Lake, and the DesPlaines River* were segments in the famous Chicago Portage, used by Marquette and Joliet in 1673.

In 1939 the flow of the Chicago River was reversed in what at the time was called one of the engineering wonders of the world. Not only were the Main and South Branches reversed, but the Skokie Channel was dug to bring water from Lake Michigan down the North Branch, to help flush the toilet. In other words, the primary reason for reversing the flow was to keep Chicago's sewage from contaminating Lake Michigan, the source of the city's drinking water.

The South Branch has several interesting bridges, and some of the buildings left are from the days when lake-going ships unloaded their cargo along the South Branch of the Chicago. After the flow of the river was reversed, large ships could no longer pass up the river, but barges still regularly ply the waters. You can round-trip it into the Loop from Ashland Avenue, or use the takeouts listed for the Main Branch. Another option—and I have done this—is to start at Ashland and paddle up the North Branch to the canoe launch at Berteau. Because the rivers passed through don't have much current, trips can be done up or downstream; paying attention to the wind direction is more often important.

The South Branch passes several boat yards, several construction material handling yards, a coal fired power plant, the Amtrak Railroad yards, and the Main Branch of the Chicago Post Office. All this before entering the canyon of buildings that line the final mile of the South Branch. The South Branch and Main Chicago River are not unique in that most of the industrial cities of the middle United States are located on rivers. But Chicago as viewed from along the river is very much one magnificent city!

Canoeing the North Branch via the Skokie River

Canoeing on the North Branch begins directly above Willow Road, by putting-in below the dam that holds back the Skokie Lagoons. Parking is along Forest Way Road, where it is about a hundred-foot carry to the put-in at the Dam. Trips of different lengths are possible via the many parks that line the North Branch's corridor. Two of the most popular trips on the North Branch both start from Willow Road. There is a 6-mile trip ending at Linne Woods Forest Preserve off of Dempster Street in Morton Grove, or those desiring a longer trip of 13 miles can takeout at Whelan Pool, located off of Devon Avenue. There are several other access possibilities, but these are the most commonly used.

The section between the Skokie Lagoons and Devon Avenue has deservedly been designated the Ralph Frese Canoe Trail. I was—like thousands of other paddlers—accompanied by Ralph on my first trip down the North Branch. For 50 years, Ralph has brought attention to the environment along the river. His was a major contribution to today's ever-improving habitat on the North Branch.

The Skokie River

The Skokie River below Lake Cook Road runs through the Chicago Botanical Gardens before entering the Skokie Lagoons. The area was a swamp known to early settlers as the Chewab Skokie. The swamp was converted to today's Skokie Lagoons. Those not wishing to hassle with car shuttles can easily spend an afternoon exploring the Skokie Lagoons. The Skokie River is sometimes referred to as the East Fork of the North Branch.

The dam outflows into a pool that provides the put-in. Parking is on Forest Way Drive, which is located off of Willow Road. Below the Willow Road Bridge, one notices immediately how small and narrow the Skokie River is, especially when compared to the lagoons upstream. This is one of the best streams in this book on which to try out small stream canoeing. It has a relatively slow current and generally low banks. The logjams and strainers are cut regularly, though you'll more than likely run into a few. There are several small dams along the river, and the first of these is located between Winnetka Road and Interstate 94. The dam only drops about a foot, but concrete side walls on both ends make the portage difficult. The hydraulic recirculation below the dam is never dangerous, but the dam nonetheless causes its share of spills. One common technique used by canoeists is to stand up in their boats while hanging onto the side wall to lessen the draft while moving the boat downstream. The dam washes out at higher water.

After passing the Eden's Expressway I 94, Happ Road is followed by a railroad bridge that has a tight passage. The first of several bridges that carry bicycle/hiking trails over the river is encountered before the North Branch joins the Skokie River. The North Branch is also called the Middle Fork of the North Branch on some maps. It is less confusing to just think of it as the North Branch. Therefore, the Skokie River ends at its confluence with the smaller North Branch.

The North Branch of the Chicago River

I put-in on the North Branch by using the Northbrook Court Shopping Center parking lot close to the Lake Cook Road bridge. This makes for a trip of 6* miles down to the Skokie River. My only canoeing experience on the North Branch had been after a 5-inch rain, and at this level it could probably be canoed even higher up. I should warn of several challenges that develop at high water. The first is a diversion into a flood control overflow basin a short distance upstream of the Interstate 94 Bridge. The wider, clearer diversion channel appeared to be the main channel. This fooled my partner, who was forced to backtrack. Next, several bridges on the North Branch are not passable at high water and require portaging. This is particularly difficult at Illinois Route 68, Dundee Road, both because of its busy traffic and because at high water it overflows the road. As the stream flows through a flood plain, brush and branches crowd the small channel, forcing the paddler to duck and dodge. Also, when in flood, the stream overflows its banks, making the channel difficult to follow. I lost the channel and had to backtrack this time, while my partner kept the correct course. When not coursing through forest preserves, the North Branch skirts a golf course, a school, and numerous houses before joining with the Skokie River.

The North Branch of the Chicago River is much wider downstream of the Skokie River. Roads cross the river at regular intervals. Most of the river corridor is through Cook County forest preserves, and at several places picnic shelters are close to the river, making for easy access or lunch stops. The forest is thick in several places, but the Chicago River Hiking/ Biking Trail stays close enough, along with the regular road crossings and various forms of concrete outflows and intakes to keep the atmosphere from feeling truly wild. Four miles downstream, the West Fork joins the North Branch in the Chick Evans Golf Course, adding considerable water.

The West Fork of the North Branch

Canoeing the West Fork could begin in high water from Northbrook Park in Northbrook on Walters Road east of Shermer Avenue. The park is home to the Northbrook Historical Society, which is housed in the 1880s Northfield Inn. The Inn was moved here from its original location at Waukegan and Shermer Roads. The town of Northbrook was first known as Shermerville. Waukegan Road follows the stagecoach trail that ran between Chicago and Milwaukee when the Northfield Inn was built. A dam forms a lake above Willow Road and requires portaging. Below Willow Road, a flood control diversion on the river's left side should be avoided, but a portage needs to be made here to reenter the correct channel.

The West Fork flows through few forest preserves, making it different than its neighboring branches. The other branches flow through flood plain forest where as the West Fork flows through several wetlands that are being rapidly overtaken by development. Though segments of the West Fork are pleasant, much of its course goes through residential communities, and is channelized to prevent flooding. This is particularly true as the West Fork passes through the downtown of Glenview. The West Fork passes through two golf courses before adding its considerable flow to that of the North Branch. The 6 miles down to the North Branch show remarkable diversity from ditch to wetland and from golf course to neighborhood, making for another stream to explore at high water.

Back on the North Branch, a second dam—that is, more of a rocky shoal—is encountered below the confluence with the West Branch. The dam is under one of three golf course bridges and most paddlers portage around the dam on river left. This is more to save wear and tear on their boats than due to any dangers presented by the dam. At high water, the dam washes out and is a bouncy ride. A mile below the dam, the takeout for the 6-mile trip can be recognized by the second concrete storm drain, sided with stone sides. This is the Linne Woods access located off of Dempster Street. The bank is steep and the carry relatively long, but parking is plentiful. Picnic shelters located between the river and the parking lot allow for a meal at trip's end or a lunch stop for those continuing downstream.

From Dempster to Oakton, the North Branch flows amidst wooded forest preserves. Below Oakton, the river leaves its forested pad. The bike path that's been close at hand on river right cuts away, staying forested while the North Branch begins to feel more like the urban river it later becomes. Another golf course is passed before the Howard Street Bridge. The third dam on the North Branch is downstream of Howard Street and can be portaged on the river's right side. The dam has a more powerful hydraulic than the two upstream, and because of this most boaters walk this one. First Touhy Avenue and then Gross Point Road are passed before forest preserves again become the dominant feature along the river. Before arriving at the takeout for the 13-mile trip from Willow Road, the North Branch passes through several more miles of forest preserves. The takeout is near the Whelan Pool parking lot, which is located west of the river off of Devon Avenue.

The North Branch is crossed by Caldwell Avenue, runs through Caldwell Woods, and passes by the Billy Caldwell Golf Course, all of which refer to Sauganash—the Potowatomi named Billy Caldwell "Sauganash, which meant "Englishman." He was the offspring of a Potawatomi mother and a Captain of the British Army. Raised on the frontier near Detroit, he could speak French and English in addition to several Native dialects. Sauganash was close to and may have been Tecumseh's nephew on his mother's side. The two fought together for the British against the Americans during the Revolutionary War and the War of 1812. Billy Caldwell acted as interpreter for Tecumseh in many of his dealings with both the British and Americans. Sauganash and Shabbona were with Tecumseh, fighting against the Americans, when he fell mortally wounded at the Battle of the Thames. Caldwell and Shabbona stood together again; along with Black Partridge, they stood watch over the Kinzie cabin after the Fort Dearborn Massacre. The presence of these respected Chiefs not only saved the John Kinzie family, but the others that had gathered there for protection.

Sauganash and Shabbona swore allegiance to the United States after the War of 1812 and were to prove—time and time again—their friendship with the Americans. In 1828 Shabbona and Sauganash and Alexander Robinson kept Big Foot's band of Winnebago, at Lake Geneva, from making the Winnebago War into a real war. All three were also instrumental in keeping the Potowatomi from participating in the Blackhawk War, and the American settlers safe after war had begun. Both the Potowatomi and Americans alike sought Caldwell's assistance in treaty negotiations. Billy Caldwell's services earned him a 1,600-acre land grant, encompassing both sides of the North Branch, in gratitude for his services. But he instead chose to join his tribe, the Potowatomi who were relocated to Council Bluffs Iowa, where Sauganash died in 1841.

If you put in at Whelan pool, it is a 1/4-mile down to the Devon Avenue overpass and about 3 additional miles down to the Interstate 94 overpass. Between these two points is a delightful stretch of fast water, just downstream of a highly graffitied railroad bridge. The North Branch winds through thickly forested preserves between Devon and I 94. Thanks again to forest preserves, these are some of the wildest miles along the river. The expressway interrupts for just a short distance and is followed by the attractive Cicero Avenue stone bridge. LaBagh Woods on river right and the Sauganash Prairie, a rare wet savanna, on river left bring the North Branch back to its last natural miles. The Cook County Forest Preserves on the North Branch end a short distance below and the river rapidly becomes urban. The loss of the Cook County Forest Preserves is also the loss of convenient access points.

Between Foster and downtown, the North Branch is enclosed by stone walls often topped with chain fences. Cemeteries are passed on river left above and below Foster Avenue, which crosses the river three times in a short distance. The next miles go through densely packed residential neighborhoods. Many streets dead-end at the river and several footbridges cross over the North Branch. The last of these foot bridges, at Albany Street, is the last chance to takeout above what is elsewhere described as "the waterfall." The waterfall is really just a graffiti-laden dam. Takeout on river right is steep and difficult, but the portage is short and the reentry to the river easy.

Below the dam, the **North Shore Channel** joins the North Branch, more than doubling the width and volume. The Skokie Channel was built to act as the flusher when the flow of The Chicago River was reversed in 1900. The flow of the North Branch was found to be insufficient to wash the sewage first into the DesPlaines/ Illinois Rivers and then on into the Mississippi. The North Shore Channel was dug to add Lake Michigan water to the North Branch as part of the Sanitary District's master plan. I've been told that canoeing on the 8 miles of the North Shore

Channel is pleasant, with much wildlife. Put-in near the Bahai Temple in Wilmette; takeout on the North Branch at Berteau Street (4200 North).

Below the dam, the North Branch instantly becomes big enough to accommodate powerboats and riverside docks, which are common along the next 1 1/2 miles, down to the access at the end of Berteau Street (west of Western Avenue and north of Irving Park Road) on the east side of the river. Parking is limited, but without this access, canoe trips on the North Branch would be substantially more difficult. Hopefully, Horner Park on the west side of the river will soon provide access. Going from Devon Avenue to Berteau is an 8-mile trip, and going from Berteau to Ashland Avenue on the South Branch means 10 miles.

The final 6 miles on the North Branch were once mostly industrial, but this is changing. Old industrial properties are being demolished or converted to shopping malls and housing. That's not to say that there are no longer industrial properties along the North Branch, but as you canoe you're bound to notice the conversion. Boat yards, material handling, and heavy industry are still the predominant features, particularly below Fullerton Avenue. Also, below Fullerton, as the scenery becomes more industrial, the bridges become more interesting. Many of Chicago's moving bridges are passed between here and downtown. Most of the bridges no longer move and several (though fixed in place) have been nicely restored.

The North Branch widens out at North Avenue to form a turning basin for the larger boats that once plied the North Branch. Below North Avenue, the river splits around the mile-long Goose Island, the only island on the entire Chicago River system. The left-hand side of the island is called the North Branch Channel.

As of this writing, access on the lower North Branch is non-existent, for most of the bridges are fenced or otherwise restricted. Even if access were available, parking downtown can be expensive. Access can be found approximately 3 miles further on the South Branch, at Canal Origins Park, located just south of the Ashland Avenue Bridge. The other takeout possibilities are at boat ramps along the lake. The last of these involves paddling through the lock, something I've never done before.

Access. As of this writing, there are a dozen or more new access sites being planned, but which ones will be completed and in what order remains to be seen. Additional information can be obtained from these sources.

Friends of the Chicago River (312-939-0490)
407 South Dearborn Street Suite 1580
Chicago, Illinois 60605 Maps and up-to-date information. They also run canoe trips.

Forest Preserve District of Cook County (708-366-9420)
536 North Harlem Avenue
River Forest, Illinois 60305
Maps of the Forest Preserves through which the Skokie River and the North Branch flow.

Chicagoland Canoe Base (773-777-1489)
4019 North Narrangansett Avenue
Chicago, Illinois 60634
Maps, books, canoe sales and rentals; a generally good source of information on the Chicago River and many of the other rivers in this volume.

The Chicago River **by David Solzman**
Wild Onion Books, 1998.
A must-own volume for those interested in the watershed.

Illinois Atlas; Page, 21 D-5; Page, 29 A-6, B-6

Bridges of the Chicago River.

Coon Creek

Coon Creek is a very wild tributary of the Kishwaukee River in Boone County. It's not wild as in whitewater, but wild as in remote and undisturbed. The put-in is east of Illinois Route 23 on Coon Creek Road, near the Dekalb/McHenry County line. Coon Creek Road is the best landing in the vicinity of Illinois Route 23.

The first several miles of this trip run through farm fields and open prairies. Coon Creek runs with a fair current over a sand and gravel bottom. In the first few miles, Coon Creek crosses four roads in close order. The last of these is Interstate 90, which is never far from the creek. You'll pass the very small berg of Riley before the first logjam is encountered. Anthony Road in Riley could be used as an alternate put-in.

Now, Coon Creek is log-jammed at the rate of about two to the mile; on most other creeks, I consider this to be too many to make for worthwhile canoeing. But on Coon Creek, we felt that this was the price of admission for a trip into the wild. What makes this trip seem so wild is that Coon Creek has a wide "corridor"; this depth makes a great habitat for wildlife, waterfowl, and even mussels. At regular intervals, marshes, wetlands, and small lakes break off of the streambed. Several islands split the already small channel.

Just when we thought that we may have been among the very few humans to have ever viewed this area, we were quickly disillusioned. First, we noticed deer hunter perches in the trees, not just one or two, but dozens. The second clue was that even though we were seven miles below the crossing of Interstate 90, every time we came to a clearing to the south the interstate was still visible. A third clue was a string of junk cars that have been used as rip-rap to fill the levied banks; if restored, some of the cars would now be considered classics. I was also surprised to note that on the map, several miles of Coon Creek appeared to be channeled; the only indication we had of this human "tinkering" while canoeing the creek the only indication was the levied banks and a "straighter" feel to the direction of the water. The tree-lined banks spanning many miles led us to believe that the channeled section still lay ahead.

Garden Prairie Road, like most of the roads that cross Coon Creek, is a roadside pull-off and could be used as an access. Below Garden Prairie Road, Coon Creek enters a wet woods or floodplain forest that turned out to be no more log-jammed than upstream. Much of the creek's flow seems to have been diverted to other channels as the width and the flow both decrease. The forest continues all the way to U.S. Route 20 (which you'll hear before you see it).

Housing on the left and Belmar Country Club Golf Course on the right are below Route 20. The golf course ends at the Chicago and Northwestern Railroad, which crosses Coon Creek downstream of an older bridge locally known as Two and a Half Mile Bridge. Coon Creek joins with the Kishwaukee River below the bridge.

The takeout is a pull-off on Route 20 where old U.S. 20 dead-ends at Coon Creek; another alternative is to take out two miles below Coon Creek on the Kishwaukee. The landing on the Kishwaukee is off of Lawrenceville Road at Red Horse Bend Canoe Access: an excellent take-out with a parking lot and a level but slightly muddy landing. This area was donated by the Pillsbury/Green Giant Company.

To paddle Coon Creek, you really have to have the attitude that logjams are a part of some really pleasant watersheds and are part of the overall experience. To me, the sharp turns into the unknown are part of the fun of running small creeks, as is the precise boat control it takes to stay out of trouble. Coon Creek provides all this and more.

Illinois Atlas; Page 19, C-6; C-5

Covel Creek

Covel Creek has it all: variety in size and scenery, and two sections, one of which has a twenty-six-foot-per-mile gradient, making it one of my personal favorites in Illinois. It reminds me of a smaller version of the Vermilion River, which parallels it ten miles to the west. Covel Creek has two distinct sections; an upper section through farmland and a lower section that seemingly becomes more remote the farther you proceed into its ever-deepening canyon. The dividing line between the upper and lower section is the LaSalle E 1800 bridge, but beware: the local landowners are rumored to be hostile toward paddlers using this bridge as access or egress. We have not had a problem here, but others have.

The upper section begins at a bridge on LaSalle County Road E 2000, one hundred feet north of N 2200. Covel Creek is hardly even a waterway at this point. It is so small that on one low water trip, I stepped off one bank into my canoe and stepped out onto the opposite bank. At optimum levels, it is about 20 feet wide at the put-in. Speaking of optimum levels, Covel is pretty tame at low-to-medium flows, but at high water, it takes on a Grade II+ nature and requires prior whitewater experience. Whitewater paddlers will likewise be disappointed in anything less than flood stage.

Don't worry about paddling on such a micro-stream, as it soon grows with the addition of four tributaries, tripling its size in the first mile. For the first couple of miles, Covel is entrenched with 4-to-6-foot-high mud banks. It eventually breaks into open pasture, making it necessary to look for barbed or electric wires in several places. The water remains swift, with occasional gravel bars, for about five miles. After the E 1800 bridge (the alternate put-in), the action and gradient really starts to pick up. A mile downstream of the E 1800 bridge, a couple of good surfing waves appear on a sharp left turn. A hundred yards or less further brings on Covel's best rapid. The drop is fairly straightforward, but it's hard to see the passage until you are right on top of it. It might be best to stop and scout it unless you have a *reliable eddy turn*, as there is always a chance that there could be a deadfall lodged in the narrow main passage.

Rock outcroppings are frequent in this area and small rapids and riffles continue past a Burlington Northern Railway Bridge, almost down to the Illinois Route 23 Bridge. This bridge is a good place to scout water levels, for if it doesn't look runnable here; there are shallower places downstream. The Route 23 bridge could be used for a landing or launch, except that the traffic is very heavy. The next bridge, N 2501, is fair, although a steep launch. And watch out for poison ivy.

Henry Hibbard moved to LaSalle County from Cincinnati, Ohio, where his widowed mother had recently been remarried to Reuben Reed. A total of fifteen members of this combined family moved to LaSalle County in 1827. Shortly after this, Mrs. Reed invited her brother from St. Louis to join them. This Mr. Hibbard seems to have been quite the scoundrel. He was accused of breaking up the marriage of his newly remarried sister in short order. Next, Hibbard, for a fee, bound his own three children out to work for other early settlers. The youngest girl was bound over to one Lewis Bailey. (*See Bailey Creek.*)

Mr. Hibbard from St. Louis seems to have had much to do with the fact that all the future marriages of the Hibbard children ended in divorce. It is also interesting that every Hibbard that moved away from LaSalle County died within a short time after leaving. Henry Hibbard settled along Covel Creek in 1828, probably after the divorce of his mother. He stayed only a few years. By 1834 the area was known as Ebersol's Grove, after its new owners.

The creek remains swift and narrow between Route 23 and the N 2501 bridges. The remnants of an old dam site create a small play hole below the N 2501 bridge. You are now on golf course property and approaching a three-foot-high dam with a runnable center chute. Run center or portage right. There is a golf tee located on river left, up the six-foot-high bank, with a cart path next to the creek. During the golfing season, you are liable to have an audience when running the dam. Below here, the gradient picks up noticeably—it's like running downhill for a short distance. The scenery is remote and spectacular. Rock walls occasionally grace the valley as it grows steeper while closing in at the same time. The rapids in this section are almost a continuous Grade II at optimum levels, consisting mainly of shallow rock gardens. Nice waves and riffles at high water, but it is hard to choose a route in low water.

About seven miles below where the rapids began, the walls close in, then open out and close in once again. This widening of the valley is one of the few places on the lower creek where human intrusion in the form of buildings is seen. This is the location where Thomas R. Covell built his cabin in 1825 and a short time later added a dam and a mill. During the 1820s, the Illinois River was the northern boundary of frontier settlement, except for the lead mining district along the Mississippi and Chicago on Lake Michigan. Ottawa, located on the south side of the Illinois River access from where the Fox River entered, was the center of a small but growing population. During the Winnebago War in 1827, Covell and about a dozen other settlers built a fort for mutual protection. This fort was used again in 1832 during the Black Hawk War. Many early settlers in LaSalle and Kendall counties were directed to prime locations by Covell who, by 1833, decided to relocate first on the DuPage River at Plainfield and later on Salt Creek in Cook County. After these buildings, the valley closes in again. Rock walls can be seen on both sides of the creek. There are large icefalls in winter that should be of interest to any ice climber. After you reach flatter, slower water, it is about a mile further to the Route 71 Bridge, the end of the trip. A pretty rock pulpit comes in sight and sandstone walls line both banks of the creek. The best takeout is on the downstream side of the Illinois Route 71 Bridge on the right side of the stream.

Illinois Atlas: Pages 34 & 35, B-4

A natural bridge in Covel Creek's final mile.

Covel is so small that on one trip I stepped off of one bank into my canoe and stepped out onto the opposite bank.

Des Plaines River

The DesPlaines River has its headwaters north and west of Kenosha, Wisconsin, and ends below Joliet where it joins with the Kankakee to form The Illinois River. I have personally canoed as far upstream as Wisconsin Highway 50. In Illinois, a put-in is available a 1/2-mile downstream of the Illinois/Wisconsin boarder on Russell Road. For those wishing to cross the boarder, put-in in Wisconsin on Kenosha County Road C for a 7-mile trip down to Russell Road. Trips this high up on the DesPlaines River watershed require the spring melt or a large amount of rain—or both. In fact, this applies to the DesPlaines River as far downstream as Oak Spring Road in Libertyville where it is more or less canoeable year round with normal amounts of rainfall.

A short 6-mile trip between Russell Road and Wadsworth Road has improved canoe launches at both ends. A hiking trail infringes on what would otherwise be a very natural section with an abundance of wildlife. Beaver and their signs are common, and I have spotted more beaver on this section than on any other in this volume. Beaver and deadfall go together so it follows that the river is blocked in more than one place along these miles. In periods of very high water, this wetlands becomes a wetland and most of the deadfall blockages can be gone around.

I should make mention here of the Des Plaines River Trail, which is the crown jewel of the Lake County Forest Preserve District. When the trail is finished in the near future, it will run the length of the county, a total of 33 miles. My reason for mentioning it is, as its name implies, it follows the river closely, sometimes along the river banks crossing over the Des Plaines River many times on rustic bridges. For the canoeist this means a shared river corridor, so expect to see people often and wildlife less often. Now I don't mean to be a spoil sport, and I realize that far more people use these trails than canoe the Des Plaines River, but they spent so much money on the trail, imagine how easy it would have been to add canoe access at a few more locations. This becomes obvious when looking at the Forest Preserves Des Plaines River Trail map. The landings the forest preserves have are excellent in design, but they tend to be located close to one another, leaving many miles in between the clusters.

Early settlers said that a string of Native American burial mounds lay along the banks of the DesPlaines River for a distance of three miles downstream of the Wisconsin/ Illinois boarder. One of these has been preserved in Van Patten Woods Forest Preserve. Only one road, Illinois 173, crosses the DesPlaines River before the improved take-out at Wadsworth Road. The entire 6-mile trip is within the boundaries of Lake County Forest Preserves.

The 5 1/2 miles from Wadsworth to Gurnee, like the trip upstream, is very natural due again to the fact that most of the route is through Lake County Forest Preserves. Much of this trip takes place through a wetlands restoration area that the DesPlaines River leaves cleaner than it enters. The DesPlaines River remains a small stream that meanders through the wetlands and marsh and offers little protection from the wind. Approximately 4 miles below the put-in, the river widens out to become more like a lake than a river, then becomes wooded. A short distance downstream, U.S. 41 is crossed and the banks become more wooded, creating occasional dead fall blockages.

The best landing in Gurnee is just south of the Grand Avenue which is Illinois Route 132. The landing is not marked from any roads in Gurnee, nor is the landing improved. However, there is plenty of parking a very short distance from the river, by the park. The park is called Vern Grove Memorial Park and to find it, take 132 east of the river to O'Plaine Road, turn south, and turn right again at the first street, McClure, and follow it one block to where it ends in the park. There are other possible takeouts, but they involve parking on narrow road shoulders or in privately owned parking lots. The last of the Gurnee area landing would be Belvidere Road Illinois Route 120 where a fishing access provides an unimproved landing with parking for about a dozen cars.

It's an 8-1/2 mile trip from Vern Grove Park to Oak Spring Road in Libertyville; these miles are mostly forested, breaking into open wetlands regularly. A new parking area is being constructed (circa Spring 1998) at Buckley Road

Illinois Route 137 east of the river. Independence Grove may become access in the future. Takeout at the very well done Oak Spring Road Canoe Access Area

The Oak Spring Road access marks the starting point of the annual Des Plaines River Marathon. The race, which was first run in 1957, takes place two weekends before Memorial Day and covers the 19 miles between Libertyville and Dam #2. The marathon draws more than 1,000 canoes on some years and the events surrounding the race take up the whole weekend.

The 19 miles that the race passes through are different than any others up or downstream, in that not only is there an ever-growing urban intrusion, but this intrusion expands just often enough to keep the Des Plaines from ever feeling remote. It's not that Lake County doesn't have parks along this section, it's that the parklands are regularly broken up by private holdings. Add to this the fact that Milwaukee Avenue is never very far to the west.

Just North of the Rockland Road Bridge, which is the first road crossed below the Oak Spring put-in, is the site of one of many natural springs that once existed in the Libertyville area. The Potawatomi Indians of the area thought the waters had curative powers. Chevalier De LaSalle was said to have heard of these waters and to have come to this vicinity in 1684 to sample the powers the water conveyed. There is no access at Illinois Route 176, but 4 miles downstream at Town Line Road there is an improved canoe launch on the west side of the river via a pond, making this a unique access. Much of the 3 1/2 miles between this landing and Half Day Road is occupied by The Captain Daniel Wright Forest Preserve, named after Lake county's first settler, whose home was north of here, between Milwaukee Avenue and the River. Captain Wright was a veteran of the War of 1812 and was helped in building his home by the Potawatomi Chief named Mettawa. Daniel Wright is buried less than 200 yards from the banks of the DesPlaines in Veron Cemetery

There are four dams to contend with, all of which have red signs signaling their approach. All four are low and wash out easily with high water, all are shallow at low water, and the author has no knowledge of conditions in between. The first of these is located a short distance downstream of Illinois 178; the next two are above and below Illinois 60. The last is downstream of the Ryerson Cabin. Beware of these dams as a hydraulic may develop, making the dams dangerous. The third of the three dams has a larger drop than the first two.

The next bridge is Illinois Route 22 Half Day Road, named for a Potawatomi Chief Aptakisic, which means Half Day. It was said that Aptakisic could—in half a day—do the work that others would take a whole day to do. Downstream of Half Day Road, Indian Creek enters on river right through an extensive wetlands. On the western end of this wetland, Marriot's Lincolnshire Resort can be seen from the Des Plaines. Native Americans occupied this vicinity for centuries. Mounds were found here, as were many Indian trails that came together in the area.

Ryerson Conservation Area is the next Forest Preserve that's entered and is easily recognized by a boarded up log cabin in a wooded clearing. The cabin was built in 1928 by Edward and Nora Ryerson, whose efforts brought about much of the forest preserve in the river corridor. The second cabin downstream contains restrooms for users of the bicycle/hiking trail that parallels the river for many miles. Park planners must think that canoeists don't need to use the bathroom, as they forgot to provide a canoe landing. If you don't get mad here, wait till you see the massive structure that carries this trail over Lake Cook Road; it must have cost millions.

There is no access at Lake Cook Road, but there is at Potawatomi Woods Forest Preserve, accessed north of Illinois Route 68, Dundee Road. There is not an improved canoe landing here, but parking is close and the banks are neither too steep nor too muddy for landing or launch. Downstream of Dundee Road, Dam #1 Woods has good parking and landings on both sides of the river. Dams #1 and #2 are unlike any other dams on the Des Plaines River in that both have access on both sides of the river and both dams have rocky, sloping faces. The rocky faces retard the development of the even hydraulic that forms at most dams, which means that both Dams # 1 & 2 are runnable, but at normal water level it's scrapie and will damage all but plastic boats.

Both dams make excellent places from which to watch the Des Plaines River Marathoners apply varied techniques in crossing the dams. Chicago Whitewater Association provides safety boaters each year to catch boaters with unsuccessful strategies. Both dams were at one time public swimming holes where on weekends folks came from miles around to swim in the clear waters of the Des Plaines River. In fact, there was a carousel, pony rides, and food and beverage stands located at Dam #1. Even before the dam was built this was the location of a country swimming hole.

The eight mile trip from Dam #1 to the Des Plaines Dam has been a yearly trip of mine for more than ten years, and some of my best trips have been on warm autumn days when the river corridor is ablaze with color. An improved canoe launch is located 2 1/4 miles downstream at Allison Woods, located off of Milwaukee Avenue. River Trail Nature Center, located just downstream of Allison Woods, can be recognized by a wood rail fence and iron retaining wall from the river, but unfortunately there is no canoe landing here. River Trail Nature Center provides a home to animals injured to the degree that they would perish without help. Outside is the home for these critters; inside are displays of things one might see along the river.

Located on a long river bend to the east, at the point where the DesPlaines bends back to the west, an Indian village stood in the vicinity of Big Bend Lake. The Village here was the western trailhead for the portage trail between the DesPlaines River and the North Branch of the Chicago River known as the Grove Portage Trail. This was one of as many as 30 Potowatomi Villages located along this northern portion of the DesPlaines River when the first white men explored the area. Dempster Street is about a mile downstream.

The DesPlaines River makes a bend to the right at Dempster Street, then makes a left turn and crosses under the Dempster Street Bridge, and immediately approaches Dempster Street Dam, which is dangerous at all but high water levels when it covers over and washes out portage river left. Stay away from river right because the wall supporting River Road doesn't allow passage, and beware that low head dams are the Number One killer of canoeists. Takeouts are available above and below the Dempster Street Dam at Northwestern Woods Forest Preserve, located on Campground Road which is off of Dempster Street and can only be accessed from the Eastbound lanes.

Downstream of the Dempster Street Dam, the DesPlaines River runs much the same as upstream. River Road is close to the river right side, and mostly Cook County Forest Preserves are on the left and crossed at frequent intervals by highway and railway bridges. I canoed this section last in 1998 and found more than a dozen Deep Tunnel construction areas alongside most of the bridges; these could perhaps increase the access possibilities in the future. Speaking of accesses, they are numerous along this section thanks to forest preserves too numerous to mention. This continues for the next 15 miles.

There are two dams besides the one at the put-in, the first of which is the Touhy Avenue Dam, located a short distance downstream of the Interstate 294 Bridge, and the last of the numbered dams on the DesPlaines River is Dam #4, located below Devon Avenue. These two and the Dempster Street Dam are of similar configuration and height and wash out at high water, but are dangerous at lower water levels because wide even hydraulics form below them. Signs are posted to warn of the approach of all three.

The town of Rosemont has a water tower painted to look like a bunch of roses that can be seen from the river. Many small creeks add their water in the five miles between Dempster and Higgins; the largest enters the DesPlaines between two office buildings. Interstate 90 is crossed and the right bank reveals the back side of the Rosemont Convention Center. Above and below Lawrence Avenue on the left side of the DesPlaines is the site of the land grant given to Alexander Robinson by the United States of America.

Alexander Robinson was the son of a Scottish trader and an Ottawa mother. He moved to the vicinity of the Chicago Portage in the early 1800s, and his tribal name was Che-che-pin-qua. His services as interpreter and mediator at many tribal council meetings on behalf of the U.S. helped to procure treaties on more than one occasion. After helping to negotiate the 1829 treaty of Prairie du Chien, he was given 2 1/2 sections of land along the Des Plaines River. Robinson, Billy Caldwell (Sauganash), and Shabbona were all given land grants at the same time. Alexander Robinson is buried along with his family on East River Road, just north of Lawrence Avenue. A historical marker here tells more about this noble friend of the early settlers.

It's a ten-mile trip between Dempster and Grand Avenue, but trips of almost any length are possible. Accesses, though numerous, are often steep, muddy, or both. The same goes for using the numerous picnic shelters; it's hard to land and launch at most locations. Hopefully, the Illinois Waterway Trail that the Des Plaines is part of will secure some better canoe launches.

The land in between the Railroad Bridge and Grand Avenue once belonged to a man of French and Indian decent named LaFramboise. The land was part of a grant given to LaFramboise for aid which he gave to victims of the Fort Dearborn Massacre in 1812.

A short distance below Cumberland Avenue, another dam appears. It is similar to the last 3 upstream in that it washes out with high water and it has a ramp to aid portaging. I should mention that these dams are among the most user-friendly in northern Illinois.

About a mile downstream of the dam, in the vicinity of Evans Field, is another Potowatomi Village. The settlement at this location is interesting in that it was built on the site of an earlier Mississippian Culture Village, of which there is no record. The five conical mounds that once stood around the area attested to the existence of Mississippian occupation of this territory.

Below Illinois Route 64, North Avenue landings are few until Madison Street where parking is allowed on the north side of the street. Madison Street can be used as access, but it's a steep climb up the bridge's concrete easement. For much of the distance between Madison Street and Cermak Road, cemeteries line the bank, but they are hidden for the most part by high banks. Interstate 290 is crossed in these miles. A few more miles and Salt Creek enters on river right. One of the best takeouts on the entire Des Plaines River is just around the bend downstream of Salt Creek at Plank Road Meadow Forest Preserve. What makes this landing desirable is a large parking area with a gravel boat ramp, which most of all saves portaging the two dams in Lyons.

The town of Lyons is easily recognized by the Hoffmann Tower and adjoining dam, built in 1908 to provide electricity for George Hoffmann's beer garden. Portage this first of two dams on the river left. The portage requires crossing 39th Street and a steep reentry into the water. By the time you put back in, the second dam is visible; this dam is easily portaged left or right. There is a tight chute on river left, but the hydraulic is wide and dangerous, making this chute a risky alternative. Every year, dams kill canoeists. Be careful, because conditions change with different water levels.

Below the two dams in Lyons, the Des Plaines River runs fairly fast and crosses one footbridge. Before leaving Lyons, the Des Plaines River passes one of the Chicago area's most historic sites, The Chicago Portage. Before Europeans ever set foot on the North American Continent, Native Americans regularly used The Portage connecting the Atlantic Ocean (via the Great Lakes) with the Gulf of Mexico (via the Illinois and Mississippi Rivers). Father Marquette and Louis Jolliet, guided by Native Americans, passed through the Portage in 1673. The history of Chicago and the Midwest was destined to revolve around events at The Portage. For instance, The Portage was considered a top military priority and was fortified on the Lake Michigan end by Fort Dearborn. It's a shame that the Chicago Portage Park doesn't connect with a Des Plaines River canoe access, but a canoe access is available upstream, off of 47th Street at Stoney Ford Forest Preserve. The Des Plaines River derives its name from the French "eau plien," meaning full of water. To a traveler of The Portage, "full of water" would mean an easy passage between The Des Plaines River and Lake Michigan, and low water could lead to a 9-mile walk.

Across the river from Stoney Ford was the one-time location of Laughton's Trading Post. Established in 1827, it served not only as a trading post but also as a tavern and ferry. The location should have been a good one as it was located at the far end of The Chicago Portage at a ford over the DesPlaines River. However, it has been said in more than one account that the tavern was shabby and unkept, so more than one traveler passed up accommodations at the Laughtons to camp down the road. Such was travel in the early 1800s.

The 8 miles between the Stoney Ford access and the Columbia Woods Forest Preserve means canoeing through one of two major industrial wastelands on the lower Des Plaines River (the other section is below Joliet). On this trip, you'll be treated to examples of transportation in the form of the Interstate 55 on river left side, railroads on the river right side, and the Chicago Sanitary and Ship Canal only yards away. The Chicago Sanitary and Ship Canal is really an extension of the South Branch of the Chicago River, and is the successor of the 1846 Illinois and Michigan Canal, this portion of which was covered over to build Interstate 55. The wildlife through these miles consists mostly of waterfowl, which is also what it smells like. To top it off, the Des Plaines River runs in a manmade channel, making this section the least desirable on the Des Plaines River. Access is just downstream of the Willow Springs Road Bridge on river right at Columbia Woods. All the access points between Stoney Ford and the Lockport Prairie Restoration access are designated canoe access areas and have some form of parking.

Seven miles below Columbia Woods, Blackpartridge Forest Preserve canoe access is located downstream of Lamont Road. In those 7 miles, the scenery improves but little, although below Flagg Creek a short stretch of green enhances the trip. Illinois Route 83—that of the accompanying noise and junkyards—gives a general industrial look to the stream side. Strong south or southwest winds can make any trip on the lower Des Plaines River a real character builder, for there are long open passages to contend with.

The next 10-mile section begins at Lamont Road and ends at the Lockport Prairie Restoration, and is by far the nicest section on the lower Des Plaines River. The riverbanks become more natural. Waterfowl—including ducks, geese, great blue herons, and snowy egrets—are abundant, as are signs of beavers. Five miles below the put-in, the river widens out and islands loom ahead. Stay to the right side, go under the Romeoville Road Bridge, and land at the docked canoe launch, and you have arrived at Isle a La Cache. Follow the sidewalk up to the Museum and enter the era of the French fur trade.

"Isle A La Cache" means Island of the Hiding Place in French, and the Museum is a hidden treasure of artifacts and reproductions of trade goods, beaver pelts, voyagers' personal items, and strip canoes, plus period artwork and a slide presentation.

Below Isle A La Cache, the river braids its way around more islands, creating narrow channels with fast water. Rock outcroppings also appear in this area, and even more frequently downstream. With all these things going on, you might not even notice the Commonwealth Edison coal fired power plant on the river left side of the islands. The next bridge downstream is private and belongs to Material Handling Corporation. A dam existed here at one time, but it was removed in 1992 and no longer presents a hazard.

The Des Plaines River widens out and becomes shallow as the Illinois Route 7 Bridge is passed. For the adventurous, the next mile and a quarter contains fast water with many riffles, and even a rapid. Yes, just above the Division Street Bridge Fishnet Rapids rates a class II+ and is a pretty straightforward series of ledges featuring waves large enough to swamp an open canoe at moderate water levels. Staying to the river left side, the largest of these waves will be avoided, but you can still expect to get some water in the boat. Recover unlucky boaters and their equipment quickly, as the takeout is upstream of the Division Street Bridge. Division Street on the other side of Illinois Route 53 is the location of Joliet State Prison, Statesville. The access here is the Lockport Prairie Restoration Project. Take-outs are scarce and unimproved below Division Street.

Fast water continues downstream of the Division Street bridge. After 1 1/2 miles, the Lockport Locks are visible on the river left side. One mile below the locks, the Des Plaines River merges with The Chicago Sanitary Ship Canal to form The Illinois Waterway. It's still the Des Plaines River, but below here barges and other motorized boat traffic are regularly encountered. Right at the confluence of canal and river, some shoals exist on river left, consisting of narrow chutes that would have been fun to run had they not been blocked by trees and other debris. A triangle-shaped railroad bridge marks the entrance of the Illinois Michigan Canal, whose channel leaves the Des Plaines River below the Brandon Lock and Dam.

Attractive iron bridges and river gambling boats characterize the impression of downtown Joliet that one gets from the river. The retaining wall on the river left side allows the Des Plaines to flow substantially elevated above the surrounding streets, making for an odd view from the river. Interstate 80 crosses the DesPlaines and is the last bridge on the river before Brandon Lock and Dam. The only takeout options that I found above Brandon Dam were where U.S. Route 6 comes alongside the river right side. (NOTE: If you takeout at the restaurant/bar, get permission to park or you may find that your car has been towed.) The other option is to proceed downstream through the locks, which I have never done.

The final section of the DesPlaines River can be accessed at a Joliet Water Treatment plant located on McKinley Street south of U.S. Route 6. This put-in is on Hickory Creek. Another access, albeit without much parking, is on Brandon Road directly off Route 6 south of the dam. If using the Hickory Creek launch, be aware that the main release chute from the Brandon Dam lies remarkably close to the mouth of Hickory Creek. Dangerous crosscurrents, along with whirlpools and backwashes that may be unavoidable at high water, exist at Hickory Creek's mouth. Under these conditions, it would be wise to use the Brandon Road put-in.

The 13 miles between the Brandon Dam and the Dresden Island Lock and Dam start out very industrial and end surprisingly natural. Below either of the put-ins is a Commonwealth Edison coal power plant that occupies both sides of the river. From the power plant on down to Interstate 55, a frequently used railroad right-of-way runs along the river left side, while the river right side features many rock outcroppings. Barges and high winds are more often than not encountered because the Des Plaines River is wide and open. The other pair of Joliet's casino gambling boats moor a couple of miles below the Brandon Lock and Dam. A few miles above the Interstate 55 Bridge, industry rears it ugly head in the form of petroleum tank farms, oil refineries, and all related forms of construction machinery and materials. Just under the I55 Bridge, a large marina and dry dock are a welcome relief from the pure industry that proceeds it.

Joliet Mound was known as such before a town ever existed in the Joliet area. In fact, the town was called Juliet first and then changed to Joliet in 1845. (Romeoville and Juliet get it.) Joliet Mound received its name from the year 1673, when the Jolliet and Marquette expedition made camp at this location. The mound no longer exists; it was dug up for the clay from which it was made—to make clay tiles. A second historical event took place here in 1769: a Native American council meeting with the Ottawa and Potowatomi tribes on one side and the Illinwek on the other side of a hunting rights dispute. The great Ottawa Chief Pontiac rose to speak to the council when the head Chief of the Illinwek, named Kineboo, jumped up, stabbed Pontiac, and then ran away like a coward. This act of treachery brought the wrath of all Midwestern tribes down upon the Illinwek, forcing them to remove themselves from their traditional village near present-day Utica, where Jolliet and Marquette had found them in 1673, to the French settlements in Illinois, around the St. Louis area. From 1769 until 1833 it was the Potowatomi tribe that white civilization would encounter and make treaties with in Northern Illinois.

The Joliet Arsenal located on the river left downstream of the Interstate 55 bridge is the location of three graves that date back as far as 1813. Nothing else is known, but the first recorded settlement in the area was Jesse Walker in 1823. (*See Fox River*) Not much past the Interstate bridge, the Des Plaines River makes an abrupt change in character. As the tank farms and the like fade from river left, a farm is visible just upstream of the mouth of the DuPage River. The Des Plaines is very wide through this area, but stay close to the navigation channel as the river right lake is silted and too shallow in many places to float even a solo canoe.

Continuing downstream of the DuPage River, The Illinois Michigan Canal reappears on river right and follows right alongside the Des Plaines River—at times even forming the river right bank. A shelter with overlook marks your arrival at McKinley Woods Forest Preserve, which has picnic tables and shelters, water bathrooms and camping. Not only is canoe access to the Des Plaines River available here, but there is also access to the Illinois Michigan Canal. It's two more miles before the confluence of the Des Plaines River with the Kankakee River forms the Illinois River, which flows for 272 additional miles to mix its waters with those of the Mississippi. Downstream of the Kankakee lies the Dresden Lock and Dam. A takeout is possible just above the dam by portaging up and onto the Illinois Michigan canal and then downstream on the canal a short distance, to the Dresden access on the canal. By road, this access is located where McClindon and Hansel roads meet.

The Des Plaines River is about as varied as any river in this volume. Its beginnings as a small stream around the Illinois/Wisconsin boarder till its end as major waterway show its extremes. The DesPlaines is for the most part canoeable year round and has sections that are outstanding—along with sections that are the pits.

Illinois Atlas; Pages 20-21 A 4-B 4-C 4-D-4
Pages 29-30 A 5-B, 5-C, 4-C, 3-D-3.
Page 36 A,-2

DuPage River

The DuPage River was named after a French fur trapper by the name of DuPazhe who worked for the American Fur Company. Little is known about him except that for a time he traded around the forks (the East and West Branches) of the DuPage River. The forks of the DuPage River were also the site of the Scott settlement circa 1830 where Bailey Hobson, the first settler of DuPage County, left his family while looking for a mill site upstream on the West Branch.

The closest and best access is one mile upstream of the forks in Naperville at Knoch Knoll Park on the West Branch of the DuPage River. The West Branch gets wider by the time it reaches the confluence with the East Branch and becomes even wider after the merge. On this trip, the river's left side is frequently occupied by quarries, while the river's right side is increasingly occupied by housing subdivisions. This and the low gradient make the 10-mile trip from Knoch Knoll Park to Plainfield one of the more mundane trips on the DuPage River system, but the history is good, as are the put-ins and takeouts.

The Scott Settlement at the Forks of the DuPage River was founded in 1830 by Stephen Scott, and contained just four families. When the Blackhawk War broke out in 1832 the settlers located here fled to the Naper Settlement (as Naperville was then called) and then to Chicago where they stayed for several weeks. When the Scotts returned, they found their possessions taken or destroyed by the Indians, as did Bailey Hobson on his return. Compare this to the settlers on the other side of Will County on Hickory Creek, who returned home to find that their farms had been tended and their livestock fed by the Native Americans.

The DuPage River below the forks is crossed by five roads at roughly one-mile intervals. I have used one of these, 111th Street, several times as an access. Park by the church if it's not Sunday morning. Book Road at one time made a good access, but the road is now blocked off. The last of the five bridges is 135th Street—it's a two-mile paddle between Illinois Route 59 and the town of Plainfield.

Walkers Grove, now Plainfield, was settled in 1826 by the Reverend Jesse Walker, a true pioneer preacher (*see Fox River*), Vetal Vermette, a French Canadian, Thomas Covel (*see Covel Creek*), James Walker (no relation to Jesse) and Reuben Flagg. At the time of the Blackhawk war in 1832, the dozen or so settlers in Walkers Grove thought that they could defend themselves and so built Fort Beggs. The fort would give the impression that it was more than it really was. Fort Beggs is named after another of Plainfield's early Methodist Ministers, Stephen Beggs, who came to help Jesse Walker with his expanding ministry. Beggs had purchased Vetal Vermette's cabin on the DuPage River. The Beggs home was determined to be the most defensible cabin in the vicinity, and by tearing down the out buildings and the pigpen, a low breast works was constructed.

Panic had swept the settlements west of Chicago as news of the Stillman's Creek battle became known. Shabbona and his sons rode over a four-county area warning the families of their danger (*see Indian Creek*) and 125 people had gathered at Fort Beggs. The odd thing is, if we can believe Stephen Beggs' 1861 book, he was a minister. Of all those pioneers gathered at Fort Beggs, only four had working guns with which to defend themselves, nor was there enough food and water to overcome a siege. Those gathered at Fort Beggs were rescued in a few days by the militia from the Naper Settlement and taken to the safety of Chicago. The marker for Fort Beggs is located by the tennis courts of Plainfield High School, near the river.

Just downstream of the Fort Beggs marker is a pull-off on River Road that is the best landing in the Plainfield area; this would make for an 11-mile trip from Knoch Knolls Park. Also, if you are passing through Plainfield, on your shuttle stop by the cemetery you'll find the graves of many of Will County's first settlers.

A 1/4-mile below the River Road landing, Renwick Road crosses the DuPage River on a rustic iron bridge. The next bridge downstream is the second Illinois Route 59 bridge, which can be used as access. In the 1820s, this was the site of a Potawatomi village of about 1,000 people.

The DuPage River continues to run wide and placid below Route 59, with riverside homes becoming a common feature. Below Caton Farm Road, Interstate 55 runs alongside the DuPage River for several miles, but the highway is only visible on one river bend. Black Road, the next bridge, indicates that the first of two access points in the Hammel Woods Forest Preserve has been reached. Water, bathrooms, picnic tables, and camping via prearranged permit are available here, as is a large parking lot—but it is a long carry. The next mile or so contains several islands and is fast and fun when the river is running high.

The second Hammel Woods access is below the islands where a concrete observation deck signals the approach of Hammel Woods Dam. Portage on the right side upstream of the observation deck.

This dam has a nasty hydraulic at high water levels and should be avoided by all. A chute on river left is narrow and not as straightforward as it looks. The main part of the dam still retains its hydraulic along the even face of the dam. If River Road in Plainfield was used as a put-in, the Hammel Woods dam would be an 8-mile trip. If putting in at Hammel Woods dam, one has a 10-mile trip down to the Channahon dam takeout.

The fast water downstream of the Hammel Woods dam carries you past the U.S. Route 52, then the third crossing of Illinois Route 59, and then through two check dams that become scrappy at lower water levels. Dolomite outcropping show themselves at regular intervals as Interstate 80 is approached. A mile below the Interstate, a sharp bend to the left signals the entrance to S Turn Rapid, also called DuPage Rapid. Chicago Whitewater Association uses this section to train boaters who are learning to paddle whitewater. S Turn is a straightforward series of Grade II—sloped ledges that are largest below the railroad bridge. Remember that the string of large waves running down the rapid usually indicates the deep water channel.

A good landing exists for those wishing to run only the whitewater on Canal Road downstream of the Shepley Road bridge. A pull-off provides parking for several cars, and it's only a few yards carry to the water. Look on the river left side across from this landing at the long-ago filled-in feeder canal for the Illinois and Michigan Canal: all that is left are the two stone walls marking the former entrance.

The rapids have settled down to an occasional riffle. The left bank of the DuPage River is a peninsula formed by the river on one side and the Illinois Michigan Canal on the other. The river again runs wide, and housing becomes more common as the town of Channahon is neared. The river slows and soon two bridges come into view. The first of these is U.S. Route 6, the second really is the Channahon Dam; portage to the left on the improved path.

Have a look around Channahon State Park: the dam had to be rebuilt in 1997 after the high water of 1996 damaged the retaining wall and portions of the canal. The lock tender's house is (circa 1998) being repaired and painted. The house and the remains of the canal lock are preserved and are a great place to reminisce about the heyday of the canal. A canal was first contemplated in 1673 by Louis Jolliet, but not completed until 1846 by the State of Illinois. Water, bathrooms, and information all are available here, as well as parking, both at the dam and below the next bridge, which is named Bridge Street.

Channahon is a Potowatomi word meaning "The Meeting of Waters," referring to the Des Plaines, DuPage, and Kankakee all coming together in this area. The final mile is one of the more natural sections on the main trunk of the DuPage River. A good takeout is a 1/4-mile upstream on the Des Plaines River. This access is on Front Street, accessible from Channahon or the south-bound frontage road for Interstate 55.

Illinois Atlas page; 28 C-2; 28 D-2; 36 A-2

Bob Tyler, Aimee Tyler, and Aimee's friend Abby Hall
cruise the DuPage at high water

East Branch of the DuPage River

This is the closest river/creek to my home and yet I have only canoed it twice. Is it because there is a high degree of pollution, is it the frequency of logjams and low bridges, or is it the close proximity of Illinois Route 53 and Interstate 355? The answer is yes. Add to this the fact that a trespassing problem exists. The first time I canoed the East Branch, it was out of curiosity, the second time was for this volume, and I'm not planning any trips on the East Branch of the DuPage soon.

Although it looks like Army Trail Road might be a good put-in, the channel is too small and too blocked to afford passage, so canoeing starts no higher up than North Avenue Illinois Route 64. Even the mile of river between North Avenue and St. Charles is often blocked. The Great Western Trail crosses over the river on an abandoned railroad right-of-way along this stretch. High tension wires are ever present throughout these miles.

St. Charles Road is the northern boundary of Churchhill Forest Preserve and is the start of a very historic mile of canoeing. I grew up across Crescent Boulevard from Churchhill Forest Preserve and played as a child in the swamps, lakes, and wetlands between Perry's Lake, where a mastodon was found, and the East Branch of the DuPage River. A river rat since my early youth.

The dam at Crescent Boulevard presents a problem, as running the dam isn't an option and the portage over the road is dangerous. Besides this, the lake that the dam created is silted and shallow. If it were not for the dam, Churchill Forest preserve would make a very good put-in. The mile below Crescent Boulevard skirts Glen Oak Country Club, the old Lombard Waste Water Treatment Plant, high tension wires, levies, and residential back yards—all blessings to the eye! Also in this mile, The Illinois Prairie Path crosses over the East Branch.

The East Branch is noticeably channelized for several miles below Illinois Route 53 and is rather uninteresting until below Butterfield Road, where riffles appear and the river returns to Du Page County Forest Preserve, which improves the situation somewhat. I should mention a possible hazard a short distance below Illinois Route 38, Roosevelt Road: Someone has constructed a pair of rock cribs that constrict the river. Not much wider than a canoe, they increase the speed of the water, along with the chance of a problem.

Below Butterfield Road, the East Branch enters first the Hidden Lakes Forest Preserve and then The Morton Arboretum. The Morton Arboretum was formerly the Morton family estate and was donated to the public by Joy Morton, the son of J. Sterling Morton. J. Sterling Morton was the founder of Arbor Day and their estate was also the site of the second Potawatomi Village on the East Branch of the DuPage. Yes, Joy Morton was the founder of the "when it rains it pours" Morton Salt. There are several small check dams to be contended with while passing through Morton Arboretum, the largest of which is located under one of the Park Road bridges. Remember I mentioned trespassing was a problem on this river? Well, Morton Arboretum is where several boaters have had a problem.

After leaving the Arboretum, Warrenville Road crosses the East Branch, as does Interstate 88. Several of the miles below here are monotonously channelized. Below Maple Avenue, The East Branch of the DuPage enters The Four Lakes Apartment complex and ski resort. The stream still remains channelized and levied, then opens up first as a golf course, followed by the Greene Valley Forest Preserve below Hobson Road. If North Avenue were used as a put-in, then taking-out at Hobson Road would make for a 12-mile trip.

Continuing downstream from Hobson Road, Illinois Route 53 is close enough so you'll never get the impression that you are in the wild. Large, hard to portage logjams tend to form along this stretch. Seventy-fifth Street, Royce Road, and the Will County Line are all crossed before the East Branch turns to the west for its final miles. Another warning: the East Branch becomes continually more log-jammed in its final few miles (this seems to happen on many small streams).

Below Royce Road, residential neighborhoods intrude on river left, while river right begins to show signs of the large quarry downstream. After a few miles, the East Branch begins to meander. The East Branch flows through manmade channels most of the time. One of these meanders will bring you to the DuPage River Park where there are toilets, water, and parking.

Small planes are numerous, as three landing strips are neighbors to the East Branch for the final few miles. Naperville Road is crossed. Go two more miles to the confluence with the West Branch of the DuPage that forms the Main DuPage River, and then two more until a takeout at the junction of Plainfield Road and Broughton appears.

In conclusion, this is a very hard paddle with no redeeming characteristics. The West Branch is nicer.

Illinois Atlas; Page 28; B-3.

West Branch of the DuPage River

The West Branch of the DuPage River (hereinafter referred to as the West Branch) looks canoeable above St. Charles Road, but these miles are tough due to frequent logjams and steep dirt banks. (If you like these couple of miles, you'll love the East Branch.) A more practical put-in would be St. Charles Road, which is 50 yards upstream of North Avenue, Illinois Route 64. It's a ten-mile trip from this point to Butterfield Road, Illinois Route 56.

The Baker Homestead circa 1843, located west on St. Charles Road, was one of DuPage County's first brick homes. Peter Baker did stone work for the Illinois Michigan Canal in the 1830s when the canal went temporarily bankrupt around 1840 and Baker moved from Will to DuPage County. Peter Baker located his house on the main road from Chicago to St. Charles. It served as a model home that demonstrated the quality of his masonry talents.

Downstream of North Avenue, the West Branch runs fairly fast and narrow, passing through prairie, wetlands, and light forest. Soon the Illinois Prairie Path crosses the river. The Prairie Path runs along the abandoned right-of-way of the bankrupt Aurora & Elgin electric railroad. It offered passenger and freight service between Chicago and several points in the Fox River Valley. The railroad brought with it the very first electricity to pass through most of the villages it serviced. Another branch of the Prairie Path/Aurora & Elgin crosses the West Branch nine miles downstream.

One of the nice things about these early miles is the amount of time that the West Branch spends passing through DuPage County Forest Preserves. In the 12 miles between Army Trail Road and Butterfield Road, you'll pass through the following Forest Preserves: West Branch, Timber Ridge, Kline Creek, Winfield Mounds, West DuPage, and Blackwell. Although these don't add to the accessibility of the West Branch, they do add to the scenery and wildlife. These county Forest Preserves form an almost continuous corridor that helps make up for the poor water quality.

Below Roosevelt Road, Gary's Mill is passed. The mill dates back to 1837 and was started by Erastus, Jude, and their sister Orinda. It was operated as a saw mill and had cut the boards for many of DuPage County's early homes.

Continuing downstream past Gary's Mill, Blackwell Forest Preserve is entered. Blackwell has a canoe launch at Mack Road that makes good access, or you can continue two miles more to Butterfield Road.

Beware of the 4-1/2 miles below Butterfield Road, as they contain three dams. The first two are run or portage affairs, depending on the skills of the boater and the water levels. Remember: every year boaters die trying to run small dams, so if you are not sure about hydraulics, *portage either dam on the river left side*. The first of the two former mill-dams is Warrenville dam, which was constructed in 1835 by Julius Warren (son of Daniel Warren, founder of the town of Warrenville) a year after he settled in the area. An inn or tavern (as they were then called) was built to accommodate patrons of the mill who needed to stay overnight. Colonel Warren's tavern had a ballroom on the second floor that was frequented by the early citizens of Chicago.

The McDowell dam downstream is only half as high as the Warrenville dam. The last of the three dams in this section is Fawell dam, the most formidable and unusual. The first problem you face as you approach Fawell dam is to decide whether or not to run one of the three tunnels, which at most levels is easier than it looks. However, at high water levels a fair-sized wave/hole develops at the out wash of the tunnels, making a clean run harder. The portage on river left is hard due to the fact that the dam burm is high and wide. The portage trail is recognizable (though long) and may also be used to scout the dam's out wash.

Continuing downstream from Fawell dam, the town of Naperville is visually entered as Ogden Avenue breaks the forest preserve corridor that the river has traveled in for so many miles. The Burlington Northern Railroad crosses over the river on an attractive stone bridge. Houses appear more frequently and nearer to the river. As downtown Naperville is approached, you'll see The Riverwalk—a well used downtown park and trail that follows the West Branch's left side. A small grade I/II rapid is formed below the first footbridge on the Riverwalk.

The Naper Settlement is a living history park and museum that is one block south of any of the Riverwalk bridges. The settlement of Naperville began with the arrival of Bailey Hobson in 1830. Bailey Hobson ascended the West Branch in search of a mill site where he planned to settle. He was followed the next year by Captain Joseph, a ship captain, and his brother John. Naper built a dam that powered both a saw and a grist mill. Both Naper and Hobson built cabins and brought their families to live there. Several other families joined the settlement prior to the outbreak of the Blackhawk War in 1832.

When the Blackhawk War started, the 30 or so families in the area moved to the safety of Fort Dearborn. Fifteen or twenty of the men under Captain Naper stayed to protect the property of the settlement. Christopher Paine, his wife, and their six children were somehow left behind. Naper and the militia escorted the Paines to Fort Dearborn, then proceeded to Plainfield and escorted settlers there at Fort Beggs back to Chicago. They then returned to the Naper Settlement and, with the help of Captain Payne and 40 additional militia, erected Fort Payne. During the construction, a volunteer from Danville by the name of James Brown was ambushed and killed by Indians. Brown was the only casualty of the Blackhawk War in DuPage County. With the added security of the fort, the settlers returned and so ended the Blackhawk War in DuPage County.

As you canoe by the football field at North Central College, look up to the top of the hill at the former site of Fort Payne.

After leaving the business district, the Hillside Road bridge is crossed—and if you look back upstream at the bridge piling, you'll see the only water gauge for canoeists on the West Branch. (0 is no longer canoeable and more than 2 feet is downright fun.)

This section of the West Branch runs fast and has frequent riffles. Homes occupy one side or the other of the river much of the time. A footbridge signals the approach to Pioneer Park, which can be used as a landing. Pioneer Park was the site of Bailey Hobson's mill. The next road that the West Branch crosses is Hobson. A large apartment complex is passed below 75th Street, and another short stretch of riffles below an island

The next two parks, Weigand Riverfront and Knoch Knoll, are both excellent landings with level gravel ramps. Two miles below Knoch Knolls, the East and West Branches merge to form the Main DuPage River.

I find all the miles of the West Branch pleasant to paddle and I easily overlook the pollution and the occasional urban intrusion.

Illinois Atlas; Page 28; B-2

Original millstones purchased
from John Kinsie for
Bailey Hobson's mill
on the West Branch.

River walk in downtown
Naperville; a delightful
run on the West Branch.

Elkhorn Creek

Elkhorn Creek's headwaters are very near those of the Leaf River; both run into the Rock River, their mouths separated by fifty miles. Elkhorn Creek, like the Leaf, has steep dirt banks for most of its length and has a longer watershed; in all but the driest times, Elkhorn Creek has enough water for paddling the bottom miles. Even after weeks without rain, this upper section still has more than enough water to paddle, along with short runs of swift water with frequent riffles.

The U.S. Route 52 bridge can be seen from the put-in, less than a mile downstream. Route 52 follows the 1831 Chambers Trail; the section where the trail crosses Elkhorn Creek was called Chambers Grove. Isaac Chambers was one of four men who controlled the early trails leading to the lead mining district centered around Galena. The other three were John Dixon, Oliver Kellogg, and Thomas Crane. Each of these men had a trail named after him except Dixon, whose namesake is Dixon Ferry, and all had a tavern/trading post along the trails prior to the Black Hawk War of 1832. It's not too surprising that all were also captains of militia during this war, for they were interested in protecting their investments.

I put-in a mile west of Brookville on the Ogle/Carroll County line at the Illinois Route 64 bridge. Elkhorn Creek is canoeable this far upstream; however, one runs the risk of more frequent logjams here than one does farther downstream. Logjams occur mainly when Elkhorn Creek heads into forested groves that pad portions of the creek. Many turns along these upper miles are so tight that they stop forward momentum when they are negotiated. Several farm roads cross over the creek and steep dirt banks line the creek sides all the way to the mouth on the Rock River.

Five miles below the put-in is the site of the first settlement in this section of Carroll County, the town of Elkhorn Grove. When most of the trees had been cut from this thickly forested area and the railroad passed to the south, the population in this small town decreased. As Elkhorn Grove declined, the town of Milledgeville, downstream, prospered. Milledgeville, as its name suggests, was one of the mill sites on the upper portions of Elkhorn Creek. Elkhorn was, in the days of water-powered mills, very much a working creek. The even but steady drop of the creek as it heads for the Rock River, along with its high banks, proved ideal for the construction of mill-dams. Other mills on Elkhorn Creek were the 1840 Isaac Chambers Mill located near the Brookville put-in and the 1837 Elijah Eaton Mill located at Hitt; later in the 1840's, this saw mill cut the beams that were used by the Grand Detour Plow Company. Further downstream once stood the 1866 Elkhorn Grove Mill at Elkhorn Grove, the aforementioned 1834 Knox Mill at Milledgeville, along with the 1837 Brinks Mill at Empire, the 1843 Harvey Mill, and the 1846 Smith and Weber Mill at Como—the last three were located in Whiteside County.

A good alternate put-in can be found in the very small burg of Hitt along Telegraph Road posted locally as Eagle Point Road. Duck Road, two miles downstream from Hitt, doesn't provide good access, but it does pretty much mark the end of the logjams. Milledgeville, two miles further downstream, is skirted but not seen, except for an old suspension footbridge, a sewage treatment plant, and the Burlington Northern railroad bridge that can be used for a takeout/ put-in. A very small check dam crosses Elkhorn Creek under the Burlington railroad bridge and a dirt access road leads to the bridge from Milledgeville Road.

Below Milledgeville, Elkhorn Creek runs through pasture and crop lands in steep black dirt banks that only occasionally level out to reveal the surrounding countryside. Elkhorn turns to the west two miles below Milledgeville, making this a good section to do on a day when the wind is blowing out of the west. By the way, the roads that cross Elkhorn Creek downstream of Milledgeville deserve mention because of their rather odd names. The first is Lovers Lane, which is fenced off and very much a part of the adjacent farm; the second is Sunshine Road; followed by Goose Road, which divides the upper portion of Elkhorn Creek from the lower. Taking out at Goose Road would mean a ten-mile trip from Hitt; putting in here would mean a twelve-mile trip down to Science Ridge Road.

About a mile below the Goose Road bridge, Elkhorn Creek runs up against a ridge which changes the water flow to a southerly direction. Through the years, Elkhorn Creek has cut into this ridge, exposing several miles of lovely moss-covered rock bluffs. By the time Pilgrim Road is reached, the bluffs are on both sides of the creek; however, this area is marred by an active quarry on creek right. The bluffs become smaller and end above Pemrose Road. Both Pemrose and Pilgrim Roads are fenced, so permission should be sought before using them as access. Elkhorn Creek continues much as above with few houses or farms seen from creek level; instead, groves of timber are more frequent and more plentiful. At this point, Elkhorn has grown to sufficient width to resist log jams. Illinois 40 is the last road crossed before the takeout at Science Ridge Road. Both of these roads are fairly busy and have parking along their narrow shoulders.

The final nine miles begins at Science Ridge Road and ends at the Rock River. This section is amazingly natural considering the close proximity of the towns of Sterling and Como. Elkhorn Creek runs through a deeply wooded corridor that is often nearly a hundred feet thick on either side of the creek. The thick forest causes a large amount of deadfall, but only once did this necessitate portaging. Several sizable creeks enter from both sides, adding their waters to those of Elkhorn. Steep banks restrict views into the woods, creating the feeling that just a small portion of the animals in the area can be observed. The only signs of humanity along these bottom miles consist of two homes and a quarry that is seen for only a short distance, but can be heard for several miles when it is operating. One small check dam, located directly above the Galt Road Bridge, is runnable through a center chute.

As one leaves this lush section of forest, an ornate iron railroad bridge and the Harvey Road bridges (Harvey Road is named after Joel Harvey who owned a saw, woolen, and grist mill along the creek) stand side-by-side and mark the start of noticeably faster water. Elkhorn Creek's dirt banks become mixed with gravel and sand. Rocks in the creek bed create frequent and often long riffled sections. Eventually, as U.S. Route 30 is neared, the camp sites of the Ruffit Campground are seen along the left bank.

Elkhorn Creek nears the town of Como below Route 30. This area was once the haunt of a large Mississippian cultural population; some of the many mounds in this vicinity were investigated in the 1800s in a somewhat "scientific" manner. Most of the early settlers found the mounds to be an impediment to farming and so just plowed them under, keeping the souvenirs that the plow would turn over each spring. Evidence exists that Native Americans inhabited this area 5,000 years ago. It's a shame that so many of these prehistoric sites were destroyed without any record having been kept of even their locations.

A mile below the Route 30 Bridge, three more bridges are encountered, all of which are connected to Interstate 88. The Rock River lies directly below the interstate. The last two miles on the Rock display a more natural setting with no housing visible until just above the takeout at a roadside park along Monoline Road.

Elkhorn Creek was an unexpected find that came from exploring the Rock River, and what a find it turned out to be. Its "small creek" habitat, along with its longer-than-average runnable season, makes Elkhorn Creek a watershed that I will visit annually.

Illinois Atlas; Page 16-17; D-4, 24-25; A-4; B-4

Ferson Creek

Ferson Creek is a delightful small urban stream that empties into the Fox River a short distance upstream of downtown St. Charles, Illinois. It is named for the Ferson brothers who moved to Chicago from Vermont.

After arriving in Chicago in 1833, the brothers became involved in the land speculation craze that was going on at that time. They purchased land at what is now Clark and Lake Streets in the heart of the Chicago Loop. Dean and Read Ferson profited substantially in just a few short months.

Read returned to Vermont along with the Minard brothers, with whom they had shared the real estate venture. Dean taught school in Ottawa, Illinois, and explored along the banks of the Fox River. In May 1834, Read returned to Chicago from Vermont and the brothers were together again.

Dean encouraged Read to go west to the Fox River with him and further explore the valley. They crossed to the west side of the Fox at the head of the Big Woods, present day Batavia. From here they headed north until they came to an Indian encampment. The Indians were camped next to the small stream that later would bear the Ferson name. They described the stream they settled on as "clear, winding, and bordered by a thick growth of blue beech."

The canoeing begins at Bolcum Road. Ferson's headwaters are drained from Lake Campton, an impoundment of the stream, via a dam just west of Burlington Road. A quick look at Burlington Road convinced me that even in high water it wouldn't be feasible to put in this far up. By the time the creek gets to Bolcum Road, the waters of Otter, Stoney, Bowes, and Fitchie Creeks have all contributed to the flow.

On two occasions, I tried to put-in higher upstream. The first time, I came down Otter Creek using Silver Glen Road as access. This was log-jammed with more than ten downed trees to the mile. The same thing happened when I tried to put in at Burr Road on Ferson Creek itself. Although shorter than the trip down Otter Creek, Ferson is very difficult this high up. These creeks all have short water sheds, so you'll have to catch them immediately after a heavy rain.

However, Bolcum Road has much better access, and with the added water of the additional creeks, there is at least four times the volume of water than at Burlington Road. Ferson Creek opens up considerably after Bolcum Road as you enter the Burr Hill Country Club Golf Course. The golf course borders the stream for quite a ways downstream. Nature returns to adorn the banks below the golf course, alternating between light flood, plain forest, and wetlands.

It is four miles between Bolcum and Randall Roads, but within those four miles, nine dams must be negotiated. Most are one-to two-feet-high check dams. But the one close to Randall Road has a much greater drop of four or five feet. Keep your eyes peeled for the horizon line of the dam as you enter an area of large homes with large backyards. It should be easily visible as you approach it.

A short distance downstream is a riffle. A 90-degree turn signals the approach of the four-lane Randall Road bridge. Expect to see more houses along this part of Ferson Creek after passing Randall Road. The flood plain that you'll be passing through was once devoid of housing but is rapidly developing. In fact, it seems that every year the housing doubles along the creek. The houses are large, expensive, and generally set well back from the stream banks. Be warned that there were dozens of new homes going up in 1996. The closer you get to the Fox River, the more homes you'll see.

The Ferson brothers would be proud of the "land speculation" going on in their name. For the most part, the speculation is close to their 1834 claim near the mouth of Ferson Creek. Less than 100 yards downstream of the Randall Road bridge is a small check dam, two to three feet high, followed by another check dam that is one to two feet high. The first formed a hole worthy of Class II whitewater. The second is still pretty rocky at high water.

The last two miles below Randall Road is fairly swift, with many strainers and a number of logjams. The two-plus miles from Randall Road to Illinois Route 31 pass quickly. After Route 31 it's a very short distance to the Fox River.

The takeout possibilities are numerous; here are a few. First, Ferson Creek Nature Preserve is located next to the creek below Illinois Route 31, with roads that come very close to the water on both Ferson Creek and the Fox River. There are also two more parks downstream on the Fox. Potawatomi Park on river left and Boy Scout Island Landing on river right. Closer to the St. Charles dam is a free city parking lot on river right. If you choose this last landing, beware: the St. Charles dam is directly downstream of the parking lot. *This dam has taken more than one life.*

This is a short seven-mile run that is good high water fun. Many local paddlers asked me to include this in the guidebook, as it is a favorite. Although none of the Ferson Creek enthusiasts that I talked to had launched above Randall Road, I found the upper four miles most enjoyable.

Illinois Atlas: Page 28 A-1

Ferson Creek is a delightful small urban stream that empties into the Fox River a short distance upstream of downtown St. Charles, Illinois.

Occasionally, you will see Jim Hart running creeks with Bob.

Fox River

When settlers first came to the Fox River Valley, it was separate and far away from the city of Chicago. As the year 2000 approaches, Chicago and its suburbs now reach out to include parts of the Fox Valley. The Fox River has its origins north and west of the city of Milwaukee where it is one of two Fox Rivers in the State of Wisconsin. The Fox River in Wisconsin is covered for the most part in *Best Canoe Trails of Southern Wisconsin* by Michael E Duncanson. If you wish to cross the state line, put-in at Wilmot Dam in Wisconsin for a 6-mile trip to the Maple Grove boat launch in the Chain O' Lakes State Park.

The Fox River flows for 116 miles in Illinois from the Wisconsin state line to the Fox's junction with the Illinois River at Ottawa, Illinois. The most northern put-in in Illinois is just downstream of the Illinois Route 173 bridge where Chain O' Lakes State Park operates the Oak Point boat ramp. These first few miles (thanks to the State Park) are the only truly natural riverfront that will be seen for many, many miles. Chain O' Lakes State Park operates a second boat ramp 3 miles downstream at Maple Grove in the main portion of the State Park. The boat ramps at Chain O' Lakes State Park are the only free public access sites on the Fox Chain O' Lakes. The Chain of Lakes Fox River Waterway Management Agency regulates boats on the lakes with a user fee. Canoes that are 16 feet or less are (as of 1999) exempt from these fees.

The miles within the State Park are marshy and reed-lined with many cattails. This continues as the Fox River empties out into Grass Lake, one of the 9 lakes that make up the Fox Chain O' Lakes. Grass Lake is the most natural of the lakes that the Fox River passes through and is shallow, with an average depth of less than four feet. Coming out onto the lake, head south toward the Grass Lake Road Bridge, which is visible from the mouth of the Fox River. An Indian fortification that enclosed several acres was once located on the peninsula where Grass Lake Road approaches the bridge. Once out on the Chain O' Lakes, stay to the right without veering into the bays. After you pass the Grass Lake Road Bridge, staying to the right will bring you into Nippersink Lake. Nippersink Lake is really a bay in Fox Lake and the two lakes are often considered one. Again, stay to the right and aim for the U.S. Route 12 Bridge. Below the bridge, Pistakee Lake is entered.

Nippersink Creek* enters on the right side below the Route 12 Bridge. Stay to the right side of Pistakee Lake—the largest of the lakes that the Fox River courses through. Head your canoe for a point on the right side of the lake to find where the Fox River exits The Chain O' Lakes. The Fox Lakes have the highest boating accident rate in the State of Illinois due to over-congestion and the ease of buying alcohol lakeside or riverside. These factors make for dangerous canoeing, particularly during warm summer weekends. Off-season weekdays are quiet. On one December weekday, there wasn't one boat visible in the 16 miles between the Chain of Lakes State Park and the McHenry Dam. Besides contending with motorboats and jet skies, wind can be a factor in crossing the wide-open lakes. The aforementioned bridges are constrictions of the channel and are high traffic congestion points. Cottages are never out of sight through the lakes, and this continues as the Fox River exits the Chain of Lakes along the southwest end of Pistakee Lake. The town of Johnsburg is marked by a bridge crossing over the Fox that does not provide access.

Access can be achieved 3 miles downstream of Johnsburg, at Weber's Park in the town of McHenry. There is a unique Indian Ford across the Fox River in McHenry. Its uniqueness is owed to the fact that it was paved with large flat rocks that seemed to have been quarried (according to one of the early county histories). It is also said that white settlers took and used these paving stones for doorstops and fireplace bases. What I can't figure out is why the Native Americans needed a flat stone bottom when they didn't use wheels in their transportation.

Two bridges cross the Fox River in McHenry, but neither has free access. There are many fee for access launching sites between the state line and Algonquin, but I managed my way down the river without using them. Most are shown in the *DeLorme Atlas*.

The only change of scenery as the towns along the upper Fox are entered is that marinas along with bars and restaurants replace the riverside housing—if only temporarily. McHenry Lock and Dam is located in Moraine Hills State Park, 3 miles below the town of McHenry. The parking lot in the park extends both above and below the dam on the east side of the river, making this an excellent access. The Lock and Dam was the location of one of several Potawatomi villages that were to be found along the Fox River.

Putting in below McHenry Lock and Dam, the Fox River is much like the miles above. The river is lined with the docks and piers that accommodate the thousands of boats and jet skies that inhabit the Fox all the way down to the town of Algonquin, 17 miles downstream. The Fox River has three distinct sections, each with its own history, character, and function. This upper section is mainly recreational. In this case, "recreational" means motorized and unnatural. Nonetheless, thousands of boats can be found between the state line and Algonquin on each summer weekend. Alas, having a quiet river all to oneself isn't for everyone.

An alternate landing 6 miles downstream of the McHenry Lock and Dam is Hickory Grove Park, which is maintained by the McHenry County Conservation District. The park has a parking lot and bathrooms, and access is through a side channel on river right that leads to a small pond. Fox River Grove, the next town downstream, has a series of parks on river left above and below U.S. Route 14 that would make great access if they were not signed "No River Access Bank Restoration." The miles down to Algonquin are much the same as those above, with a lot of motorized traffic and riverbanks that are lined with cottages and piers. In the summer, the Fox River turns green—not with envy but with algae. Fertilizer nitrates have worked, along with impoundment, to produce an unusual amount of algae growth in the summer months. This is true of the Fox River throughout its miles in Illinois.

The best takeout above the Algonquin Dam is on the west bank of the Fox River, a couple of hundred yards above the Dam/ Illinois Route 62 Bridge. This access is really just a riverside parking lot, but most of the riverfront is private property. Without this access, one would be forced to pay a fee to use one of the private marinas. Algonquin marks the end of the upper recreational section and the beginning of the middle industrial section. Algonquin Dam is the first of 13 unlucky dams that block the Fox in the 46 miles between Algonquin and Yorkville. Most of these (11) are located in Kane County. These dams on the Fox River *regularly* take the lives of those who don't know of or believe in the dangers existing in the hydraulics that are created below the dams! Algonquin Dam can be portaged with some difficulty on river left if you're not taking out at River Front Park.

Less than a mile below Algonquin Dam, on river right, is Buffalo Park, a campground with free canoe access. The Fox River is noticeably different as it leaves Algonquin. For one thing, the motorboat traffic is drastically reduced, and shoals (particularly below the dams) create fast water. The Cottages thin out and a natural pad is created by the natural flood plain, along with many Kane County parks, including The Fox River Trail, a 41-mile hiking and biking trail that runs on one side (or at times, both sides) of the river.

Carpentersville Dam, the first of the Kane County dams, is located 5 miles below Buffalo Park. When I started canoeing in 1984 access at the dam was marked "no trespassing" and "no parking," but have times changed. Nowadays, the dam is not only a park with a large parking area, but it features signs that interpret the history of the site, along with a gazebo that overlooks the dam. The dam at Carpentersville supplied water to several different mills, each having its own race, or water supply. The dam is most easily portaged on the right, near the gazebo.

The towns of Carpentersville, East Dundee, and West Dundee run together as viewed from the river. East and West Dundee are divided by the Fox River. Some of the old industrial buildings along the river between the Dundees have been attractively restored for new functions. West Dundee was home to Allen Pinkerton, one of the first detectives in America. Pinkerton was a cooper and came to Dundee to engage in the business of making barrels for the areas mills. In 1853 Pinkerton caught a counterfeiter. This led to his finding the printing press used to print the bogus money. The printing press was located on what came to been known as Bogus Island. The island was covered over by the backwater of the Carpentersville Dam. Pinkerton went on to greater fame as the first head of the U.S. Secret Service, acted as chief of intelligence for the Army of the Potomac during the Civil War, and organized groups of men known as Pinkerton Men who he would hire out to anyone willing to pay. It was

Pinkerton Men who where hired to break early attempts to unionize. It was also Pinkerton Men who captured several of the Western train robbing gangs of the late 1800s.

Approximately 3 miles downstream of the Carpentersville Dam, on river right and within sight of the Interstate 90 Toll road, is Voyager Landing, a Kane County Park with a boat ramp. An offshoot of the Fox River Trail crosses the Fox on a footbridge under the toll road. After the toll road bridge, Tyler Creek* enters on river right after passing through Judson College. The Elgin Dam 3 miles further downstream is best portaged along the left bank. A 10-mile trip between the Algonquin and Elgin dams is a pleasant journey and is typical of the miles the Fox travels in Kane County. Elgin Dam can also be used as access via The Gail Borden Library parking lot adjacent to the Elgin Dam.

The next 10-mile section begins at the Elgin Dam and ends at one of the many takeout options above the St. Charles Dam. There are two islands below the Elgin Dam; both are city parks. A short distance downstream, one of Illinois riverboat gambling operations takes up more than half of the Fox's riverbed. It's hard to believe that the Fox River, which in the summer can barely float a canoe, can float ships the size of these casinos. Popular Creek* Enters on river left 2 miles downstream of the Elgin Dam. Two miles below the mouth of Poplar Creek, the South Elgin Dam requires portaging, which is best done through Panton Mill Park on river right. Panton Mill Park has parking and can be used as access.

Two interesting side trips lay in the next mile. The first is the Fox River Trolley Museum, on the west bank and up the hill. The museum deserves a look around, if you can catch it when it's open. The second is Blackhawk Forest Preserve, where General Winfield Scott's army camped during his pursuit of Blackhawk in August of 1832. Two unknown soldiers of that army were buried here and the park has a monument to these two Black War veterans.

These miles on the Fox River flow steadily through the mid-sized towns that line the Valley, but the scene remains natural when viewed from the river. Downtowns are the exception, with roads crossing at frequent intervals and the backsides of many of downtown businesses visible, along with concrete walls that retain the river. But the common occurrence of spring flooding has kept buildings at a distance outside of the downtowns. This—along with the Fox River Bike Trail and other interconnecting parks—has created a green way through which the Fox River flows. Because of the towns, road crossings, dams, bike trail, and parks, you'll not have the river to yourself. I can't remember a trip down the Fox in Kane County, even in rainstorms, when I didn't meet people walking, biking, and fishing.

Plenty of tightly packed takeout options are available above the St. Charles Dam. The first two are located off of Illinois Route 31. Ferson Creek Park is the first and the best, with the shortest carry and the least congestion. Boy Scout Island is the next choice (although very crowded on weekends) with powerboat and jet-ski launchings from the boat ramp. The next access, and the closest to the dam, is Pottowatomie Park on river left. This is the most extensive of the three parks above the dam. Pottowatomie has softball, golf, and tennis facilities, along with a refreshment stand and paddlewheel boat rides around the dam backwater. Of course, parking and bathrooms are also located here, but it is a longer carry to the river. There are parking lots on either side of the river above the dam; these can also be used if spaces are available. The portage of the dam at St. Charles is fairly easy on river left by taking-out downstream of the statue of Ekwabet (Potawatomi for "Looking Over")—dedicated to the Potowatomi Indians who inhabited the Fox River Valley at the time when the first white pioneers came to settle. Complete the portage by taking the narrow stairs just below the dam back down to the River.

The towns of the Fox River Valley grew up at the mill locations along the Fox River. The early communities along the Fox River were first settled within a few years of each other. 1833 finds Dean and Read Ferson moving in upstream of St. Charles at the mouth of Ferson Creek, along with Chris Columbus Paine (got to love that name) at Geneva and Earl Adams at Yorkville. In 1834, Sam Gillilan arrives at Algonquin, Angelo Carpenter settles Carpentersville, Batavia is inhabited by Col. Nathan Lyon, and Capt. C.B. Dotson, along with the brothers Sam and Joe McCarty, move into Aurora, In 1835, George Tyler and James Gifford build cabins at Elgin and an inter-married family of Gilbert's and Collin's settles at South Elgin. Circa 1835-1836, the valley fills out with too many settlers to mention. The Fox Valley grew on the industries powered by the Fox River, which was by far the hardest working river in Illinois. While Chicago grew up as a shipping center having no water power available. By the late 1800s, steam power had more than leveled the playing field and the industrial base of the Fox Valley slowly declined while that of Chicago grew.

The next access below the St. Charles Dam is at Mount Saint Mary Park, but the carry is long. The Old Piano Factory located on the Fox, between Illinois and Prairie Streets, has parking for customers only, but it's a lot closer to the river. The two miles between St. Charles and Geneva are lined with houses and apartments. This, along with the close proximity of roads, makes these miles pretty urban. Riverside Park is on river left, halfway between St.Charles and Geneva; this can be used as an alternate landing. Islands that have been increasing in number since Algonquin become a regular feature from Geneva to the mouth of the Fox River in Ottawa.

The Geneva dam is easy to portage on river left. There is a display regarding the Bennett Mill, which operated at this location for more than a hundred years. Their best known product was a self-rising pancake flour. Just under the Illinois Route 38 bridge is the Mill Race Inn. This building was the first blacksmith shop in Geneva. Mill Race Inn, like other restaurants located along the River, can make for some interesting lunch or dinner stops. Mill Race Inn is particularly convenient because it's located near the portage. Prairie State Canoe Club had a full moon dinner cruise along this section of the Fox River.

The next few miles are novel even for the already unique Fox River. Parks and gardens, along with the bike path now on both sides of the Fox, make this area quite congested. Fabyan Forest Preserve (formerly the Fabian Family Estate) contributes much of this distinctive character. The park has a functioning 100-year-old, 68-foot-tall windmill, a Japanese Ceremonial Garden, a museum, and all the other amenities that you would expect of a well appointed park—including canoe access.

One mile down river of Fabyan Forest Preserve, dolomite rock outcroppings on river left signal the approach of the Upper Batavia Dam, which can be portaged on the river right side of the dam, on what appears to be an island. The far right-hand channel is an old millrace and is a dead end. If you're taking-out here or want to visit the Batavia Historical Societies Depot Museum, follow the right channel. The left side of the Batavia Dam is run by the very best paddlers and rates a Class 4+ rapid at runnable levels and a Class 6 (death or injury probable) when higher. The dam is only runnable with a few inches of water flowing over the dam face. The Batavia Dam can be portaged on the river right side where another whitewater channel opens up at flood stage.

A good put-in is located just downstream of the Batavia Dam, near the Batavia Police Station. Downstream, Island Park consists of three islands connected by footbridges, a short distance below the Upper Dam. A second dam in Batavia is less than a mile downstream from Island Park. Like its upstream partner, it is runnable at certain levels by those with the appropriate skills who have thoroughly scouted routes. An island forms the center of the dam and is the easiest place to portage. The lower Batavia Dam has a sloping face and a drop of about 3 feet. Below the Lower Batavia Dam, islands become thick from here on into Aurora.

Batavia was the location of another of the Potawatomi villages. Located along the west bank of the Fox River was the village of Waubonsie. Waubonsie, a Potowatomi Chief over 6 feet tall, along with Shabbona (*Indian Creek*) and Sauganash (*Chicago River*), was instrumental in preventing both the Winnebago War in 1828 and warning settlers in time for them to save themselves in the 1832 Blackhawk War. Waubonsie's village was located on the Fox River across from what was then known as the Big Woods. The Big Woods extended several miles from the river and was a well-known landmark on the Fox.

The return of Dolomite rock walls (one with a pointed wooden overlook built on it) marks the location of the Red Oak Nature Center, which features trails and an interpretive center newly remodeled in 1999. Cave of the Evil Spirit, also known as the Devil's Cave, is also located downstream in the Red Oak Nature Center. The cave has an Indian legend associated with it that was most likely embellished or invented by the early pioneers. The legend concerns a young brave who was banished from Waubonsie's Village for harassing the Anglo settlers with whom the Chief was trying to stay on good terms.

A considerable time afterward, members of Waubonsie's Village were occasionally found murdered under mysterious circumstances. The superstitious thought that the crimes were committed by the devil or ghosts. After one of the killings, footprints were found and traced to the mouth of this cave. The culprit was smoked out and held to account for his devilish crimes.

Downstream a mile below the cave, the North Aurora Dam can be portaged on either side of the river, but I prefer the river left side since it's through a park. Illinois Route 56 Butterfield Road passes over the Fox below the dam. The last 3 miles continue through wooded banks backed by the remnants of the industrial Fox River Valley. Islands are nearly continuous and the Interstate 88 toll road crosses on a high bridge, as does Indian Trail Road, before an excellent takeout at Illinois Avenue Park. The park (if you can believe it) is located on an island that is split by

Illinois Avenue. Parking and boat ramps are available both up and downstream of the Illinois Avenue Bridge. Illinois Avenue Park would end a 10-mile trip from St. Charles.

Putting-in at Illinois Avenue Park and taking-out at the Yorkville Dam means a trip of 13 miles, but several alternate access points are available. Warning: when putting-in at Illinois Avenue, only the farthest right (or westernmost) channel allows for canoe passage. The channels on either side of Stolp Island lead to dangerous dams located on the upstream portion of the island. The dams on either side of Stolp Island have drops of six or seven feet. The hydraulic that is created by the dam is a killer at all water levels. The second of the Fox River's casino gambling boats and its associated land-based structures are situated at the top of Stolp Island. The ship is on the left side of the river right channel, above the dam and opposite the Canoe Chute.

The Aurora Canoe Chute has been controversial for being over budget and not functioning properly. As of Spring 1999 the chute is undergoing a reconfiguration after being flooded in 1998, and promises to be more functional in the future. A second dam on the Fox lies a 1/2-mile below the Stolp Island Dams, and herein lies the mystery: Why build a Canoe Chute on what was formerly an impassable dam when the North Avenue dam also develops a potentially dangerous hydraulic and is difficult to portage?

The North Avenue Dam only drops about one foot but a hydraulic though broken at a few narrow outflows is still present at most levels, although it washes out at very high levels. This necessitates portage at a place where the Fox is walled in, a very hard prspect. At very low water levels, the portage is easy at the edges of the dam.

Below the North Avenue Dam is Hurd Island Park where access can be found for those not wishing to deal with the two Aurora dams. Hurd Island Park has restrooms, a playground, and is 11 miles upstream of the Yorkville Dam. Between Hurd Island and Oswego, landings are frequent; they are less than a mile apart and usually located at city or county parks. These parks are easy to locate because Illinois Route 25 closely follows the east side of the Fox River. Two miles below Hurd Island, the Montgomery Dam can be portaged on both sides, and as a bonus, whichever side you choose has a park with a playground and access (if desired). Both U.S. Routes 30 and 34 and the Kane /Kendell County line cross the river in the 4 miles between Hurds Island and the town of Oswego. Waubonsie Creek enters on river left beside the business district of Oswego. Waubonsie Creek also marks the site of an Indian Ford of the Fox River that was used by the early pioneers.

In the 7 miles from Oswego to Yorkville, housing, though not absent, noticeably thins out. Saw-wee-kee Park is the only intermediate landing in these 7 miles. Wooded islands lend to the increasingly natural environment that the Fox River courses through. This effect is aided because the roads back off a bit. Houses are still passed regularly, as are sections with overgrown banks backed by forest, leading to uplands supporting farmland. The valley is steep, which is noticeable as Yorkville is entered. Approach the Yorkville Dam with caution, as its reputation for being one of the deadliest dams on the Fox River is well deserved. A list of its victims is posted on the river left side, along the portage route. If taking-out here, parking is available along Hydraulic Avenue.

If putting-in at Yorkville, there is a better launch sight just downstream of the Illinois Route 47 Bridge. The second launch is also on Hydraulic Avenue south of Illinois Route 47, and next to the post office. It is operated by the town of Yorkville and allows you to pull your vehicle up to the water's edge. The 8 miles from Yorkville to Millbrook are the miles on the Fox River that I most often paddle. Both the launch and the landing sites are exceptional for their ease of use rather than their extensive facilities. Below the Yorkville put-in, the town fades rapidly after passing a waste treatment plant and the mouth of Blackberry Creek* on river right.

The Fox River runs through its most island studded miles below Yorkville. The islands range from barely large enough to pitch a tent on to the better portion of a mile long. By passing on different sides of the islands, totally different views can be encountered. As a rule, the far river left channel yields the more natural trip. Waterfowl are plentiful, particularly Great Blue Heron. Duck blinds are not uncommon and are usually located at the ends of islands. Gravel shoals create fast water when the water is high, and at low water make finding the deep water channel difficult. Summer moonlight trips are easy on the wide, safe section below Yorkville.

A power transmission line marks the boundary line of Sliver Springs State Fish and Wildlife Area. The main portion of the park is on the river left side. The State Park can be used as an access or a lunch stop, and has bathrooms, playgrounds, and picnic tables. The best landing is on the river left side, just above the modern bridge that carries Kendall County Road 15, which leads to the town of Plano. Across the Fox River from the Silver Springs Canoe access is the Farnsworth House, which was designed by world-renowned architect Mies van der Rohe in

1950. The house allows for very little privacy because its outside walls are made of glass. The house is the only residence he designed in the United States and may be toured if one has reservations. (Call 630-552-8622.)

Directly downstream of the bridge and the Farnsworth house, Big Rock Creek* enters on river right. The triangle of land between Big Rock Creek and The Fox River was the location of the village of Main Poche, whose warriors took part in the Fort Dearborn Massacre on August 15, 1812. Main Poche's name meant Swelled Hand, referring to a deformed hand that the Chief claimed was the mark of being touched by the Great Spirit. This must have been what kept him from being pursued after killing the garrison of Fort Dearborn on the dunes of Lake Michigan.

A mile below Silver Springs a dam remnant marks the sight of the 19th century Millhurst Dam. The old mill, which existed for years as a shell without a roof, has recently been refurbished and is now a livable residence. The dam is breached on river left, creating fast water with some larger waves and strong eddy lines. Good boat control and a center route should get you through.

A mile below Millhurst Dam, the double bridges at Whitfield Road come into view. A park that includes the old iron bridge that formerly carried Whitfield Road across the Fox and into the town of Millbrook is there. This is great canoe access, but no other amenities are available here. The landing is river right upstream of the two bridges.

The Fox River passes the unincorporated towns of first Millbrook and then Millington with no more than bridges to mark their locations. It is a 9-mile trip from the Millbrook Bridge to the town of Sheridan. Wildlife, islands, and minor gravel shoals are plentiful throughout this section of the Fox River. Roads on either side of the river are far enough away to go unnoticed, but several small trailer/cottage communities mar the otherwise rural Fox. The Millington Bridge on the LaSalle/Kendall County line is the only bridge encountered between put-in and takeout and is not good access. This section of the Fox River is often overlooked for the higher profile sections up and downstream and therefore is rarely canoed.

The takeout is on the upstream river left side of the LaSalle County Road E2603 Bridge, called Robinson Road in the town of Sheridan. There are two parking options if using this bridge, but there are no parking signs along the road on both sides of the river. The first option involves paying the small fee to use the launch site at the bar on the downstream side of the bridge. The second option is to park away from the bridge or take your chances, as so many fisher-persons do. The next landing is U.S. 52, 4 miles downstream, which is the alternate put-in for the renowned "Dells of the Fox."

Across the river from the Robinson Road put-in, Somonauk Creek* adds its waters to those of the Fox. A Potowatomi Village was located on one of the islands near the mouth of Somonauk Creek. The first of the rock bluffs on this section are found about a mile downstream at the next bridge, which is Main Street in Sheridan. There is not access here, but on the upstream right side of the bridge there is a small stand of rare Red Pine trees. The bluffs are widely separated for the first few miles. Mission Creek enters on river left, within sight of the U.S. 52 Bridge.

Mission Creek is named for the ministry of the second white settler in LaSalle County. Jesse Walker was a Methodist missionary who came to this creek to bring Christianity to the Potowatomi Indians who had several villages in the vicinity. One of these villages was located on an island by Somonauk Creek*, another was located up on Indian Creek*. Jesse Walker came in 1824, starting a mission school as part of his ministries. Neither of these efforts worked out very well, for the Potowatomi did not wish to assimilate into white society. In 1826, Walker moved his mission to Plainfield, still continuing his Indian mission. This move made Walker the first white settler in Will County, as well as the second in LaSalle County. Jesse Walker had far better success bringing the Gospel to early settlers than he had with the Indians. Walker was a circuit rider, his mission being all of northern Illinois. Soon other ministers joined in splitting up the territory. Jesse Walker ended up in Chicago preaching the gospel to the rapidly growing city. He died in Chicago and is buried in Plainfield.

The U.S. Route 52 Bridge is directly downstream of Mission Creek and can be used as access, although parking is limited as of this writing. There is a campground just downstream of the Route 52 Bridge. The Campground has a trailer near the river that sells snacks and sandwiches on summer weekends. The campground could also serve those wishing to make multi-day trips. Only one short bluff graces the Fox in the next 3 miles.

A telephone line crossing over the Fox River above an island marks the beginning of the heart of the Dells of the Fox. The bluffs deserve close-up viewing because some of the formations are unusual and unique plant life can be seen from the river or by hiking back from the river. From this point on, rock bluffs, though not continuous, are always in sight. Indian Island, one of the largest on the river, has bluffs along both channels. The longest continuous rock wall along the

Fox is located along and downstream of Indian Island. This wall supports a community of swallows whose nests are built on the rock face of the bluff.

Stay to the river right side below Indian Island, not only for the rock walls, but for the upcoming cave, which can be easily seen from the river. This is a favorite stopping place either for lunch or just exploring. There are other caves in the area, but this is the only one that is so identifiable from the river. The cave is about fifty feet deep and the floor is often, muddy which is typical in caves since they are usually formed by seeping water. Just downstream, there is a hose that drops water into the Fox from a quarry that serves to remind you that this is silica sand land.

After a half-mile break, the most spectacular mile of the Dells is on river left. Indian Creek* enters opposite the bluffs. Ayers Landing, a campground/canoe rental, charges a small fee to use the landing, which is very convenient. Opposite Indian Creek, an old Indian fort—more than 1,200 years old—was excavated at an early date. The fort covered quite an area and was strategically located at the top of the bluffs with the Spring Branch on one flank.

The Wedron Road Bridge has no access, and the stories-high Wedron Silica Facility, which can be seen from a long distance, is passed directly below the Dells on river right. The second takeout option is at Chet and Mary's Fox River Tavern and Canoe Rental. Parking is along the road above the bar. This is the landing I have most often used when paddling the Dells. Please don't park in the bar's parking lot; it's for the bar customers, and they even make their canoe renters park on top. On nice summer weekends, expect to find the "Dells" section busy.

It's 3 more miles—all dam backwater—from the Fox River Tavern down to Dayton Dam. The two short rock walls in these 3 miles are hardly worth the portage at the dam. The Dayton Dam can be portaged with difficulty on either side of the dam. Beware of the river right channel as it leads to the intakes at the powerhouse. The 20-foot-high Dayton Dam is the highest dam on the Fox and was built for power generation. The Dayton Dam is the hardest dam to portage on the Fox River. The carry is long and unrewarding on either side of the dam.

John Green came here in the summer of 1829 seeking a mill location and bought the claim of William Clark, who stayed only long enough at the rapids of the Fox to erect a cabin before moving on to settle on the DuPage River. Green returned to Newark, Ohio, with twenty-four others; they loaded their wagons and crossed the wild country of Indiana and Illinois. They arrived in the summer of 1830 and by the end of the year John Green had both a flourmill and a sawmill operating. As one of the first mills operating in Northern Illinois, Green's Mill drew long lines during harvest. The wait was sometimes more than a week, and the farmers often slept under their wagons at night.

There is access below the Dayton Dam off of Dayton Road on the west side of the river, near the power house. The carry is long and the put-in is downstream of the light Class II rapids below the dam. It's 6 miles from Dayton Dam to the Fox River's mouth on the Illinois River at Ottawa. The final miles continue to be scenic, with islands and rock walls still visible. Interstate 80 is passed, as is the bridge carrying Illinois 71 and U.S. 6. The Riverside Inn has a stairway that leads up to the restaurant from the dock on the downstream side of the aforementioned bridge. You have now entered the town of Ottawa. Ottawa is the County seat of LaSalle County and in 1823 Dr. Davidson chose the confluence of the Fox and Illinois Rivers to be the first site settled in LaSalle County.

A short distance below the last bridge is a railroad bridge, followed directly by the Illinois Michigan Canal Aqueduct. The Fox River Aqueduct no longer carries water, but two aqueducts that do are on the Little Vermillion River and Aux Sable Creek. Both are restored and are worth visiting.

Several marinas are passed in the last 2 miles, all of which charge a fee for access. The last rock wall on the Fox supports the Main Street Bridge, from which the Illinois River can be viewed. A fee-free landing can found on the opposite shore of the Illinois River at Allen Park. There is a pair of boat ramps, but landings can be found elsewhere along the parking areas.

ILLINOIS ATLAS; PAGE 20-A-2; B-2; C-1; D-1
PAGE 28-A-1; B-1; C-1; PAGE 27-C-7; C-6;D-6; D-5; PAGE35 A-5; B-5; B-4

Fox River below the Carpentersville Dam.

Franklin Creek

Lee County's Franklin Creek flows through two distinct sections as it winds its way down to meet the Rock River at Grand Detour. The first section, six miles in length, flows mostly within the boundaries of Franklin Creek State Natural Area. This upper section must rank as one of Northern Illinois' most beautiful creeks. Majestic bluffs, some complete with caves, grace Franklin Creek's steep narrow valley. Because Franklin Creek is only twenty feet wide in most places, it has more than the usual number of logjams; however, while trying to take in all of the beautiful scenery, I hardly noticed the blockages (an average of roughly two per mile). Such was not the case along the lower section of the creek where a five-mile stretch boasted no bluffs and about ten to fifteen logjams per mile.

Obviously, the upper six miles make the best trip; also worthy of note is that Franklin Creek is best run at absolute flood stage. I ran Franklin Creek only one day after a three-inch rain; there was enough water to canoe, but most of the logjams fully blocked the channel. I could see by the matted down grass that the water had been three feet higher the day before; this additional water flowed around instead of through many of the logjams, making this six-mile stretch much more maneuverable at absolute flood stage.

When negotiating a put-in site, I'd caution against using Illinois Route 38; it's steep, lacks a trail to the water, and is likely to be muddy when Franklin Creek is runnable. A better put-in would be Iron Springs Road which is just to the west on Route 38. In this area, rock walls are frequent right from the start and some are truly breathtaking. Some of these walls are comprised of the oldest exposed rock in the state of Illinois; the rock is believed to be over 500 million years old.

Franklin Creek's valley is narrow, steep, and crooked, and wildlife is plentiful. I saw many deer, including a ten point buck, along with several beaver and muskrat, a fox, two species of owl, as well as blue heron and ducks. Trails that are part of Franklin Creek State Natural Area come noticeably close to the creek at several places. In addition, the nature preserve has four or five picnic areas alongside Franklin Creek, making for easy lunch stops. The last of these is Mill Springs Day Use Area: a large facility with a shelter, a playground, drinking water, and bathrooms. This facility is located just upstream of the Sunday Bridge, which carries Old Mill Road over Franklin Creek.

Mill Springs and Old Mill Road conjure up visions of the days when a farmer, his wagon loaded with grain, might take a day or two to turn his crop into a consumable form. The Franklin Creek Grist Mill, part of the Franklin Creek Natural Area, has just recently been restored to full working condition, making it the only true water-powered, operational grist mill in Illinois. This mill, built in 1847, is powered not by the waters of Franklin Creek, but by those of the Mill Spring. The Franklin Creek Mill is best accessed from the creek at the park's main office, next to a campground. The park office building can be seen from Franklin Creek and is about one half-mile below Old Mill Road. An equestrian trail crossing the creek marks the location.

Although there are a few more bluffs below the Trust Road bridge known locally as Monday's Bridge, now that you're moving out of the upper section and into the lower five-mile stretch, the logjams increase rapidly. The next bridge at Naylor Road marks the end of the rock bluffs and the start of canoeing through flood plain forest as Franklin Creek twists and turns along low banks. At several places, the logjams I encountered were nearly continuous, and to make matters a bit more interesting, some of the offending trees are crab apple, which have plentiful two-inch thorns. This stretch of Franklin Creek is one of the most difficult sections in this volume. A small dam blocks the channel at a private cleared area, and when Franklin Creek is runnable, this dam creates either a whirlpool above the outflow tube or a small waterfall at the dam; if, however, you have made it this far, this small obstacle shouldn't bother you.

Lost Nation Road is the last road to cross Franklin Creek before it enters the Rock River. Somewhere in these last few miles, the French fur trader Pierre La Saillier operated his trading post beginning in 1818, the year of statehood for Illinois. La Sallier married a Native American, like most of the early fur traders did. A daughter of their union married Joseph Ogee who operated the ferry at Dixon before selling out to John Dixon (*see the Rock River section for more information*).

The last few miles on Franklin Creek pass slowly as the logjams continue; consequently, the mouth of the Rock River is most definitely a welcome sight. The takeout is about two hundred yards upstream at a roadside park across Illinois Route 2 from the John Deere Historic Site in Grand Detour.

The portion of Franklin Creek that runs through the State Natural Area is the only section that would interest the canoeist. Even these miles require not only skill, but also perseverance; however, that's the price of admission to one of the prettiest creeks in Illinois.

A small investment by the State of Illinois Department of Natural Resources to clear the miles within the nature reserve of logjams would open this section to family trips, but even then, easy passage would still require high water. Perhaps the six miles above the Rock River are best left alone.

Illinois Atlas; Page 25; B-7

The 1847 Franklin Creek gristmill has recently been restored and is open on some weekends.

Franklin Creek cuts its course through rock believed to be over 500 million years old.

Galena River

Le Sueur, the French trader/explorer, noted a river that entered the Mississippi on the east side from the north in the year 1700 and called it the River of Mines. The Indians called it Mah-cau-bee, which meant "fever that blisters" (small pox), which was changed to La Fever River and later Anglicized to Fever River. Fever River was once again changed because the name conveyed that of an "unhealthy condition" to newly arriving settlers; it was renamed the Galena River in 1827 after the type of lead that was mined here in those days. Lead mining was solely responsible for distinguishing this area as one of the first two locales settled in northern Illinois—the other being Chicago. In fact, the Galena area population far outnumbered the small burg of Chicago from the 1820s until the 1850s.

The first put-in on the Galena River in Illinois would be Birkbeck Road, located off of Council Hill Road (which can also be used as a put-in). The twelve-mile trip from Birkbeck Road to the town of Galena is very scenic and wild. The river courses through a narrow valley and into an even narrower river bed. Like some other streams located in northwestern Illinois, steep banks make access at many bridges challenging, though not impossible. The first few miles feature many rock outcroppings and, if you look carefully, you can still spot the occasional signs of mining that at one time enveloped this and the surrounding valleys. The miners used the river water to wash the ore before smelting took place.

The Sac and Fox Indians were aware of the lead that was to be found here even before Marquette and Joliet found their way into the Mississippi Valley in 1674. Both the Spanish and the French were aware that there was lead to be found south of the Wisconsin River and east of the Mississippi River during the 1700s, but the first white traders that entered the area to trade with the local tribes were never heard from again. Nothing more is written of early American settlements until the 1820s, when several mines operated on lands leased from the United States government. By the 1840s, this entire valley and those nearby were filled with mining camps.

While canoeing down the Galena, one can easily conjure up images of miners searching the crevices along the rock bluffs next to the river. The current is fairly fast in the first half of this trip, and riffles are common. Buckhill Road, where access is typically steep but usable, is about six miles from town. The next bridge downstream is Stagecoach Trail. My last trip down this section was in Spring 1998 and this bridge was under construction; the river's accessibility remains undetermined at this point.

As one approaches the town of Galena, the river widens and the current slows; gone are the riffles and the rock walls, replaced by steep mud banks and a sluggish flow. On river right, a large levee with floodgates protects the historic town of Galena. The left bank is occupied by Grant Park for several blocks, but the banks are steep and the carry out is long. The best landing in town is just downstream of the U.S. 20/Decatur Street Bridge, where there is a parking lot and a short carry to the water. If you have time, check out the Jo Davies County Historic Society Museum and other historic sites in town. It is also important to remember that the town of Galena was honeycombed with mines and its surface was covered with smelting furnaces.

The final trip on the Galena River ends up on the Mississippi River and is mostly backwater, which means that unlike the upper river, the lower may be canoed year round. The lower river is wide, the current slow, and although the valley is still steep it has more rounded hills than on the upper river. The captain of one of the early paddlewheel steamboats on the Mississippi said that the Galena River was four times wider before there was mining in its valley. Mining altered the river by silting up the channel; this becomes apparent from above the town to the mouth of the river. The lower river channel was also straightened to accommodate the ever-increasing size of the steamboats plying the waters of the Mississippi.

If the upper section brings up visions of miners, one can easily picture a steamboat rounding one of gentle bends on the lower river.

Railroad tracks follow the river through its narrow valley, eventually curving off to the north to join the line that parallels the Mississippi River. This location is and was known as Portage and was the location of the 1821 trading post of Colonel George Davenport, after whom the Iowa town is named. After crossing under a railroad bridge, the Galena River branches out into a "T" and leaves the paddler with a choice of directions. Go right (north) and it's a little over a mile to Gears Ferry Landing, which is equipped with a full boat ramp. Don't park along the shore, for those spots are reserved for the members of the marina. Instead, park along the road or in the turnaround.

Taking the river left channel at the railroad bridge (south) also leads to the Mississippi River. The last three miles runs in between the railroad and a long thin peninsula that separates the Galena from the Mississippi. The peninsula becomes so narrow that for the last mile or more you can see the Mississippi River by standing up in your canoe. After coming out on the Mississippi, the next takeout is six miles downstream at Blandings Landing, and comes complete with an Army Corps of Engineers' boat ramp and campground.

Although the upper portion is small, the Galena River grows from small stream to river in the few miles where it flows through Illinois. The river is fairly wild, supporting much wildlife, and signs of human intrusion are few. As is the case with other streams along the Mississippi flyway, spring and fall provide spectacular views of vast numbers of migrating birds, further increasing Galena River's many assets.

Illinois Atlas; Page 15 A—1

Lead was found along the Galena River in seams like these.

Swallows build nests in the banks along the Galena River.

Green River

The headwaters of the Green River are close to those of Steward and Kyte's Creeks, separated by only one ridge. Unfortunately, all three have been altered by the hands of man; the Green River in particular has been diverted and changed to drain wetlands and swamps for use as farmland. To this end, the river has been channeled, levied, and made to flow where required, often in a straight line for tens of miles. Not only is the Green channeled, so are the streams that flow into it, resulting in a view of levied banks for most of its length.

U.S. Route 30 provides the farthest upstream put-in that I personally have used, but I am sure the Green is canoeable further upstream. The put-in at Route 30 was once located in what used to be known as Inlet Swamp; if you look around, you'll notice that that land rises in all directions, in a soccer-shaped configuration. The Inlet Swamp and the Winnebago Swamp down river on the Green were both drained to increase farm acreage.

A limestone up-cropping in the southwestern corner of the swamp used to hold back the waters. Since the up-cropping already formed a natural dam, this spot was chosen for the location of the Dewey Mill and Dam. When the local citizens decided to drain the swamp in the 1870s, their biggest obstacle was breaking through the rock under the mill. Once this was done, a steam shovel was mounted atop a barge, which began digging a channel deeper than the surrounding land. The steam shovel dug a channel wide and deep enough for the barge, a channel that sometimes followed the natural channel of the Green River and sometimes cut directly across the open prairie; the material dug out of the channel was used to form the levy walls. When this project was finally completed, the Green River was reduced to a manmade channel sunk into the prairie with twenty-to-thirty-foot-high levy walls to keep in all the water, formerly retained in the swamps, from flooding the surrounding farmland.

Swamps made poor ground for the villages of Native Americans; consequently, no settlements are to be found along the banks of the Green River. The swamps did however provide excellent hunting grounds, and Native hunting camps have been located on higher ground in the Green River's shallow valley. The French trader Le Sallier, who operated a trading post on Franklin Creek near the town of Grand Detour, was also known to have trapped and traded in the valley of the Green between 1818 and 1830.

Between Routes 30 and 52 the eight mile trip constitutes the most natural section of the Green River. However, these are far from pristine as they, too, have been channeled and levied. A Yogi Bear Park Campground is on river left at Green Wing Road, which is the second bridge downstream of Route 30. Two miles further downstream, the third bridge at Searls Road marks the berg of Binghampton where a second mill, the 1844 Dexter Mill, was located.

Senator David A. Shapiro Park is three more miles downstream and has restrooms, a picnic shelter, a playground, and parking, with only a short carry from the river. The park is on U.S. Route 52 on the south edge of the town of Amboy.

The next eleven-mile trip begins at U.S. Route 52 via Shapiro Park and ends at Illinois Route 26. The first several miles feature more riffles than one might expect. At this point, the Green River is enclosed in high banks, with no visible sign of the town of Amboy. The steep riverbanks are thick with growth; few views of the surrounding agricultural fields are present. Unfortunately, the steep banks leave too thin a corridor for much of the usual riverside wildlife to exist, as well.

The first bridge encountered is Rockyford Road. The Rockyford area, specifically the high ground south of the bridge, holds historical significance as the second oldest settlement in Lee County. The first settler in the valley of the Green River was a French Canadian trapper with the first or last name of Filamalee who was the only white settler prior to the Black Hawk War. The first American settlers made mention of an oak tree stump in front of Filamalee's cabin remains that was hollowed out to form a mortar which he used to grind various grains. Rockyford was also the site of the town of Shelburn, first settled by Tim Perkins, who erected the first sawmill on the Green River. Today, Rockyford Road is preceded by a large waste treatment plant that adds water of a distinctly different color (green) and odor (not pleasant). Rockyford Road is fenced and provides no real access, but the next three bridges have adequate roadside parking and short carries to the water. The last of these roads, Illinois Route 26, marks the end of the most popular section for canoeing on the Green River.

Now, I have to admit that the Green River is the only stream in this book that I have not canoed for its entire length. The reasons for this are several, but the most prominent is that the fifty miles between Illinois Route 26 and Interstate 80 are just plain boring. I didn't give up on the Green until I had scouted most of the bridges in between Route 26 and Illinois Route 82 and found it all to be pretty much the same.

I did paddle the final thirteen miles that lead down to the Rock River. This section, starting at the E1200 bridge in Henry County, has been channeled all the way down to Interstate 80. The Hennepin Canal crosses the Green River a mile east of the town of Green River. I expected to see some sign of this intersection, but was amazed when I passed the E600 bridge leading to the town of Green River and realized that I was already past the Hennepin Canal junction. The Hennepin Canal crossed over the Green River in an aqueduct that was rusted through when the State of Illinois made the canal into a state parkway. Instead of foot-bridging over the Green River (as was done at Bureau Creek, where another aqueduct was also beyond repair), the Green has a foot trail that just ends on either side of the river. The water from the canal flows under the Green River and comes up on the other side via an inverted siphon that drains water from an elevated pool on the upstream side and releases it at a lower point on the opposite side of the river.

The Interstate 80 bridge is about a mile below the town of Green River. Downstream of the interstate is a short natural section that is crossed by a rustic iron railroad bridge. A trailer park on river right is all that is visible of the town of Green Rock as the river passes to the south. Two bridges are crossed, though neither one makes for easy access. The first bridge is N2200 at the trailer park; the second is Illinois Route 84; followed by another railroad bridge.

The final three miles below the town of Green Rock look more natural but are marred by the close proximity of Interstates 280 & 74, less than half a mile to the south. Here, the river makes a couple of sharp turns before finally emptying out into the Rock River. The takeout is located at the mouth of the Hennepin Canal, one-fourth of a mile upstream on the Rock River. A boat ramp is located here. Though it's not marked on the map, follow the road that parallels the Hennepin Canal out of the town of Green Rock and it will lead to a large parking area at Lock 29 where the Hennepin Canal empties into the Rock River.

I had long debates with myself about including the Green River in this volume. The long straight sections along with the channeled banks was not enough of an inspiration to paddle those middle fifty miles. Sadly, the manmade nature of the Green River makes it easier to compare to its close neighbor the Hennepin Canal rather than another river. The canal is actually a more pleasant paddle because its lower banks allow for more picturesque views than the Green.

On the other hand, the Green River does show what all rivers might look like if the Army Corps of Engineers and farmers had their way.

Illinois Atlas; Page Pages 24-25, C-7,6,5; D-4
Page 32; A-4,3,2,1; Page 31; A-7,6

Typical scene on the Green

Hickory Creek

Hickory Creek is the last major tributary entering the Des Plaines River from the south or left bank before the Des Plaines joins with the Kankakee to form the mighty Illinois River. Like many of the creeks I describe in this book, the runoff is extremely fast and it must be canoed a day or two after a couple of inches of rain have raised the water levels.

Taking that into account, Hickory Creek has a lot to offer. For the adventurous, the upper miles are wild, crossed by few roads and with few signs of man's intrusion. The middle section is well suited to recreational and family canoeing. The six-mile lower section features some honest to goodness white water with a rating of Class II-III.

The farthest upstream I dared to launch was at the U.S. 30 Bridge several miles east of U.S. 45. Here, Hickory Creek is small, intimate, and blocked regularly by fallen trees for the first six miles. If you can put up with the need to portage endlessly, these miles are rather pristine.

At times I felt as if a jungle surrounded me, as the woods were deep and lush. The only visual intrusion came when passing under the Route 45 Bridge and the Wolf Road Bridge. The Will County Forest Preserve District owns most of the forested land along both banks.

A better put-in for an easier, less debris-congested trip would be at Schmuhl Road. The creek has widened out somewhat, making canoeing easier, while continuing to course its way through forest preserves for several more miles. A footbridge carries a bicycle path across Hickory Creek—it quickly fades from sight. Soon, the close proximity of the Rock Island Railroad on your left signals the approach to downtown New Lenox and the Lincoln Highway, U.S. Route 30.

You will more than likely see at least one train pass by on this portion of the trip because Hickory Creek and the railroad run parallel for several miles. The New Lenox train station is close enough to the creek for one to check water levels from the platform.

Downstream from New Lenox, Hickory Creek becomes noticeably more polluted with the addition of New Lenox's treated wastewater to that already contributed by Frankfort and Mokena. Pollution is one of the more disturbing factors of canoeing Hickory Creek.

After passing under the Interstate 80 Bridge, you are now as close as you will come to one of Will County's most historic areas. These sites are better visited from Francis Road than from Hickory Creek. Four historical markers, two on Francis Road, and two where Gouger Road crosses Hickory Creek, will tell much about the history of Will County.

The two on Francis Road are the most interesting. First, there is the French Fort located at Pilcher Park Forest Preserve as part of the Joliet Park District. There, on a small parking lot, is a trail about a quarter-mile in length that leads to the perimeter of the old fort's walls.

The fort was built and garrisoned near the junction of two Indian trails, around the year 1729 or 1730. It was constructed as part of an effort to stop the Fox Tribe, Enemies of the French, and their allies, from migrating around the southern end of Lake Michigan. (*See the chapter on Big Rock Creek.*) It also served as one of a string of French forts, from Niles, Michigan, to Green Bay, Wisconsin, used to serve the fur trade.

The University of Michigan excavated the site in the 1970s. Besides finding French artifacts, evidence of earlier mound builders was also uncovered. On the trail leading to the fort, it becomes apparent that this was a strong location as it commanded high ground and also used a small tributary of Hickory Creek to protect one flank.

Across Francis Road from the old French Fort parking lot, and 50 feet back in the woods, is the site of the first permanent white settler's building in Will County. This was Aaron Friend's trading post circa 1829. Built 100 years after the French fort, it served many of the same functions. The trading post and the fort had the advantage of lying astride two ancient Indian trails. This again illustrates how game trails became Indian trails, which in turn were used by our pioneer forefathers and eventually became today's U.S. Route 6 and U.S. Route 30.

Soldiers from Fort Dearborn were known to have traveled this far to attend parties thrown by Aaron Friend at his trading post.

Another thing to ponder while at this location is that during the Black Hawk War in 1832, frightened settlers fled the area, first for Fort Beggs on the DuPage River, and then on to Fort Dearborn in Chicago. Upon returning after the scare had subsided, the settlers found that the friendly local Potawatomi Indians had watched over and had taken care of the farms and cabins of their pioneer neighbors in their absence.

Enough history for now. A mile or so below the Interstate 80 Bridge, Gouger Road Bridge is reached. Upon landing at the bridge, a short walk will take you to the last two historical markers, with one on either side of the creek. A hike of about a city block through Joliet's Pilcher Park woodlands will bring you to the Bird Haven Greenhouse. The park's nature center features displays of native species of fish which may be of special interest to Hickory Creek paddlers. The creek flows through Pilcher Park for approximately two miles to a dam.

For those wishing to takeout in Pilcher Park, the dam should be no problem. Stay along the right bank as slack water is reached, for there are several parking areas above the dam that come within ten feet of the water.

On the other hand, if planning to continue downstream, you must stay to the left side of the island above the dam to be able to portage. The island ends only twenty or so feet from the lip of the dam. There are concrete walls on the right bank, making portaging there impossible. The portaging on the left is difficult, but doable. This route exists along an active railroad right-of-way, so keep your eyes and ears open for trains while portaging.

Rapids occur immediately below the dam and continue intermittently from here down to the second Interstate 80 Bridge, a mile upstream of Hickory Creek's mouth. I counted four that I would rate at Class II, and one located near the lower I-80 Bridge that is Class III.

After departing Pilcher Park, the scenery remains natural for a time before gradually giving way to the backside of industry and warehousing. This gives way to residential neighborhoods. Walls begin to appear, first on one side of Hickory Creek, then on the other, and finally a ten-foot wall with a fence on top encloses both creek banks. The current remains fairly quick through this section and soon the lofty interstate bridge looms ahead.

One will also notice that the gradient is very steep while approaching the bridge. This is caused by several small ledges, followed by larger ledges at the bottom of the rapid. This final drop of about three feet formed a nice surfing hole on the day I ran it, but that hole might get grabby at higher water levels.

Below I-80, Hickory Creek flattens out and the scenery becomes dismal, consisting of dumps, waste treatment plants, and a porta-potty storage area. At the mouth, the Brandon Road Lock and Dam on the Des Plaines River come into view. I took out near the wastewater treatment plant just above the mouth.

After reflecting on my experience of running hickory Creek, I have two concerns. One is that the creek has three distinct sections that are all short. For instance, whitewater boaters would be attracted to the lower section's Class II and III rapids, but probably would not be interested in the upper or middle sections. Families that would enjoy the middle section, especially through Pilcher Park, would not want to risk the rapids on the lower section or bother with the logjams on the upper. And with the 19 miles described broken into three sections, each segment is relatively short. My second concern is the pollution. This applies particularly to those interested in the whitewater section. I personally know of boaters who have gotten sick after accidentally swallowing water on the Vermilion River in LaSalle County. Hickory Creek seems to have an even lower water quality, so be careful not to ingest any.

Illinois Atlas: Pages 28 and 29; D5; D-4; D-3.

*For those wishing to takeout
in Pilcher Park, the dam
should be no problem.
Stay along the right bank
as slack water is reached,
for there are several parking
areas above the dam that come
within ten feet of the water.*

Indian Creek

Indian Creek's upper section is accessible at Shabbona Grove Road, which is just below the dam on Shabbona Lake. This was near the site of Chief Shabbona's village, located in a large grove of trees along the banks of the creek. Shabbona fought for the British during the War of 1812. However, after the Battle of Fallen Timbers, Shabbona swore allegiance to the United States, an oath he never broke. He repeatedly risked his life to save the settlers of Northern Illinois—but more about this as we move further downstream.

The creek at this location is small, only about 20 to 30 feet wide, and much of this upper section is channelized, running through alternating landscapes of light forest and farmland. The channelized portions of the creek run fast with few obstructions, and support healthy populations of muskrat, beaver, mink, blue and green heron, and I even spotted a ground hog. Logjams are occasionally found in the wooded sections. A few miles downstream, Stone House Campground appears on the right, just before the Suydam Road Bridge. The Smith's own the campground; they are canoeists, and also local history buffs. Indian Creek assumes a more natural appearance below here; more woodlands, less farmland. Four miles downstream is the Svendson Road bridge, eleven river miles from Shabbona Grove Road. Another two miles will bring you to a good landing at the Hyde Road Bridge, for a total of thirteen river miles.

Using the Hyde Road Bridge as a put-in, the first few miles were heavily obstructed by deadfalls. These became less frequent as we got closer to the town of Earlville, but were replaced by homes as the creek skirted the eastern edge of Earlville. Passing under a railroad bridge, one enters the Earlville Country Club grounds. There is one low clearance footbridge to negotiate in this nine-hole golf course. The next bridge encountered is the Union Street Bridge. A short distance downstream, Sutphens Run enters from the right and adds considerable volume, as have other small tributaries, so that in the five miles traveled since Hyde Road, Indian Creek has doubled in size. There are fewer logjams downstream from here.

Just as the creek starts to look inviting, a landowner just below the Route 34 Bridge has claimed the creek as private property via at least a half a dozen warning signs. We thought we would be cute and ignore the signs. Less than 100 yards below the bridge, this landowner has erected an insurmountable barricade across the creek and up both banks. This barrier consists of four-foot-high upright steel posts, well-anchored and positioned two feet apart, with five strands of barbed wire strung horizontally. This was more than we wanted to tackle. Threatened by the specter of arrest, we turned upstream and paddled back to the bridge. We then walked the three miles to where we had planned to take out at the N4225 Bridge, which was the site of one of the few good landings.

This is the start of the most hostile waterway in this volume. From Illinois Route 34 downstream, most of the bridges across Indian Creek and many of the properties alongside are posted. Some say **No Trespassing**. Some say **No Canoeing**. And many of them say **Violators Will Be Arrested**. This condition continues all the way to its mouth at the Fox River. The hostility the present day inhabitants express along the lower creek has historical roots in the valley. For starters, just upstream of the N4225 bridge is a park commemorating the victims of the Indian Creek Massacre. Despite warnings from Shabbona, who was riding like Paul Revere all over Northern Illinois to warn settlers of the raiding Sauk, Fox, and Potawatomi war parties in the area, the little settlement of Indian Creek lay dormant, and on May 20, 1832, the settlement was attacked.

William Davis was the first one to settle at this location along the creek. In 1830, Davis set himself up as a blacksmith and built a dam on Indian Creek, which was crossed by the Sauk Trail. Soon others joined Davis and a small settlement developed. Residents of an Indian village six miles upstream found that fish could no longer migrate upstream in high water because of the dam. The Indians went to Davis to protest, but were turned away. They returned and tried to dismantle the dam, but Davis discovered them and drove them off, capturing one whom he beat unmercifully with a hickory stick. This all took place shortly before Stillman's defeat on May 14, 1832. The Indian victory (*See Stillmans Creek*) had made all the young warriors bolder.

Shabbona had gone to the Indian Creek settlement specifically to warn Davis to seek shelter at Fort Winnebago (in the present day city of Ottawa) because of the beating. Davis didn't want to leave because he had been talked into leaving the year before and didn't want to waste his time again during spring planting. Besides, he thought that they had a large enough community to defend themselves. On the day of the massacre, Shabbona once again came and warned them that the hostiles were close at hand in the nearby woods.

When the Indians attacked, two of the settlers were in the blacksmith shop, two were at the mill next to the dam, and the two Davis boys were half a mile off in a field planting corn. The women and children were in the house when the Indians suddenly rushed in and started shooting. They overwhelmed the settlers, without loss to themselves, and then proceeded to scalp and dismember the victims. Even the children were cut to pieces, and the women hung by their heels to the outside of the cabin. The four men who were working outside of the main buildings escaped.

Rachel and Sylvia Hall, ages 13 and 17, were held captive for 11 days, but were later ransomed near Beloit, by Chief White Crow accompanied by their brother, J. W. Hall, who also survived the attack. A seven-acre county park commemorates the attack on the Indian Creek settlement, and contains the common gravesite of all 15 victims of the massacre. The memorial of the incident was erected in 1877, and in 1902 Shabbona Park was established to preserve the grounds. Although the creek comes within 50 yards of the monument, a barbed wire fence and "No Trespassing" signs discourage visitation of this historical site from the water. The N4150 Bridge is only 100 yards downstream

Below the park, canoeing is done in a hostile countryside to this very day. And it is a real shame since much of the course is in an easterly direction, a blessing when a west wind is blowing. It is two miles from Shabbona Park to the next bridge on N4101. Another two miles farther is Illinois Route 23. It was at the next bridge on E1925 that I received a lecture on trespassing from the local landowner.

The next few miles are lightly forested with frequent riffles. Then Little Indian Creek enters on the left and adds considerable volume to the waterway. Sandstone bluffs adorn the last few miles to the Fox. Native red cedar and white cedar or Arbor Vitae, a state endangered species, crown these rocky outcrops.

The area around the confluence of Indian Creek and the Fox River has several caves of historic interest. One cave is of particular interest, as it has not one but two maps dated 1822 that show the Indian Creek watershed. It has been theorized that these cave drawings were made as part of a land survey that was to be the plot of land to be ceded to the veterans of the War of 1812. The Illinois Michigan Canal was surveyed at the same time. These maps not only show the Indian Creek watershed, but also the location of those who had already settled in the vicinity.

The High Ridge Trail crossed Indian Creek close to its mouth on its way from Chicago to Ottawa. This was an old Potawatomi trail that was also used by the earliest pioneers. Across from the mouth of Indian Creek on the Fox River is the site of an old Indian fortification estimated to be 1,200 years old.

In retrospect, Big Indian Creek is an enjoyable enough canoe trip *but is not worth the risk of being arrested.* Therefore, I recommend trying one of the other area streams. The Little Vermilion or Big Rock Creek both come to mind as better canoeing streams.

Illinois Atlas: Page 26, B-4. Page 26, C-4; D-3. Page 27, D-4. Page 35, A-5.

A seven-acre county park commemorates the attack on the Indian Creek settlement, and contains the common gravesite of all 15 victims of the massacre. The memorial of the incident was erected in 1877, and in 1902 Shabbona Park was established to preserve the grounds.

Kishwaukee River

The main trunk of the Kishwaukee River begins north and slightly east of the town of Marengo in McHenry County. The north and south branches join above Millstream Road and are also covered in this volume. Kishwaukee was a word in both the Sauk and Potawatomi languages that translates to "sycamore tree." The South Branch of the Kishwaukee was called the Sycamore River at one time. Millstream Road is an acceptable access, as is Deer Pass Road a couple of miles downstream. The trouble with this upper portion of the Kishwaukee River is that much of this section flows through a wet woods or floodplain forest. Philip Vierling's guidebook *Landings: Kishwaukee River* states that it took him seven and a half hours to canoe a 4 3/10-mile section. Well, I didn't take the warning, figuring that my slowest canoe trips averaged no less than two miles per hour. And I beat Phil's time by a lot, managing to cover the eleven miles from Millstream Road to County Line Road in about seven hours, a new "slowest trip record" for me. Trees and logjams are what make this into such a sluggish trip. When I describe this section to others, I talk about pulling my canoe over a tree in the river. When I looked upstream, I could see the last two trees I had portaged over, and looking downstream, I could see the next two blockages that would require me to exit my boat to get over them.

All of this translates into a finding a more practical put-in. That would be County Line Road, on the border between McHenry and Boone Counties. Downstream may be blocked once or twice in the next ten miles down to Belvidere Park. The Kishwaukee doubles its size with the addition of Coon and Piscasaw Creeks and hence loses its small stream character. (*See section on Coon & Piscasaw Creeks.*) The river does come out of the floodplain forest more than a mile above County Line Road, but there are no access points in between.

Downstream of County Line Road is the border between Boone and Winnebago counties. The Kishwaukee River runs twenty to forty feet wide while passing through a combination of forest, marsh, and farm fields. These natural features are broken up by a couple of campgrounds, some farms, and a gun club, along with a railroad and U.S. Highway 20 in close proximity. Care should be taken when passing the gun club, as the skeet shooting range backs up to the river. During my more than twenty trips down this section, the gun range has never been in use, but one never knows…

A whistle attached to your life jacket can be useful at these times. Above the gun club, the first of several islands on this section appears in high water; take your choice, but at low water go with the greatest flow because some of the side channels become unnavigable.

Both campgrounds on this section have altered the river with dams. The first campground is located upstream of Garden Prairie Road and the dam is runnable through a center chute. The second dam, the Epworth Dam, is located downstream of Epworth Road and has two sections divided by an island; each section has concrete dividers that look as if they were meant to support a walkway, but they don't. The dividers tend to catch debris, so find one that is clear and paddle hard over the two-foot drop. Below the dam, choose your channel carefully at low water, as it's hard to stay in deep enough water at this point. The Chicago Northwestern Railroad now forms the river left bank. High banks also form river right, creating a narrowing of the streambed; this continues down to where Coon Creek enters on the left, crossing under a picturesque bridge just upstream.

Coon Creek adds a substantial amount of water to the Kishwaukee River; as the river turns away from the railroad, it becomes wider and open. On windy days, when the wind blows from the west, these last few miles can become challenging. A good takeout eight miles below County Line Road is to be found at the mouth of Piscasaw Creek. The Red Horse Bend Nature Preserve and Canoe Access have improved parking and a level entry to the water, make putting-in or taking-out easy. Just downstream of Piscasaw Creek, the bridge that carries U.S. Route 20 over the river marks the border of the town of Belvidere, Boone County's largest town.

On a hill overlooking the Kishwaukee River where Belvidere stands today once stood the unusual grave of a Potawatomi chief. Chief Big Thunder died early in the 1830s, and the grave was noted for its unique nature by early travelers and settlers alike along the Chicago/Galena Road. The Big Thunder grave described the Chief as sitting upright in a chair facing south; the chair sat on top of a six-foot-high platform built upon a dirt mound. A palisade surrounded this structure, six feet in diameter and high enough so that Big Thunder wasn't visible from the outside. The wall was cut out on the south side to provide the Chief a view of the prairie landscape, where it was thought that a battle would take place someday. It was believed that Big Thunder would see the battle and rise from the dead to lead the warriors against the enemy.

The chief sat wrapped in a blanket and was said to have the appearance of a mummy. As was common custom in Native American burials, on the platform with Big Thunder were his knife, bow and arrows, and hunting spear, and on his lap was a supply of tobacco. For a time, the grave went unmolested, but one by one items were taken as souvenirs until not a bone or stick remained. A mill erected along the banks of the Kishwaukee in 1846 and operated until 1923 was known as Big Thunder Mills.

Three good access options exist in Belvidere; the first is a concrete boat ramp with parking for about a dozen cars and a porta-potty (in season), located off of River Drive and Burgess Street. One half-mile below the boat ramp is the second landing on the river's left bank; this access point requires taking-out above the unrunnable Belvidere Dam on the left side where parking is found along the park road to Belvidere Park, which is located off of Locust Street.

The park has restrooms and the first of many playgrounds along the Kishwaukee. If continuing on to the third access option, the Belvidere Dam can be portaged on either side, but the left side has the playground. Beware not to get washed over the Belvidere Dam when portaging; good boat control and hugging the shore are a must. A fast riffle below the dam continues more or less all the way down to Spencer Park, the third option for access.

The seven-mile stretch between Spencer Park in Belvidere and Baumann Park in Cherry Valley was at one time deemed by local landowners to be private property. The case was decided in the courts and the Kishwaukee River in Winnebago County was declared to be navigable and therefore canoeable. From Belvidere on downstream, the Kishwaukee has enough water to be runnable year round, although it may be shallow in dry years. The first several miles below Spencer Park are wooded and uncrossed by roads. A fence at the Interstate 90 Bridge marks a pasture that occupies a mile-long stretch down to the U.S. Route 20 Bridge where a second single strand fence marks the other end of the field.

Below Route 20, the Kishwaukee River enters the quaint town of Cherry Valley. An original log cabin that was moved down from Wisconsin stands on the river left side of the State Street Bridge. This structure is an excellent example of an 1830s settler's cabin. State Street is the main street in Cherry Valley and has a gay 90s look with gaslights, cobblestone streets, and an old town clock.

Baumann Park in Cherry Valley is the best landing on the Kishwaukee River. It features a playground, restrooms, and play fields, and is only one block from Cherry Valley's State Street business district. The canoe launch in Baumann Park has a circular drive only a few feet from the river. The next eight or so miles down to Seth B. Atwood Park in New Milford is arguably the most popular trip in Northern Illinois, rivaled only by the "Dells" section of the Fox River. One of the elements that make this trip so popular is the number of Winnebago County Parks that line the Kishwaukee River. Many of these parks have picnic shelters, playgrounds, parking, and improved canoe ramps. Kids love parks, and my daughter Aimee has named this section the "Kids Waukee" since we always stop a couple of times to play at the parks on our family trips.

This trip begins in Cherry Valley; housing lines the right bank for a ways but soon thins out. The Kishwaukee is rural but never wild through these miles; power lines, railroads, roads, and the frequently encountered parks and campgrounds keep the signs of man never far from sight. On the other hand, having year-round legal access to paddle water that is wide and safe enough for beginners, the absence of dams, the abundance of parks, and the fast shoals all contribute to a delightful trip. The Kishwaukee is the most popular river on the Prairie State Canoe Club's trip list; consequently, these trips are also some of the best attended, at times drawing as many as eighty people. The first road crossed is Perryville Road, right above the confluence with the South Branch of the Kishwaukee; a dolomite rock wall marks the South Branch location as well as the Blackhawk Springs Forest Preserve. From here on downstream, the Kishwaukee River grows substantially wider.

Early descriptions of the Kishwaukee River Valley below the junction with the South Branch make mention of hundreds of burial mounds between here and the Rock River. The mound builders or Mississippian Indians left no written word, and the tribes in existence when the first Europeans entered the Midwest had no knowledge of the mounds or their builders. So archaeological excavations of the burial mounds themselves have uncovered what is known about the Mississippian culture. Most mounds were looted for artifacts and leveled by farmers long before science had a chance to assess the artifacts that lay within. More than a dozen mounds still remain within Blackhawk Springs Park; they are more easily located between late fall and early spring when the underbrush is less dense and the poison ivy is not active.

The next road downstream is Blackhawk Road, with an additional access available at the Kishwaukee River Forest Preserve and playgrounds located on either side of the river. As you leave the park, a small check dam creates a fast chute that forms the biggest waves on this section. A few more miles and the Kishwaukee Gorge is entered, evidenced by the how steep the valley is, growing to a depth of one hundred and sixty feet and, by the U.S. Interstate 39 bridge, crossing high over the river at the gorge's steepest point. The gorge is at its most spectacular in fall colors, but winter is the best season for viewing the dolomite walls that line it. A couple more miles and a suspension bridge marks the takeout at Seth B. Atwood Park. The takeout is directly below the bridge on the south bank and has an improved landing with parking only feet away on the park road shoulder. The river right side of Atwood Park was used as a rifle range for troops bound for World War I; some bunkers still remain.

The final six-mile trip is wide, slow, and marred by levied banks and the close proximity of the Greater Rockford Airport. A few miles downstream, life improves below Belt Line Road.

A mile or so downstream, the Kishwaukee divides around an island and stays in two separate channels for almost two miles, rejoining at the takeout at Hinchliff Memorial Forest Preserve. The river left, or south channel, is my favorite because it has faster water, a narrower channel, and the entrance of Killbuck Creek. Hinchliff Forest Preserve does not have a canoe landing and does have a long steep carry to parking on a pull-off on Kishwaukee Road. This takeout is one-tenth of a mile above the Kishwaukee's mouth on the Rock River.

I canoe the Kishwaukee River often and with good reason; the ease of access, water quality, and variety of scenery all contribute to the appeal. Sure, there are areas that are less than scenic, but when the neighbors with rusty paddling skills are coming along, or my daughter wants to bring along friends, I can't think of a better choice.

Illinois Atlas; Pages 18-19 B-5; B-4; B-3 C-2

North Branch of Kishwaukee, McHenry County

The north branch of the Kishwaukee in McHenry County is a micro stream compared to its counterpart, the south branch. I started at U.S. Route 14 by the Woodstock Conference Center, which is located on a small dammed lake at this location. The family that runs this facility is friendly and has a half dozen canoes on the lake.

I put in close to the dam so I could paddle the fast water below it. The first four miles were very narrow, fast, and full of obstructions. I have to admit that somehow this combination caused me to be swept sideways into a strainer and capsized, something that had not happened to me in my several years of paddling small creeks.

The area had five inches of rain in the two days prior to my trip. Even with this much rain, most of the stream was still within its banks. While this river needs this kind of water level to be runnable, its steep gradient causes it to become challenging at high water.

All small streams require constant maneuvering and exacting control of the craft. One of the things I like about canoeing them is the need to be alert every moment and the full range of paddle strokes required to get downstream safely. On the north branch of the Kishwaukee, all of this happens at breakneck speed. The canoeist is forced to duck tree branches while at the same time making 90-degree turns at speeds rivaling those attained in whitewater runs. This makes for a very challenging trip. So I highly recommend that those who would attempt to canoe any micro stream have advanced canoeing skills. Now that the warnings are out of the way, let us continue.

Another thing I love about small remote streams like the upper branches of the Kishwaukee is the natural appearance of the landscape. This is best noticed at logjams. Most streams have a lot of human-generated trash built up behind river blockages such as fast food containers, Styrofoam cups, plastic swimming pools, and rubber balls that I take home to my dog. The scarcity of such trash on these smaller streams is always noticeable.

The other great thing about small streams that are not often canoed is the abundance and variety of wildlife. On my only trip down the north branch of the Kish, I saw the largest pair of beaver that I've ever seen. They let me get within ten feet of them before noticing me. I also came upon my first badger on this trip, plus the usual mammals, deer, mink, muskrat, and an opossum. The fowl included blue and green herons, barn and great horned owls, and several species of ducks and geese minding eggs in their nests. Frogs and turtles (representing the reptiles and fish) were present, but went unidentified. Spotting this amount of wildlife in one ten and a half mile trip can only make me think that these small creeks support the last thin thread of nature that represents what Illinois must have been like 200 years ago.

The north branch of the Kishwaukee flows under four road bridges on this trip. All are modern structures with plenty of clearance even at high water. But beware of the one at Collins Road, for there are two electric fences directly downstream. There are also two farm bridges to consider, one of which needs to be portaged.

Garden Valley Road is the fourth bridge and signals a changing character for the north branch of the Kishwaukee. After the Garden Valley Bridge, the river widens out onto a flood plain. At times, the channel was hard to follow or sometimes find. It mattered not whether I was in a forest or in a field—it was water, water everywhere. This continued all the way to the takeout at Millstream Road. Incidentally, parking for the takeout is best on the adjacent Kunde Road.

Millstream Road got its name from the 1836 sawmill built by Robert and John White. It was located between Millstream Road and the confluence of the north and main branches of the Kishwaukee.

Illinois Atlas: Page 19; B-6.

"I saw the largest pair of beavers that I've ever seen. They let me get within ten feet of them before noticing me."

South Branch of Kishwaukee, McHenry

The Kishwaukee River has two major branches, the North, originating in McHenry County, and the South, originating in DeKalb County. However, in McHenry County, we also find a north and a south branch of the Kishwaukee. These two headwater feeder streams don't seem to have a lot in common with each other. The south branch isn't as steep or narrow and does not have the same abundance of wildlife. Towns and roads are never far away and are often visible from the river.

On the other hand, the south branch of the Kishwaukee has a great deal going for it. First, because it is wider and carries more water than the north branch, it is more canoeable. Second, it's pristine. It has excellent water quality and almost no trash on the banks. The south branch also flows past the Illinois Railway Museum with its five miles of track, and several dozen steam, electric, and diesel engines. This museum is probably the best of its type in the world. The problem is that it takes the better part of the day to see everything. In the nearby town of Union is the McHenry County Historical Museum, which can be visited in a couple of hours.

I put in at the Seeman Road Bridge, a mile or two southeast of the town of Union. The south branch flows through open grassland country, which then gives way to farm fields, giving the visitor a splendid panorama. This is the way the Prairie State must have looked 200 years ago: Long stretches of open prairie, only occasionally broken up by a grove of trees. These groves often took on names as landmarks on the endless prairie.

A mile down river of Seeman Road, there are three low farm bridges that require portaging. By the time you reach Hemmingsen Road, the town of Union and the Illinois Railway Museum are clearly visible. They will continue to be seen for the next several miles.

As you approach the next bridge downstream, six tall willow trees, picnic tables, and a small playground mark a riverside park. This is High Bridge Road, although no high bridge exists here. High Bridge Road is about the closest the south branch comes to the Railway Museum complex, which stays in view until after you pass North Union Road.

The south branch continues much the same as before, until it approaches Illinois Route 176 where homes can be seen close to the river. After Illinois 176, the town of Marengo is close by, but it never intrudes on the scenery.

In the next mile, the south branch of the Kishwaukee changes character from open fields to wet woodlands. I should probably explain what is involved in paddling through what I call "wet woods."

A wet wood is sometimes called a floodplain forest. These are forested areas where the river has very low banks. This allows the river to overflow its banks whenever the water rises. The water then picks up anything that will float. The river may widen out for hundreds of yards in flooded periods and flow through the trees, weeds, and underbrush.

What this means to the canoeist is a channel that is extremely hard to follow. To make paddling even more difficult, abundant forest debris has floated everywhere. Logjams, causing the paddler to leave the main channel, very often block the channel. Once out of the river channel, it may be difficult to find the channel again since maneuvering a boat through the trees becomes the problem. This is a good place to use a pole. If you lose the channel, keep an eye on the current. It is the best indicator of where the river is going. Good luck and remember this is a learning process. The more times I paddle through floodplain forest, the easier it becomes to read.

By the time Dunham Road comes into view, you will have traversed a mile of wet woods. A couple of hundred yards will carry you on to the main branch of the Kishwaukee. If you think the channel will be better on the main branch of the Kishwaukee, you are wrong. The two miles on the main branch below the confluence with the north branch will continue to head through a floodplain forest and will bring you to Deer Pass Road, where there is a good landing. The day I paddled this section, there wasn't enough clearance for a canoe under the Deer Pass Road Bridge.

This trip on the south branch of the Kishwaukee is seven and a half miles long if you take out at Millstream Road. If you takeout at Deer Pass Road, the trip is nine and a half miles in length. Although this trip makes for fairly difficult canoeing, it is much easier than attempting the north branch of the Kishwaukee. Be sure to try to take advantage of the nearby museums in the area.

Illinois Atlas: Page 19, C-6.

A view upstream of the dam at the put-in on the North Branch of the Kish.

A view on the North Branch of the Kishwaukee River.

Takeout on the South Branch of the Kishwaukee River.

South Branch of the Kishwaukee, DeKalb County

Kishwaukee is an Indian word meaning "sycamore tree" and at one time the south branch of the Kishwaukee was originally called the Sycamore River. The headwaters of the south branch are close to those of Big and Little Rock Creeks, Big and Little Indian Creeks, and Somonauk Creek—all tributaries of the Fox River. However, all branches of the Kishwaukee run into the Rock River because the watersheds are separated by a single ridge. Canoeing on the south branch is a mixed bag of rural farmland, urban small towns, and forest preserves. It's not a bad mix: the river has some very pristine sections, lots of wildlife, and best of all, accessible entry via almost all of the bridges crossing the river below DeKalb. This ease of access allows for trips of varying lengths along any particular section.

The furthest upstream I have put-in was Elva Road where the stream is very small and requires quite a bit of water to be considered canoeable. A large beaver dam two and a half feet in height looks like it has been there for many years and is found only yards upstream of the Keslinger Road Bridge. The first few miles are channeled through cornfields and only begin to meander above Gurier Road. The next few miles are very pleasant, marred only by the close proximity of the Interstate 88 and its tollbooth (these are more often heard than seen). After the south branch crosses the toll road, it crosses Fairview Road then winds its way through the River Heights Golf Course. The river flows through open grassy fields until you pass the Chicago and Northwestern Railroad bridge, followed quickly by the Illinois Route 38 (Lincoln Highway) bridge, followed by the campus of Northern Illinois University. The next few miles run alongside and through the campus and are paralleled by a bike path, the Kishwaukee Kiwanis Pathway. A view of the campus buildings from the river is restricted in all but the highest of water conditions because sides of the river channel are quite deep as it runs through university property.

DeKalb, the heart of Illinois corn country, was also the town where the idea of barbed wire fencing took form. At the DeKalb county fair in the year 1873, a man by the name of Henry Rose exhibited a patented wooden fence of his own design. The thing that was different about Rose's fence was that it had metal points—or barbs—poking through the wooden strips to keep cattle or whatever from pushing the fence over. Rose's invention was designed not as a fence but rather as an attachment to a fence. Three men stood together in front of Henry Rose's exhibit, not discussing it, but rather contemplating its uses or maybe its improvement. In the next year, all three men—Joseph Glidden, Jacob Haish, and Isaac Ellwood—would hold patents for varying types of barbed fencing. Ellwood and Glidden joined forces using Glidden's patent and were the most successful. DeKalb was not only the birthplace of barbed wire, but also the center of its manufacturing. The DeKalb Park District operates the Ellwood House & Museum and a portion of the museum is dedicated to the story of the barbed wire fence.

Hopkins Park downstream of Northern Illinois University marks ten miles from Elva Road. These are the least scenic ten miles on the south branch, but they are also the only miles that have a "small stream" feel to them. Shy canoeists should avoid this section, as there is no way to avoid contact with other humans when canoeing through DeKalb. The takeout in Hopkins Park is at the end of the park road where a parking lot is available. Load or unload next to the river; the riverbanks are steep but not overgrown.

On leaving Hopkins Park, several footbridges are encountered, as is the Kishwaukee Country Club Golf Course. The next two roads crossed, Bethany and Coltonville, are both busy and, as the town DeKalb continues expanding out in this direction, are bound to get busier. It is a six-mile trip from Hopkins Park to Illinois Route 64, and fifteen miles to Baseline Road. The landing at Route 64 is the best landing to be found on the south branch of the Kishwaukee; there is a large roadside pull-off right along the river and a fairly level entry to the water.

The river takes on a more rural feel downstream from DeKalb, becoming wider with occasional housing appearing (mostly where roads cross the river). The east branch of the Kishwaukee joins the south branch a mile downstream of Illinois Route 64. The confluent waters add to the width and flow of the south branch and canoeing opportunities increase with the additional water. A sportsmen's club with a shooting range is on the river's right side. The shooters are unaware of river users; if you hear shots, be sure to make your presence known. Blowing a whistle on my life jacket is the method I use to let others know I'm out there when shots ring out.

Downstream of Aldrich Road, the river flows with farm fields on one side and quarries on the other. Now you might think that this would make for a pretty unnatural setting, but the river has a narrow corridor that contains an amazingly diverse and populous animal community. Deer are seen on most trips, and fox, beaver, muskrat, porcupine, and woodchucks are regularly spotted. An unused railroad right-of-way crosses the south branch before housing marks the approach of the landing on Baseline Road. The best launch site is on the northwest corner of the Baseline Road Bridge. Parking can be found at Knute Olson Jr. Forest Preserve, located on the east side of the river downstream of the Baseline Road.

The next five miles between Baseline Road and Illinois Route 72 are uncrossed by roads, although one low water bridge used for a gravel quarry spans the river and requires a portage. The south branch eventually enters a forested section on a wide bend of the river, indicating the entrance to Russell Forest Preserve; this portion of the river is one of the more scenic on the south branch. A park road could be used to gain access, but it's not one of the better landings. A park trail crosses over the river on a footbridge. Two more miles after Russell Forest Preserve, you'll come upon Illinois Route 72 where better access is available at David Carroll Citizens Park.

The south branch of the Kishwaukee passes under Route 72 and then the Illinois Central Railroads Bridge before turning its course from north to west for the first time. The next three bridges can be used for access, but Five Points Road in the small town of Kingston is the one I've used most often. Kingston Park has parking on both sides of Five Points Road along the north bank of the river. The park is closed in the off-season, at which time it's best to park your car in Kingston and then launch from the park. Kingston is nine river miles downstream of Knute Olsen Forest Preserve on Baseline Road.

The next section, beginning at the town of Kingston, never wanders far from Illinois Route 72 or the Illinois Central Railroad; river, road, and railroad all follow the same course for the next eleven miles down to a good takeout at Irene Road. The trip can be shortened by a mile or two by putting-in at Glidden. The road and railroads proximity mar this section, along with riprapped banks and a waste treatment plant located at Pearl Street. Where they've been left alone, the banks manage to maintain a more natural state. Kirkland Road in Kirkland is not a good access point; the north side of Pearl Street is better.

Once past Kirkland Road, the south branch of the Kishwaukee enters a more forested area twice dividing around islands. These islands are the only place below DeKalb where I've ever encountered log-jams. The second island signals the entrance of Kingsbury Creek and also McQueen Forest Preserve, where you're more likely to run into wildlife than people. The takeout is Irene Road; the shuttle is quick and easy using Illinois Route 72.

The final section of the south branch is also eleven miles in length, starting at Irene Road and ending at Black Hawk Springs Forest Preserve. On this last trip, the south branch again changes its direction from west to north. As with the upstream sections, cropland, pasture, and natural prairie are all part of the scenery. County Line and Edison Roads are close to one another and each can be used as access, as can Blomberg Road. County Line Road marks the border of DeKalb and Ogle counties; the next bridge at Edison Road marks the Ogle and Winnebago County boundaries. The south branch of the Kishwaukee spends less than one fourth of a mile in Ogle County.

Below Blomberg Road, the south branch flows around an island that is more than a mile long. The last few miles are through prairie and are very reminiscent of what the area must have looked like before the arrival of the Europeans. Black Hawk Springs Forest Preserve is where the south branch joins the main Kishwaukee River. It is also the site of several dozen Mississippian Indian burial mounds. The confluence of large rivers was often considered sacred ground to the Mississippians, and therefore a suitable place to bury departed loved ones. Downstream, where the Kishwaukee joins the Rock River, was the location of yet another area of numerous mounds. Black Hawk Park has parking and a rather long carry. If takingout here, do not go too far below the Perryville Bridge, as you'll just increase the carry to the parking lot. If you're looking for the mounds, they are easiest to spot between late fall and early spring when the underbrush is down.

The south branch of the Kishwaukee River has no fast water, no rock bluffs (except at its mouth on the Kishwaukee), and has waste treatment plants emptying their effluents. The upsides, however, are plentiful: several good access points, amiable relations with local landowners, lots of wildlife, and several nice forest preserves. For most of its length, the south branch is in close proximity to farmland, which supplies food. Meanwhile, the river's corridor supplies shelter for the wide diversity of wildlife surrounding. The south branch is unrivaled in its wildlife even by rivers in more remote settings; this distinction alone makes it worth paddling.

Illinois Atlas; Pages 26-27; A-4; A-5, 18-19; D-5
D-4, D-3, C-3

Killbuck Creek

This small stream is the last tributary to feed into the Kishwaukee River before it enters the Rock River. The spelling of the name alternates between Kilbuck and Killbuck on various maps. I chose to use Killbuck, for I think it is more likely to signify the origin and meaning of the name.

Killbuck Creek is very small at Illinois Route 64 where I put in. The first several miles go through open agricultural fields. Watch for the ever-present barbed wire and electric fences across the stream.

The section below Mowers Road is wooded and this leads to a series of logjams, as bad as any I have ever encountered. It was so bad at one point that I had to carry my canoe the distance of several city blocks across a field to avoid more than a dozen bank-to-bank blockages. These blockages continue until you reach the Chicago Northwestern Railroad Bridge, followed by the twin bridges of Interstate 39, beyond which the logjams thin out.

Houses appear as you approach the town of Lindenwood. Don't expect to find a business district, as the community of Lindenwood is more a cluster of houses than a full-sized town. You'll be treated to viewing backyards from the stream.

In the next five and a half miles from Lindenwood Road to Illinois Route 72, Killbuck Creek is crossed by only one bridge, on Big Mound Road. These miles pass uneventfully with the scenery alternating between open agricultural fields and lightly wooded banks. Illinois Route 72 is a practical access site.

The next ten miles seem very wild and untouched, with tree-lined banks shading much of the stream corridor, although I must say that all three trips I have taken on this section have all taken place during the summer months. This summer greenery may have obstructed signs of human intrusion, but I don't think there could have been very much.

There is a low water bridge that crosses Killbuck Creek about a mile downstream of the Illinois Route 72 Bridge. At normal water levels, this can be run or scraped over. But at low water, you'll be forced to portage over the road. The eight miles from Illinois Route 72 to Illinois Route 251 can take you back to a time before there were roads and towns here. Signs of human habitation are brief and rare. Wildlife can be spotted if you are quiet, but I have never found the wildlife to be abundant.

Civilization returns in a most obnoxious manner: in the form of power lines and landfills as Illinois Route 251 is approached. A third of a mile below the bridge is a dam that can be run at some levels. Be sure to check the hydraulic below the dam to make sure of a safe run. If you are not familiar with what I am talking about, it is probably best to portage around the dam.

This dam was part of the Johnson Mill, which was built in the 1930s, partly to generate electric power. Milldams on Killbuck Creek were also located near Lindenwood, Illinois Route 72, and the South Bend Road in past years.

Mills were as essential to the local economy of the earliest settlers as they have been to later residents. The first mills on the prairies of Illinois were built to accommodate the basic needs of food and shelter. To these ends, gristmills and sawmills were the first to be built. These mills were vital because the lack of roads and the lack of cash prevented pioneers from traveling long distances to secure their services.

So, it was inevitable that some enterprising settler would come up with the idea of damming the local watershed in the name of commerce. The dam could be erected with local labor, but a millwright was required to install the machinery for the saw or millstones.

Millwrights were specialists in an age of self-reliance. Most millwrights hired out their services. They would work on a mill as long as required, and then move on to the next project. Some millwrights would build and then operate a mill for a time before selling out.

The millwright was also needed to convert an existing mill for a new function. If the local timber supply ran out, the sawmill might be changed over to a gristmill. A mill might change functions many times during its operating years. Most of these early mills also changed owners regularly.

The advantage of building a mill on a small creek instead of on a major river should be obvious. Smaller creeks were not only easier and cheaper to dam, but they also flooded less often. The downside was that the smaller creeks could not always supply enough water during some seasons. As manufacturers started to use waterpower, a more reliable source of power was required, so locations on larger rivers were needed. Eventually, hydroelectric plants supplied power more widely so there was no longer a need for each plant to have its own dam.

The Johnson milldam is not an old dam, but it is interesting in that part of its machinery is still visible. It is also unusual in that part of the dam face is made of iron.

Below the dam, the gradient increases and the riffles are numerous. After you have traveled under a railroad bridge, you will have entered Kilbuck Bluffs Forest Preserve, a Winnebago County Park. While there are several possible landing sites here, my favorite is just past South Bend Road. Kilbuck Bluffs Forest Preserve has a fairly level access with parking close by. Water and picnic shelters are also available here. Note that the county prefers "Kilbuck" to the "Killbuck" spelling on the map.

It is about a mile further to the mouth of Killbuck Creek. When you reach the confluence of creek and river, it becomes difficult to distinguish which is which. The Kishwaukee River, although much larger than Killbuck Creek, has split its channel around an island upstream, with the greater flow going to the other channel. This means that the first small stream you encounter that enters on the right is, in fact, the Kishwaukee River.

If you have paddled as far as the mouth, two more miles down the Kishwaukee will carry you to Hinchliff Memorial Forest Preserve and a good landing. A steep carry uphill on river left will lead to a small parking area along the Kishwaukee Road.

The thing I liked most about Killbuck Creek is the long uninterrupted stretches of nature. It is easy to imagine yourself traveling in times past when evidence of modern living is masked from view. Killbuck Creek's water is also very clean because it runs through no condensed population areas.

The other thing that I find attractive about Killbuck Creek is its accessibility to several rural interstate roads. Interstates 88, 39, and 90 are all close by. Paddlers from many areas can reach it easily without following elaborate directions.

Illinois Atlas: Page 18, D-2; C-2.

Kilbuck Creek as it runs through   Johnson Dam,
Kilbuck Bluffs Forest Preserve.   Kilbuck Creek.

Kytes Creek

Kytes Creek or the Kyte River is a small tributary that enters the Rock River from the east two miles upstream of Castle Rock State Park in the community of Daysville. It is navigable as far up as the town of Rochelle, if you don't mind paddling on an urban sewer that's not as nice as the DuPage River. Launch on the east side of Rochelle on Route 38, the Lincoln Highway.

The river winds through the neighborhoods of Rochelle for the next few miles. It was somewhere in this area that two of Ogle County's first settlers took an unexpected winter plunge into Kytes Creek. William Cochrane had settled here in 1836 with his family—the second white family to settle in Flagg Township. Mr. and Mrs. Cochrane were returning from Hennepin, where they had gone for additional supplies to see them through the winter.

The water had been very high when it iced over and it had frozen to a substantial thickness. But the water level had dropped by the time the Cochranes tried to cross it in January, and the hollow shell of ice broke when they were halfway across the stream, submerging both of them in the frigid waters. Their clothing was frozen solid by the time they arrived home. In addition, most of the goods they had gone for were damaged, making it a wasted trip.

Just before leaving town, you will pass the sewerage disposal plant on your right where you will be able to view the waste treatment process. This is followed by a few miles of dredged channel with levies on both banks. Interstate 88 comes within visual range at one point just before Steward Creek enters from the left on the Dekalb/Ogle county line, doubling the flow. Although Steward Creek has enough volume to be canoeable, it appears to be a channelized ditch and looks uninteresting.

The next bridge to appear is Brush Grove Road, which is followed shortly by Beach Creek coming in on the left. Two more miles will bring you to Illinois Route 38 where there is good access. Homes are dense for the next four miles down to Skare Park off of Flagg Road. With a trip length of 12 miles so far and the best the creek has to offer in the next 12, I see no reason to ever canoe this section again.

Skare Park is a great access site for it is an easy carry to the water and there are picnic tables and a wooden stockade. But the next two items are what make it unique: a golf driving range and a barn. So leave the hackers behind to shag some balls while others are doing the car shuttle.

From Skare Park, the creek reverts back to nature. Gone are the canalization, the levies, the waste treatment plants, and even most of the homes. This is more what you would expect 70 miles from the city. Small rolling hills and a well-forested corridor give the feeling of another time, perhaps when the Sac and Fox hunted this land before white settlement. There aren't any bridges interrupting the six miles between Flagg Road and Chana Road, which is unusual for any small stream in Northern Illinois. This has given the local wildlife an ideal habitat and breeding ground. Mink, beaver, muskrat, blue and green heron, ducks, geese, frogs, turtles, and more are all there for the nature lover to enjoy. That is, if you are *quiet enough* not to scare them off! I often travel alone, and am able to travel silently for miles. If you can't, then you'll think the area devoid of what I've described. As quiet as I try to be, I suspect that even I miss more than I see.

The only memorable things I encountered in the first six miles were one beaver dam, one hand-operated cable trolley that crossed the creek, and whitewater. The rapids are of the small Class II type and should be no problem for the average recreational peddler.

After passing the Chana Road bridge, watch for barbed wire: you are entering a pasture. If it is windy on the day you paddle this section, you will notice it. The next few miles are mostly open fields separated by sparsely wooded sections. As you approach the end of the stream, typical flood plain forests dominate the scene. The last few miles also contain a few deadfalls.

Before I discuss the choice of takeouts, I would like to talk about the bandits of the Rock River valley. In the early years of settlement, there were always some who thought it easier to take from others than to reap the rewards of their own labor. This was fairly easy to accomplish, as neighbors were usually miles apart. It wasn't uncommon for whole families to be found murdered, their stock and belongings missing, and no witnesses.

The locals suspected certain families of being involved in the gangs that perpetrated these atrocities, but were unable to prove their complicity. The main gang was known as the Banditti of the Prairie. As the area became more populated, the citizenry resolved to put a stop to the lawlessness by force of action.

To this end, vigilantes, who called themselves Regulators, began their own reign of terror. Certain farms mysteriously caught fire while the occupants were away. The identity of the suspects and the intended punishment were made known. It was in this climate that a father and his four sons, a family by the name of Driscoll, were given twenty days notice to leave the country. Being of a contrary nature, instead of leaving, they murdered John Campbell, one of the leaders of the Regulators.

The Regulators apprehended two of the Driscoll boys, William and Pierce. Next, they forcibly took the father, John Driscoll, from the custody of the jail at Oregon, Illinois. A trial was shortly convened with 111 Regulators as jurors. Pierce Driscoll was released because of his youth. John was shot by 56 men; William by 55. This all happened at Washington Grove, less than a mile away from the river. The Regulator judge and a jury of 12 men were later tried for the two murders but were acquitted.

This brings us back to the different takeout options. Rocky Hollow Road is a good takeout for a 9-mile trip. The one I've used the most is the Honey Creek Road. This would make for a trip of 12 miles from Skare Park. Those wishing to extend the trip by two more miles could land just north of Daysville on Daysville Road. This is one-half mile above the mouth at the Rock River. Daysville was the main trading post for this part of the Rock River Valley in the 1840s and 1850s

The next takeout would be at Castle Rock State Park, five miles downstream on the west bank of the Rock River. Castle Rock was a noted landmark on the Rock River for the Indians and the French. In fact, almost every early written account of travel on the river makes mention of it. The State Park has paved boat ramps, making for an *easy landing*.

Illinois Atlas: Page 26, A-1 A-2.

Leo Krusack and Eric Grundin, along with Bob Tyler,
enjoy a winter paddle on Kytes Creek.

The Leaf River

The Leaf River in northwestern Ogle County is more a creek than a river, though rumor has it that its runnable year round, and that alone qualifies it to be called a river. "Runnable year round" applies below Mud Creek during normal periods of rainfall. The Leaf River's name most likely came from a viewing of autumn leaves floating on its surface, or so legend has it.

I accessed the Leaf River a few miles upstream of the town of Leaf River where Pond Road crosses the river. There is a wooden marker here stating that the farm located north of this point was once owned by Clarence Mitchell who authored a book called *River Hill Solioque,* about both this farm and this river. After Clarence Mitchell's death, the farm was willed to the University of Illinois.

After putting-in on Pond Road, the Leaf River parallels Illinois Route 72 closely for several miles. Mud Creek merges on river left just north of the town of Leaf River.

The beginning of the town of Leaf River coincides with the decline of the town of Lightville. The town of Lightville was founded by John Light; in the early 1840s, it was located one mile north of the confluence of Mud Creek and the Leaf River. Lightville grew to be the mercantile center for the immediate area, but in 1880 the Chicago, Milwaukee, St. Paul, and Pacific Railroad passed a mile south of Lightville, sealing its fate. J.B. Bertolet, Lightville's largest merchant, was the first to see the "light" and move the mile south to be closer to the railroad. On the other hand, when you look at today's town of Leaf River, you'll see that it once supported three hotels. Many towns across the county were missed by the railroad and died as a result.

Leaf River Road crosses over the Leaf River below Mud Creek and is a steep but otherwise acceptable landing. Another mile of paddling brings on Illinois Route 72. Below Route 72, the Leaf River turns south as it heads toward the Rock River, and the Leaf River valley is noticeably steeper in these miles. This is more evident on the shuttle than on the river.

I should mention here that the banks of the Leaf River are similar to those of the Pecatonica River and Stillmans Creek, two nearby streams, in that the banks are made up of thick black dirt and are 6 to 8 feet in height. The bottom of the river, on the other hand, is for the most part made up of sand.

One more thing: Over the years, some kind soul notched out most of the logjams. These passages, though sometimes narrow, are the only reason the Leaf River remains canoeable. Stillmans Creek on the east side of the Rock River is about the same size, and has the same type of mud/dirt banks and several logjams per mile. I saw frequent chainsaw cuttings and was grateful for the clear passage on the Leaf.

Town Line Road edges up alongside the Leaf River and access is again possible; the best put-in seems to be at the small wooden bridge at this location. Several uncleared logjams were located just above the next bridge, Townhall Road. It's a little more than a mile from the Town Hall Bridge down to the Illinois Route 2 Bridge and the mouth on the Rock River. There is a good takeout at a roadside park less than a quarter-mile downstream on the Rock River.

Illinois Atlas: Page 17-C-6 and D-6

Little Indian Creek

I started canoeing down Little Indian Creek above the town of Leland. Put-in north of town on Leland Road or two miles upstream on LaSalle County Road N4800. The stream passes through open farm fields, but has nothing extraordinary to offer for the first few miles.

After passing under the Route 34 Bridge and past a few houses, the scenery becomes more natural; an inclined tree-lined corridor borders the creek. This masks the agricultural uplands that surround it. The creek soon winds its way around a large and nicely appointed campground. This is the Hi Tide Campground, which is located on E2200, which is the road that parallels the east side of the stream at this point.

The next bridge you come to is the N4500, and from here to the confluence with Indian Creek, there is very little human intrusion except for bridges. Wildlife was abundant, as were small shoals. Beware: when approaching pastures, there usually is barbed or electric fence wire on the upper and lower boundaries. Such wire will generally appear on blind turns, in fast water, or when you're not paying enough attention. Stay alert! Deadfalls also are numerous (as they are on most small creeks).

Eight more bridges cross Little Indian Creek at intervals of about a mile each, allowing for possible alternate landings to the N4000 Bridge. When I finished my trip down Little Indian Creek, I found the landowner at the N4000 Bridge to be hostile toward trespassers. A quarter of a mile further downstream of N4000 is the confluence with Indian Creek.

Little Indian Creek was a very pleasant canoe trip for the 16 miles I canoed. The only problem is taking-out, because the N4000 Bridge cannot be used and the surrounding Indian Creek farmlands being labeled "No Trespassing" can cause a problem in finding a takeout before the Fox River.

This is a good place to discuss what makes landowners hostile toward canoeists. This concept is best illustrated by three stories I've heard.

The first story was told to me by the next-door neighbor of the man who placed the impregnable barricade across Indian Creek below Earlville. This man had just completed the construction of a gazebo on his property near the banks of the stream. One day, this man went to town and, upon returning home, found that three or four canoes had landed, and their occupants were having lunch, which included a good quantity of beer. The landowner pleasantly informed them that they were on private property, at which time the canoeists became abusive, even going as far as throwing a can of beer at the resident. Because of a few fools, all are now forbidden passage.

The next story involves, of all things, a Boy Scout troop. The scout leader had brought along a pair of wire cutters to cut all the fence wire that the troop encountered on Indian Creek to facilitate their passage downstream. The result was a whole lot of cattle wandering around LaSalle County, including some prize-winning livestock. It was days before all was restored to normal. Many people who raise livestock think of it as more than a hobby; it's also their livelihood. Just check out the state or county fair livestock competition and you'll appreciate what a big part of their lives it is. Many of the farmers I've encountered have cited fence cutting as the main reason for not wanting canoeists to cross their property.

My last story involves a property on Little Indian Creek where the landowner was sued because a canoeist was injured while landing, slipping on the bank, and breaking a limb. This very landowner waited at my van and told me I couldn't take out there! I think the bag of garbage I had picked up on the way downstream was the only reason he let me land, but not before I received a half-hour lecture on the relationship between canoeing and private property. And a promise not to use HIS property as a landing again.

As a good citizen and a canoeist, have the same respect for the landowners along these creeks and rivers that you would expect another individual to have for your property.

Illinois Atlas: Page 27-D4

Nippersink Creek

Glacial Park, located below Wonder Lake, near the junction of Keystone Road and Barnard Mill Road, is the starting point for trips down the Nippersink Canoe Trail on the tame little Nippersink Creek—and that is an appropriate name. The evidence of glaciers is everywhere in Northern Illinois if you know what to look for. At Glacial Park, there are two large conical hills that are called kames. One of the kames is on the right side of the creek, a little more than one mile downstream of the put-in. It is partly eroded, exposing the sand and gravel that the kame is composed of.

A glacier is formed when more ice and snow accumulates than melts. Over the years, this pack gains weight and the weight pushes down hard enough to cause the ice to move. As the ice and snow are building up, large amounts of melt water are generated in warmer seasons. Kames are formed when melt water on the surface of the glacier finds its way downward through the glacier ice. This seepage can grow to stream or river size and is called a moulin. Where these streams exit the glacier, ice caves are often formed. The sediments carried to the bottom of the moulin sometimes form kames. When the sediment forms a long ridge instead, it is called an esker.

Another glacial formation that is present in the area is called a moraine. Moraines are ridges formed at the sides of a glacier. As the glacier moves forward, it plows up the land in front. Some of this, in turn, is pushed to the side, forming hills that parallel the path of the glacier.

> *"…as you are canoeing down Nippersink Creek, see if you can spot any signs of what took place here more than 10,000 years ago. The best opportunity to do this is in the first five miles, as the land is more open and affords longer views."*

So, as you are canoeing down Nippersink Creek, see if you can spot any signs of what took place here more than 10,000 years ago. The best opportunity to do this is in the first five miles, as the land is more open and affords longer views.

The Nippersink Canoe Trail was created by the McHenry County Conservation District via the unprecedented action of acquiring permission from all of the private landowners along the stream to allow canoeists access through their lands. Since so many of Illinois' scenic little waterways, like the Nippersink, are off-limits because of Illinois' antiquated laws, one hopes that this precedent will open other streams for such use in future years.

The first few miles have been ditched through pastureland that once belonged to Northern Pump Farms, a cattle operation. It has overgrown to the point where it looks like a very natural prairie, excluding a couple of farm bridges. All of these have plenty of clearance, even at high water. The last of these is an old railway bridge that carries the McHenry County Prairie Trail north. This bridge has many rows of old bridge pilings, and the current through here is swift. A little caution and a slow approach will get you through safely. The creek flows through some lovely oak woodlands as it approaches Illinois Route 31. This is the first major road that has crossed the creek in the four miles since the put-in. I love the long stretches of solitude in natural surroundings.

Below Illinois 31, Nippersink Creek flows through a rural farmscape for about a mile before you come to Pioneer Road. Here is Pioneer Park, the second access point on the Nippersink Canoe Trail. The park has a water pump and bathrooms, and makes an excellent lunch stop. A stairway leads from the creek up to the park.

From here, the Nippersink runs through several pastures. There are fences here, but they are the friendly kind, allowing safe and easy passage. The north branch of the Nippersink enters from the left in the last of these pastures before encountering the U.S. Route 12 Bridge. This area above and below U.S. Route 12 contains the best riffles the Nippersink has to offer.

Around the bend below U.S. Route 12 is a riffle with a name. Any riffle that has been given a name deserves to be called a rapid, and this one is called Five Inch Falls. The buildings that are visible around U.S. Route 12 indicate you have reached the town of Solon Mills.

For the next few miles down to the town of Spring Grove, civilization is never far away. There are the roads on either side. Even when the roads are not in sight, the traffic is still audible. Homes are seen regularly along the banks. This doesn't mean that all the wildlife is found only upstream. Muskrats and waterfowl seem to be even more abundant in the stretch between Solon Mills and Spring Grove.

Spring Grove is the location of the third landing on the Nippersink Canoe Trail. The Lyle C. Thomas Memorial Park is located at Blivin Street and the creek. Blivin Street crosses U.S. Route 12 at a stoplight, so it is pretty easy to find. There is a state operated fish hatchery located here. The Spring Grove landing is a little more than seven miles from Glacial Park.

The last landing on the canoe trail is the Nippersink Canoe Base, four miles downstream of Spring Grove. Nippersink Creek slows its pace in these last few miles as it winds endlessly through a wetland wilderness. Although it parallels U.S. Route 12 the whole distance and the sound of traffic can be heard, the natural surroundings and the wildlife make this a pretty section of stream, one not to be missed. Below the Canoe Base landing, Nippersink Creek empties into Pistakee Lake, the lower of the Fox Chain of Lakes. The miles downstream of the Nippersink Canoe Base are mostly natural, with cottages, resort homes, and boat yards starting a short distance above U.S. Route 12. Takeouts are mostly private after Nippersink Creek empties into Nippersink Lake, one of the Fox Lakes. (*For takeouts, see Fox River chapter.*)

The Nippersink Canoe Trail is the perfect introduction to canoeing small streams. It has many of the things that make small stream canoeing challenging, without any really dangerous hazards. Like with most streams in this volume, high water levels add to the fun.

Illinois Atlas: Page 20, A-1

The evidence of glaciers is everywhere in Northern Illinois if you know what to look for. At Glacial Park, there are two large conical hills that are called kames. One of the kames is on the right side of the creek, a little more than one mile downstream of the put-in. It is partly eroded, exposing the sand and gravel that the kame is composed of.

The North Branch of Nippersink Creek

The town of Richmond on the Wisconsin border is where I started my trip toward the main branch. The best thing about the North Branch is that eventually you'll come to the mouth, where the obstructions end. Although they're not as bad as Spring Creek, that's only because Spring Creek was longer. You might ask why someone would keep putting himself and his friends on unnavigable streams again and again. Well, I do scout before starting out. But scouting at 5 or 6 bridges allows a look at only a couple of hundred yards of river (out of many miles). This leaves most of the mystery to be solved from your boat.

One thing to look out for when scouting is what I call a wet woods or wooded flood plain. The problem here is that the trees in these woods aren't deep rooted because there's enough water near the surface. So the roots grow wide rather than deep. Then when the area floods and the ground loosens, the trees fall down, usually across the channel. This creates lots of deadfall, so much so that you find yourself…pulling the canoe over one tree…while looking back upstream at the last two pullovers and downstream at the next two. This makes for extraordinarily slow going.

A couple of hints for dealing with dead falls, log jams, beaver dams, or low bridges, all of which are encountered on the 6 miles of the North Branch.

First, if there seems to be enough clearance to get under, approach slowly to make sure that there is. It's important that you keep the boat parallel to the current as you test the clearance. If the boat doesn't clear, but only by an inch or two, shift your weight toward the front of the boat. This will reduce the profile of the boat by inches. Sometimes you can stand in the boat, and while holding onto the obstruction, walk across the boat. This keeps the weight (i.e., you) at the point that needs to be cleared. When you get to the end of the boat, you can lay down on your back in the bottom and push with your hands if necessary. This method also works well for all types of low bridges (provided that there is enough clearance).

Another trick that works on obstructions that are low to the water is what I call the "teeter totter method." This involves getting the weight (once again, you) to the stern—or back—of the canoe. This raises the bow—or front— of the canoe; with luck, added speed will propel the boat up and over the obstruction. Of course, if the front of the boat wasn't out of the water enough, an abrupt stop can be expected. This trick works best with canoes that are made of plastic. Some amount of rocker in the design also helps.

If none of this has worked, look to the two banks, as there is often a sneak route located there. Although these are often brushy, and introduce a variety of insects and spiders as passengers of your boat, they are still faster and easier than portaging. The last resort before portaging is pulling up over the obstruction. This is where an 8' or 10' rope tied to the bow and stern comes in handy. All of this of course takes practice, good balance, and common sense. Many canoeists tip at obstructions. This can be fatal. Getting washed under a logjam or strainer drowns many boaters each year. So be careful.

Back to why the subject of obstacles needed discussing: the North Branch of the Nippersink. I put-in at a very nice park that is off of May Street in Richmond. May Street intersects U.S. Route 12 on the south end of town.

I put-in where the creek comes closest to the shelter in the park. This was a bad choice, for I had completed 5 portages before my van was out of sight. Most of these are low footbridges; some private, some belonging to the golf course on river left. After the golf course fades from view, the creek stays in a wooded corridor. U.S. route 12 is close by but is rarely seen or heard. At one point where the creek edges up next to Route 12, it starts to meander, and continues a winding course the rest of the way to the mouth. It's about 3 miles from Richmond to where the North Branch crosses Route 12.

Just after the Route 12 Bridge, a picnic or lunch area has been built by a factory or office building. There's also an upturned footbridge that required a difficult portage on my part. From here to the mouth, there isn't much that is memorable. The closer you come to the main branch, the more you're paddling through pasture. In many places, thick black topsoil can be seen at depths of four feet or more.

Route 12 is crossed again soon after entering the main branch. Several takeouts are available depending on your desired trip length. I took out at the Nippersink Canoe Base off of Route 12. This makes for a trip of 12 miles. (*See Nippersink Creek for alternate landings.*)

ILLINOIS ATLAS; Page 20-A-1 & 2

Pecatonica River

The Pecatonica River enters Illinois a mile or so above the town of Winslow, Illinois, where there is a public boat ramp. If you want to canoe across the state line, as I did, find the main northbound road out of Winslow and continue on this road across the state line. In about a mile, a bridge crosses the Pecatonica and a reasonable canoe access is found. Canoeing above this point is described in *Southern Wisconsin Canoe Trails.*

The name Pecatonica means "muddy waters" in the Winnabago language. "Muddy" describes the banks of the river from the state line to the mouth of the Rock River. The Pecatonica River also meanders incessantly through those same miles, earning its reputation for being crooked. It is so crooked that when the sun is out, you'll find that within a few miles, the sun has been on all sides of you.

The good things about the Pecatonica are that it always has enough water, and it has long natural stretches. Add to this the fact that the shuttle miles are shorter than the river miles.

The drab thing is that those long uninterrupted stretches sometimes leave you with access at inconveniently great distances. The high muddy banks are the other inconvenience; they make landing ashore for any reason a messy affair.

During the lawless 1840s, Winslow was the victim of a frontier crime committed by "Prairie Pirates." A well-known group called the Winslow Vigilantes was established to counter the effects of this crime wave. (*For more on vigilantes, see Kytes Creek.*)

Below the town of Winslow, the river runs flat, with a steady current. These most northerly miles contain high hills that the river meanders in between. The next town downstream is McConnell, which is more of a crossroad than a town. West of town, there is a bridge and boat ramp located downstream on the southeast side of the bridge.

Below McConnell, the river continues to course its way between towering hills. Now and then, rock outcroppings appear.

As houses and trailers come into view, so does the Cederville Road Bridge. The access here is not great because all sides of the bridge are occupied by the yards of the adjoining properties; this makes the next possible landing five more miles away, at Winneshiek Road. The best takeout at Winneshiek Road is 100 yards east of the bridge. One bend in the river upstream of Winneshiek Road, Richland Creek adds considerable volume to the Pecatonica. (*See Richland Creek.*)

Winneshiek Road is named for the Indian Chief whose village occupied the present day site of Freeport. He was a leader in the 1827 refusal of the Winnebago tribe to sell their lands adjoining the lead mining district to the U.S. Government. The Winnebagos absolutely rejected the proposed sale. Their unwillingness to even enter into negotiation of the sale was termed by the whites as "The Winnebago War." It's interesting to note that after refusing to sell the land, Chief Winneshiek was seen attempting to gather lead (albeit unsuccessfully).

It is 10 miles from Winneshiek Road to Illinois Route 75 in downtown Freeport. The hilly terrain is replaced by a flat flood plain. Freeport edges the river for a surprisingly short distance. Access in town is limited to two bridges and neither is very desirable.

A man named Baker opened a trading post and ferry next door to Chief Winneshiek's Winnebago village. It has been claimed that Baker's wife complained about the failure of her good-natured husband to charge visitors for services rendered. She claimed that the place was a "free port."

From Freeport to U. S. Route 20, the constantly meandering river doubles or triples its course by winding around more than usual. Yellow Creek enters on river right, about halfway between Illinois Route 75 and U.S. Route 20. (*See Yellow Creek.*) The only other interruption in the 15 miles between Freeport and Ridott is the small community of Browns Mill.

The bank of the Pecatonica around Browns Mill is noticeably higher than it is anywhere else for miles around, making it a perfect mill site. The first mill at this site was erected in 1853. Browns Mill went through many transformations of functions, from sawmill, to gristmill, and finally to electrical generation before falling into disuse.

Browns Mill is not good access because all the roadside property appears to be private. The mill, dam, and building create a Class II-plus rapid. The old mill walls on the river right provide the most challenging route. As always, dams are dangerous and conditions change with different water levels. So scouting is highly recommended.

An abandoned railroad bridge crosses the Pecatonica a short distance below Browns Mill and is similar to one just above Freeport. The miles downstream to Ridott pass pleasantly. The landing is north of Ridott on River Road upstream of the Rock City Road Bridge.

From the River Road landing to the Farwell Road bridge is 6 more miles of winding forest-lined river. Below Farwell Road, you come within audio range of the town of Pecatonica. This noise is generated by the Deans Foods nondairy creamer plant. I was told that it's the dryer blower motor that makes all the noise.

As the town of Pecatonica is approached, the Winnebago County line is crossed and soon the Winnebago County fairgrounds come into view. One of the two landings here is located directly behind the fairground grandstand. Between this first landing and the second lays the remains of an old dam. Even on the *Delorme Atlas* map, a rapid is indicated at this location. The largest part of this rapid is down the center, while a narrow passage can be found through the remains of the old mill. The rapid at this location is larger than the one upstream at Browns Mill, and probably rates a low Class III. Always scout for yourself before running it.

The town of Pecatonica deserves a look around. The turn of the century Victorian, gingerbread houses are the attraction here, along with the antique stores. Also, look along Pecatonica Road on the east side, downtown, for a sign indicating the prior existence of an opera house.

If putting-in or taking-out in Pecatonica, one has a choice of whether or not to run the dam, as there are paved boat ramps both up and down stream. As the river leaves town, it quickly reverts back to its natural state and continues much the same as before. The next three takeouts all have paved boat ramps, and good access, as do all Winnebago County Parks. The first is Pecatonica River Forest Preserve, about six miles downstream from the town of Pecatonica. This park is closed during some seasons. The next takeout is seven miles further downstream at Trask Road Bridge Forest Preserve, and (again) provides access and parking. Twelve more miles brings on Two Rivers Forest Preserve, located between the towns of Harrison and Shirland. It's called Two Rivers because the Sugar and Pecatonica Rivers merge at this point. (*See Sugar River.*)

This leaves one more 9 1/2 mile section down to the river's mouth on the Rock River. Only one bridge, Meridian Road, crosses the river in these final miles. A good landing is located at Macktown Forest Preserve, right at the confluence of the Rock and Pecatonica Rivers.

Macktown Forest Preserve is home to a couple of historic buildings in the location formerly known as Macktown, a village founded by Stephen Mack, the first white settler in Winnebago County.

Mack entered the area in the year 1829 with the intention of becoming a trader to the local Winnebago village, located 1 1/2 miles from the mouth of the Pecatonica on the Rock River. Stephen Mack refused to trade guns or liquor with the Indians, which seems to have bred hostility, as two attempts were made on his life. Both attempts were thwarted by the intervention of an Indian maiden named Hononegah, who it seems was smitten with Mack. After the second attempt on his life, Mack returned Hononegah's affection by marrying her in a traditional Indian ceremony. Even after he married the daughter of a chief, a robbery and a murder were attempted on Stephen Mack, this time by ambush. They were again foiled by his new wife, Hononegah Mack.

After the Blackhawk War, Mack became instrumental in the early settlement of the area. Besides running the trading post, Stephen also started a ferry in 1838, which he replaced four years later with a drawbridge. He also filed claim on some of the best land in the county. Eventually, the town of Rockton waxed as Macktown waned.

There are many takeouts downstream of the Pecatonica on the Rock River. One bears the name Hononegah, Stephen Mack's wife and savior.

Illinois Atlas, Page 16-A-4; 17-B-5; B6; 18-A-1

Pecumsaugan Creek

Until I ran LaSalle County's Pecumsaugan Creek, I thought that Spring Creek in that county was the worst canoe trip experience I ever had. Its not that Pecumsaugan was any harder going. It wasn't. It was the fact that local land owners got so angry at us for going down the creek, they called the County Sheriff who caused our vehicle at the put-in to be towed. It was taken 20 miles away at our expense!

Even this incident would not have ranked Pecumsaugan as the worst trip, but I discovered there were more than ten logjams per mile! In addition to this, half of the trees blocking Pecumsaugan are of the variety that has thorns. Thorny trees take away many of the options for negotiating deadfalls. If all of this isn't enough to discourage the heartiest explorer, then let me go on.

Two more factors that add more aggravation to a really bad trip are fencing and gradient. The fences appear about a mile apart and were more elaborate than on most other creeks. By this I mean that many of the fences we encountered had multiple strands. One strand might be barbed wire. The others at the same location would be electric. All of them supported by 3/8 steel cable where they extend all the way down to the waterline. Either these landowners take their fencing seriously, or the livestock they own are smart enough to get through a lesser barricade.

The last factor was gradient. This is particularly true below Pecumsaugan Falls. Below the falls, Pecumsaugan Creek drops more than 50 feet per mile. This means a careful approach to each bend in the stream. Fast water, plus possible deadfall equals danger.

We launched at LaSalle County Road 3150, just south of the Utica blacktop, State Route 178. There is no way you would want to repeat the mistake we made in starting here for the landowners are not friendly to canoeists. They consider canoeists criminal trespassers that should be dealt with by local law enforcement authorities. The next bridge downstream is Interstate 80, which isn't usable as an access point. This leaves U.S. 6 as the only other possible access road before Pecumsaugan Creek enters the Illinois Michigan Canal.

A couple of my friends were almost arrested trying to launch at the U.S. Route 6 Bridge in 1991. At that time a farm occupied the area around the bridge. Since then a golf course has been developed on the property. There were two reasons for wanting to put in farther upstream. First is the fact that the area around the U.S. Route 6 Bridge is very open, making it hard to launch on the creek inconspicuously. Second is that Pecumsaugan Canyon is less than 1-1/2 miles long, making it too short a trip for my taste.

Now I know you're probably wondering why I thought this might be a great little creek to explore. While researching other streams in the area, Pecumsaugan Creek's name kept popping up with references to an 1833 mill site and mining that took place in the later 19th century. The name Pecumsaugan seems to be a variation of the Potawatomi name for "tomahawk." This is even more curious because the next watershed to the west is Tomahawk Creek.

Whitewater boating friends had told me about a high water run in the canyon section just below U. S. Route 6. During the winter months, two of us took a hike through Pecumsaugan Canyon down to the Illinois Michigan Canal. The hike through the canyon convinced me that I should paddle this section some day.

Pecumsaugan continued to be impeded by fences and logjams, all the way past Interstate 80 and down to U.S. Route 6. Below Route 6, the character of the stream changes abruptly. As you pass under the Route 6 Bridge, Pecumsaugan picks up speed as it starts to drop very fast. Two golf course bridges are encountered as you race toward the old Crosair mill site followed immediately by the scenic six foot Pecumsaugan Falls.

The falls can be run almost anywhere, but the landing is difficult. The problem is the lack of a plunge pool. Scouting on creek right had made this apparent, but I decided to run it anyway to get the photo.

Simon Crosair arrived in LaSalle County in 1826, one year after Thomas Covell, and Lewis Bailly. (See Bailey Creek and Covel Creek chapters). Crosair settled on the south side of the Illinois River around Cedar Creek, becoming an Indian trader. A few years later, he built and operated a mill on the Cedar Creek location, which he sold in 1840.

In 1833, Simon Crosair erected his second mill, this time on Pecumsaugan Creek. For several years Simon Crosair was running mills on both sides of the Illinois River. Simon and his wife lived at the Pecumsaugan mill site for only about a year. They next moved to Utica as Simon Crosair thought that a town at the head of navigation on the Illinois River would surely prosper in the future. The old LaSalle County histories bear testament to the kindness the Crosairs bestowed on others. The Crosair family continued to own the property on Pecumsaugan for more than 100 years. In the 1850s the family sold the canyon to a mining interest.

Once below Pecumsaugan Falls, you will enter the canyon proper. The walls are close together and about 50 feet in height. The current is fast, requiring the utmost caution rounding bends. If you can find an eddy, catch it and stop to look around. The beauty of this canyon rivals that of any in Starved Rock State Park. The walls are so steep and narrow that they block out the sunlight from the bottom of the canyon.

About half way down, the first real rapid appears in the middle of a long bend, the only rapid in the canyon proper and I would rate it as a class II+ or class III−. Unfortunately, the day we ran down Pecumsaugan, three trees were down across different portions of the rapid, so we were not able to run even part of the it. But, it looked like it could be a lot of fun.

A side stream enters via a 12-foot unrunnable waterfall, on the left side at this location.

Below this rapid Pecumsaugan Creek continues fast and narrow, with an occasional deadfall to dodge. As you proceed downstream, cave openings begin to appear on both sides of the creek, These are not actually caves but remnants of old mining operations that were started in 1869 or 1870 and continued past the turn of the century. The cliffs consisted of dolomite, which was crushed and processed into hydraulic cement. This cement had to be brought into the region from a great distance at great expense, hence the need for a local source of supply for cement. So that's the reason for the over 30 mineshaft openings on two levels, with caverns extending a quarter of a mile into the bluffs. Many are refuges for the endangered Indiana brown bat. There are also remains of historic building foundations and old brick kilns used in the manufacture of the hydraulic cement at the junction of Pecumsaugan Creek and the Illinois Michigan Canal

Pecumsaugan Creek flows through the Illinois Michigan Canal channel on its way to the Illinois River. To continue on to the river through floodplain forest with its numerous logjams and then have to travel several miles on the river to an access either at Utica or LaSalle seems impractical. The logical choice here is to follow the canal west two miles and you'll end up at the takeout for the white water section of the Little Vermilion River. (See Little Vermilion River.) Or, if you go east two miles via the canal, you'll end up in Utica, where several options for taking out are available. The one we used was across the street from the LaSalle County Historical Society museum, located in an old stone canal warehouse structure.

To conclude that even the scenic last mile of Pecumsaugan is enjoyable canoeing would be a misconception for the best this creek has to offer is spoiled by deadfalls. In addition, the lower canyon and mine shafts are a state-protected game preserve for several species of bats. The upper section has absolutely nothing going for it. Pecumsaugan is best left to the birds. (And bats.)

Illinois Atlas; Page 34 A-1

The old Crosair Mill site is followed immediately by the scenic six foot Pecumsaugan Falls.

Pecumsaugan canyon is less than 1-1/2 miles long, too short a trip for my taste.

Pine Creek

Pine Creek is a tributary of the Rock River located in western Ogle County. Pine Creek is formed of branches that come together south of Illinois Route 64; it flows south 17 miles to join the Rock River between Grand Detour and Dixon. There are trespassing issues on Pine Creek both at White Pines State Park and with landowners along its course. Too further impede access bridges both up and downstream of the State Park are fenced off and posted no trespassing.

Since most of the upper miles are through pasture fences are too be expected, particularly above Oregon Trail Road, the last road before entering the State Park. 7 miles downstream of Route 64 Pine Creek enters White Pines State Park where there are No Canoeing signs posted at the park entrance. A few miles above the State Park Pine Creek begins cutting through a series of glacial ridges. White Pines State Park is where Pine Creek finds its way though the first of these ridges, forming steep valleys with bluff walls, lining the creek side for nearly half a mile. White Pines State Park was formed around the southern most stand of white pine in the country. Its a shame that a State Park which accommodates hiking, biking, fishing, camping, and picnicking, can't see the recreational value of a canoe trail.

The first of the park personal I ask why canoeing was not allowed in the park responded "because its the rule." Later asking another the response was that the fords in the park were not passable and local landowners had called the county sheriff on trespassing canoeists. This was a better reason, but it still didn't stop me from putting-in at the Pine Road Bridge, the parks southern boundary.

Below the State Park, Pine Creek turns to the east for a ways, before turning back south and cutting through a second ridge. Riffles are frequent as are rock bluffs. The bluffs are never as high or long as those at White Pines. Pine Creek remains in a steep valley past the Columbian Road Bridge, which is fenced and posted, not allowing for access. A couple of additional miles brings on Henry Road which looked user friendly. There was a newer footbridge upstream of Henry Road. A mile downstream of Henry Road, Penn Corners Road crosses Pine Creek, followed by Edgewood Road after another mile.

Below Edgewood Road Pine Creek flattens out onto the plain of the Rock River Valley. When I ran Pine Creek the Rock River was running high and this backed up at least the last mile of Pine Creek. Once out on the Rock its about 2 miles down to Lowell Park on river right. Lowell Park has boat ramps along with all the facilities expected of a well thought out park.

Pine Creek is a nice high water run. Too bad state parks like Apple River Canyon and White Pines can't see the light of developing the great recreational value of canoe trails. If the private property issues bother you try nearby Elkhorn Creek* or Franklin Creeks upper 6 miles if you don't mind a few log jams per mile. Both are also exceptional.

Illinois Atlas; page 17, D-5; 25, A-6

Piscasaw Creek

In 1996, the Prairie State Canoeists planned a club trip down the Piscasaw and were threatened with arrest while trying to launch near Chemung. They wisely chose to canoe the main branch of the Kishwaukee River downstream of Cherry Valley instead. Now, I personally haven't been stopped, but then again I paddle mostly on weekdays and alone. There are fences, however they are not the type that landowners who hate canoeists put up. But small creeks are considered not legally navigable in Illinois so one must be careful not to get arrested.

The put-in is Illinois Route 173, just west of the very small community of Chemung. There is a park located a few blocks downstream which offers a more secluded put-in but is a substantially longer carry to the water. The park is where the canoe club was stopped. Above Illinois 173 Piscasaw Creek splits into three branches that all look too small to paddle. The Piscasaw meanders incessantly for much of its course.

The first few miles are very open and never wander very far from Route 173. If it is windy the day you paddle you'll find that it doesn't make much difference which way the wind blows from, as the creeks meandering will put the wind in your face at least part of the time.

Piscasaw Creek can best be described as a farm creek. Farm homes and barns are passed frequently as are pastures and fields of corn and soybeans. Cattle are often found cooling themselves in the creek on hot days. At times Piscasaw Creek enters wooded areas where trees occasionally block the course. These stretches are never very long and soon you are back out in the open. Because of this, logjams are infrequent even though Piscasaw Creek is a small stream.

After passing under a few bridges, a series of small dams interrupt the stream. The first of these has a four to five feet high drop. But the dam face is very irregular and broken making a clean run hard to accomplish. The next three dams have obvious chutes with drops of less than two feet and are pretty straightforward. All of these dams are formed by large chunks of concrete.

Riffles and access roads are frequent. Most of the roads crossing Piscasaw Creek's upper miles can be used as access. Stimes Memorial Park is encountered a very short distance above Mill Road. Stimes Park is small, but every year it seems to have some new improvement added to the grounds. One year it was a parking lot; another year it was chemical toilets. This park might make a good lunch stop if canoeing down from Chemung.

The mill that the road was named after was the Bonus Mill built in 1849, which was located in this same vicinity. Roads are never far removed from Piscasaw Creek. They are either along side paralleling the creek or crossing over at too frequent intervals. This is partly due to the fact that most of Piscasaw Creek is surrounded by open fields making the roads visible for quite a distance.

Piscasaw Creek, more than any other stream in northern Illinois is a typical prairie stream in the Prairie State. Most of the earliest visitors to this part of the state made comments on the lack of trees and the openness of the country. It was called a treeless wasteland, and a prairie desert. Piscasaw Creek is as representative of this picture of open country as can be found on any northern Illinois stream.

The prairies every few years would burn in huge prairie fires several miles wide. Fires would light up the night skies for miles around. During the daylight hours, the smoke rising would give warning of the oncoming inferno. It is known that many Indian villages were located on the east side of streams and rivers. The hope was that the fires would be retarded by the natural firebreak the streams created.

Any of the three bridges below Mill Road provide good access. From Illinois 173 to Capron Road would be an eight and a half mile trip; to Denny Road, a ten mile trip; to Russellville Road, an eleven and a half mile trip. The Russellville Road access has four conical mounds just off the creek right bank.

The nine miles from Russellville Road to the mouth on the Kishwaukee River are similar to the eleven upper miles, with the exception of a long wooded section between Squaw Prairie Road and Marengo Road. Several horse trails come up along side or cross Piscasaw Creek in these woods.

The bridge at Woodstock Road has fencing on both sides of the bridge all the way down to the waterline and across the stream. The fence is made of heavy gauge wire crossed in six inch by twelve-inch squares. This goes all the way up the side of the bridge from water line to the railing. The corners of the bridge are treated with barbed wire.

When I came upon this obstacle I was completely dumbfounded as to what to do. Can't go over, can't go around, can't even get to the road to take out. The only alternative I had was to sink my boat and push it under the fence and then I too was forced to pass under this fence, getting very wet in the process. Once under the bridge, I was forced to repeat the procedure to get out the other side.

This fence was erected by someone who doesn't want fishermen, canoeists, or anyone else to pass under this bridge. The good news is that the high water of 1996 at least partially destroyed the barricade. Whether or not it is to be rebuilt remains to be seen, but it seems to me that anyone who put that much effort into constructing the barricade would not hesitate to do it again.

The odd part was that it should have been a warning as to the logjams ahead. As happens on many small creeks, the deadfalls are being continually pushed on farther downstream. So below Woodstock Road you can expect to see more trees across the streambed.

The takeout should be at Lawrenceville Road where a small parking area is just east of the bridge and right at the mouth on the Kishwaukee River. For two years this area was gated and posted No Trespassing. 1997 finds it again open and usable. Land donated by Pilsbury/Green Giant now has a canoe launch called Red Horse Bend at this location.

Piscasaw Creek is starting to have an access problem and it would be a shame to lose the twenty miles that I consider some of the nicest paddling in the Kishwaukee watershed. The openness of Piscasaw Creek and the surrounding countryside is unique and one that is highly recommended.

Illinois Atlas: Page 19, A-5; B-4

Plum River

The Plum River flows into the Mississippi on the south end of the town of Savanna. Its headwaters are very close to Yellow Creek in Stevenson County, separated only by the ridge where the settlement of Kellogg's Grove was located beginning in 1825 (see section on Yellow Creek). The furthest upstream put-in I dared to access on the Plum River was the Carroll Creek put-in on Jacobstown Road. I'll warn you as I was warned once by a local and once by a friend—the miles of Plum River downstream of Carroll Creek are brimming with logjams. The first two miles of this seven-mile trip are on Carroll Creek (which is spectacular) between Jacobstown Road and the town of Mount Carroll.

At the confluence of Carroll Creek and Plum Creek, the two streams are about the same size. Plum River runs in a steep narrow valley complete with several rock bluffs; the scenery is pleasant but the steady portages over and around blockages do not allow for the enjoyment of nature. No roads cross the river in this section. Although Georgetown Road comes alongside of the Plum River at one point, the banks are far too steep to make a practical landing.

The first take-out would be the Illinois Route 64, U.S. Route 52 Bridge where steep banks and distant parking provide only fair access. If you use this access, park either at Old Mill Park on the south end of the bridge or on the dead end road just north and west of the bridge. The best side of the bridge to launch or land is the northeast but be warned of one last logjam only yards above the bridge. Old Mill Park was the site of Plum River Falls, which limited steamboat navigation on Plum River. Also, as the park name implies, mills were located here between 1836 and 1885. The first family to settle in Carroll County, the Davidson's, built a cabin near here in 1828 and boarded travelers who traversed several roads that ran by here on their way to the lead mining region.

If you continue past the Route 64/52 bridge, the next section of the Plum runs nine miles down to the Mississippi River, directly downstream of the Savanna city boat access. The Plum River is more easily canoed below Route 52 as most of the logjams are upstream. The river is wider, the banks less steep and the current steady as one approaches the Mississippi flood plain. Access can be had at several places along Scenic Bluffs Road or at Illinois Route 84 to avoid the major logjam that obstructs the river below. This logjam is old; it has vegetation growing out of it and the Plum River flowing under it. It seemed at first that the river had just come to an end; I looked around for another passage but found none. The obstruction is about a block long and is divided into two sections. The blockage is not of great height but what retards passage is that almost everything is floating and can't be stepped on. Muddy banks add to the difficulty, as does thick growth along the banks.

Several miles of river remain downstream of the log jam; most of these run through the Upper Mississippi National Wildlife and Fish Refuge, continuing that natural corridor that began with the initial junction of the Plum and Carroll Creek. The Burlington Railroad Bridge marks the end of the Plum River and the beginning of the Mississippi River as one nears the town of Savanna. The Savanna boat ramps are located only a hundred yards upstream; however, the Mississippi is swift and it took hard paddling to ascend the short distance to the take-out.

If the Plum River's upper section was less obstructed this would make a remote and scenic trip, but as it stands, this section is just too much work. The lower nine miles would also be a pleasant paddle except for that one long logjam.

Illinois Atlas; Page 15 D-3; 16 A-1

Poplar Creek

Yes, this is the one they named the music theatre after. You say, "No way!" I say, "Yes way!" The theatre is now long gone, but Poplar Creek keeps flowing.

Although Poplar Creek has more than its share of logjams and low bridges, the scenery more than makes up for the difficulties. This is without a doubt the most clean, and natural appearing stream east of the Fox River and west of Chicago.

The put-in I used was Bartlett Road. I had scouted upstream one bridge but that inspection gave me second thoughts about starting there. As it turned out, it was probably a good idea to put in at Bartlett Road, as there was more than a days supply of blockages downstream. Enough discussion of what's difficult about Poplar Creek.

The distance to the water is short and the parking is good on the wide paved shoulder at Bartlett Road. Below the Bartlett Road bridge, Poplar Creek runs through Poplar Creek Forest Preserve, part of the Cook County Forest Preserve system. It is this protection that keeps the first four miles pristine.

About a mile below the put-in, Poplar Creek flows under three closely spaced bridges. The first is a foot or bridle path and has ample clearance. The second is Illinois Route 59, a very low span, which often requires portaging, although portaging is often hampered by the heavy road traffic. The third is Illinois Route 58, also called Golf Road as well as the Evanston-Elgin Road in these parts, where there is plenty of clearance.

This upper section is unusual in that most of the portages that are required are caused by man instead of nature. In the mile below the Route 58 Bridge, three old low farm bridges are encountered, requiring a short pull over. Other than the man made obstacles, Poplar Creek remains fairly open. Although constant maneuvering is required, full creek blockages are rare.

The scenery is without comparison for the Chicago metropolitan area. The banks are low, a grassy floodplain that extends quite a ways back from the creek bed. Farther back still, woodlands border Poplar Creek's valley. This landscape makes Poplar Creek one of the most natural appearing creeks in this volume.

After flowing three miles through this natural preserve, the stream again flows under Route 58, Golf Road. Downstream of Golf Road is another section of Poplar Creek Forest Preserve and you are back into nature as before. By the time you pass under a beautiful single arched railroad bridge, you will be leaving the forest preserve.

The next short stretch has both houses and a golf course. The golf course naturally has a few low footbridges to portage, but that's par for the course. Illinois Route 19, Irving Park Road or, as it is sometimes called, the Chicago-Elgin Road, passes over the stream about one mile below. Elgin High School is on the left side of the creek, a short hop downstream, its athletic fields are on the right.

Now, you would think that as Poplar Creek enters Elgin proper it would become very urban in appearance. It does go past some less than spectacular homes and some busy roads, but for the most part it stays pretty and natural. The thing that does change is the nature of the portages. Prior to this point they were caused by man.

Poplar Creek winds its way around through forest and wetland as it passes under U.S. Route 20. Much of this section was jammed with logs and debris, with much garbage caught behind the blockages. The waterway continues like this past Illinois Route 25 to Raymond Street, which is a great takeout. There is a parking area here for the two-bike/hiking trails that intersect here, the Illinois Prairie Path and the Fox River Trail.

Raymond Street was named after Benjamin Raymond, a two-term mayor of Chicago, who was instrumental in Elgin's rise as an industrial center. Through his influence, the Chicago and Galena Union Railroad crossed the Fox River at Elgin. He invested in, or owned many, of Elgin's early heavy industries. What Elgin should remember Benjamin Raymond for is his decision to bring the Elgin Watch Company to Elgin. In 1864, watch making was the cutting edge of technology. As president of the National Watch Company, the decision as to the location of the factory fell on Benjamin Raymond. The Elgin Watch Company became a main employer in Elgin for more than one hundred years.

Of the three creeks around Elgin, Poplar is the tamest. The other two are Tyler Creek and Ferson's Creek where fast water increases the difficulty. Don't get me wrong! Poplar Creek is by no means easy. But the scenery more than compensates for the difficulties. If you're thinking about trying one of these three, such as Ferson or Tyler Creek, it might be best to try Poplar Creek first to get a sample of small creek paddling. Its eight miles can be shortened at several bridges if desired.

Illinois Atlas: Page 20, D-2; D-1

Richland Creek

Richland Creek is a miniature version of the Pecatonica River, which lies only a few miles over to the west. Both run through rolling countryside, have high dirt banks and pass through quaint, rural villages. Richland Creek forms just below the Illinois/ Wisconsin state line where several branches join to form a stream with enough flow to be navigable. The first possible put-in is Illinois Route 26; however, it's a busy road with a long carry, and steep banks make for a tough entry to the water. You'll also save yourself a half a dozen logjams (but don't worry, there are plenty more downstream of Orangeville). Orangeville Road is the main street in the town of the same name; the firehouse is adjacent to Richland Creek and has a large parking lot.

Whichever put-in you use, all the bridges between here and the Richland Creek's mouth on the Pecatonica River are farm roads and make acceptable take-outs, so trips are possible from one bridge to another. It's sixteen miles from Route 26 to the mouth on the Pecatonica River. The Chicago, Madison and Northern Railroad's abandoned right-of-way follows Richland Creek closely through the mill towns of Orangeville, Buena Vista, Red Oak and Scioto Mills. These mill towns were built in the 1840's and 1850's. The railroad connecting these towns came through the valley in 1883.

The miles between Orangeville and McConnell Road are mostly pastureland through which Richland Creek meanders within steep cut dirt banks. The abandoned railroad stays close to the right bank and is often visible; it crosses to the left bank just above the small-unincorporated town of Buena Vista where McConnell Road intersects. The best riffle on Richland Creek is fifty yards upstream of the McConnell Road Bridge. Dairy cattle are the most common animals seen in these upper miles and logjams are a regular occurrence.

Continuing below McConnell Road, Richland Creek runs straight and possibly channeled for a little more than a mile before returning to its tight winding nature. Wildlife is thick from here to the mouth due to the abandoned rail bed and a steep valley that keep civilization at arm's length. We saw deer, muskrat, beaver, mink and a groundhog, plus all of the usual waterfowl. The stream courses its way through the steep valley with light forest along the banks for most of the bottom ten miles, creating a number of additional obstructions.

The right bank rises to a considerable height just above an old set of wooden bridge pilings that tend to catch trees forming yet another log jam. Cedar Creek, the largest tributary of Richland Creek, adds its waters below Cedarville Road although many small creeks downstream add water, continually enlarging the streambed. The mouth of Cedar Creek was the sight of another of Stevenson County's Winnebago Indian villages. The largest Winnebago village in the county was that of Chief Winneshiek, located on the Pecatonica River where the city of Freeport now stands. This area was the approximate western border between the lands of the Winnebago tribe and Black Hawk's tribe, the Sauk, further to the south and west.

County roads cross at about two mile intervals; the last of these is Scioto Mills Road in the small rustic town of the same name. Below Scioto Mills, Richland Creek changes its character, entering a floodplain forest. Several fishing camps are located below Scioto Mills along with more logjams, especially at low water. Richland Creek ends at the Pecatonica River where a few hundred yards produces the take-out on Winneshiek Road. The take-out is just a pull-off on the road where the Pecatonica River comes alongside Winneshiek Road.

Richland Creek is small and log jammed at more than one to the mile but the wildlife, remote country setting, small mill towns and friendly people make this an interesting and worthwhile paddle. The old railroad right-of-way has been turned into a hiking/bicycle trail in 1998. If at the same time they would spend a few dollars more clearing out the logjams, they would also have an excellent canoe trail.

Illinois Atlas; Page 17, A-4

Steep banks make for a difficult put in on Richland Creek for Jim Hart.

Big Rock Creek

Big Rock Creek is truly a gem yet to be discovered by many paddlers. There are possible access problems at some of the bridges, as several are posted and fenced, but I've used these without being hassled. In spite of this and one mandatory portage at a dam, I have nothing derogatory to say about the 15 miles I paddled.

I launched at Price Road south of the town of Big Rock and traversed a mile of pastureland till Granart Road. Below Granart Road, Big Rock Creek develops a different character from its upper reaches. It has a steeper valley with dolomite outcroppings, and frequent riffles attest to the increase in gradient. Granart Road is a good place to scout water levels. Look downstream at the shoal below the bridge which is similar to other shallow areas downstream and evaluate whether or not it is canoeable.

Big Rock wastes no time cutting a steep valley. This helps shield the creek from encroachment from its agricultural surroundings and the roads that continually parallel the stream. This doesn't necessarily mean it is remote, as houses are seen at regular intervals. These homes deserve mention. Although farmhouses are occasionally seen, expensive country estates are more the rule. These appear infrequently and add another dimension to the trip.

Two miles pass quickly and soon the Jericho Road Bridge comes into view. Jericho Road has never been more than a mile away from the creek as far upstream as Route 30 on the West Branch.

Two miles below Galena Road, a building of a camp or retreat of some sort is seen on the left. This is a warning sign that a small three-foot high dam is directly ahead. I have always run this dam, usually scraping down the sloping face left of center. *Remember that dams can kill, and that close inspection of the hydraulic hole below one is mandatory.* Another half mile further will bring you to the Henning Road Bridge. This would be a good access for those who wish to do a shorter trip. The trip from Price Road to the mouth at the Fox River would be nine miles. A trip starting from Henning Road to the mouth would be a little over six miles.

There is a variety of streamside scenery from Henning Road to the town of Plano. A gravel quarry intrudes for about 100 yards.

When you notice the current slowing and the creek widening, you are approaching a dangerous dam. This dam is unrunnable at high or low water levels. A portage would be quick and easy on creek right. The millrace splits off to the right at this point.

Riffles and fast water continue for the next half-mile down to Klatt Memorial Park in Plano. Plano was first settled by a John Matlock who laid claim to the land and built a cabin here in 1833. Across the road from the park is an old stone building that was part of a mill built shortly after the Burlington Northern Railroad came through in 1853.

The park features lights for night baseball. This was found out on a *late afternoon* trip. Everyone miscalculates once in awhile. The lie I tell at home most often is "Oh yeah, I'll be home in plenty of time for dinner, honey." Followed, sometime after 9:00 p.m., by a plethora of excuses of all the things that went wrong. Anyway, the park was well lit.

Just beyond the park is the stone masonry bridge of the Burlington Northern Railroad. The railroad, which crosses all the Fox River tributaries in the area, is deceiving to those who paddle these creeks. Trains can be heard five or six miles off, leading you to believe that you are farther along than you actually are. From the railroad bridge to the Route 34 Bridge is about a hundred feet of fast riffles, followed by an area that has unnatural banks, the result of quarrying and channelization.

It seems the most deadfalls and strainers on small streams always seem to appear on the final few miles above the mouth. Hale Road marks the start of these final few miles.

The left side of Big Rock Creek near the Fox River was the site of Main Poche's village, which contained about 50 warriors. This chief and his band were participants in the Fort Dearborn massacre in 1813 and went unpunished for their deeds.

The next road to be crossed is Kendall County Road 15. This is the road that leads south to Silver Springs State Park from Route 34 in Plano. Maramech Hill is on the right side of the creek after you pass under this bridge but is hidden from view by the undergrowth. According to local legend, the destruction of the Fox Nation of Indians took place on this hill in 1730.

The troublesome Fox Tribe seemed to find it easier to make enemies than to make friends. By 1728 they could count the Sioux, Ottawa, Potawatomi, Illini, Mascouten, Iroquois, Peoria, Huron as their enemies. Even the Kickapoo and Sauk, who had previously helped and given aid to the Fox, had turned against them. But the most dangerous foe of the Fox was the French. The French had long sought peace with the Fox, as the continued warfare interrupted the fur trade. The Fox harassed the French and the neighboring tribes so much that the French decided to make an all out effort to destroy the Fox once and for all.

Now the Fox were being harassed on all sides and were being forced from their lands, finally asking the French for peace. But the French, sensing the weakness of the Fox Nation, refused and attacked, inflicting a decisive defeat on the Fox at Butte Des Mortes in Wisconsin. The Fox then asked if the Iroquois would forgive past differences and take them in. The Iroquois apparently were going to allow this, but the Fox would have to pass around the bottom of Lake Michigan through a hostile area. This reminded me of the movie *Warriors* where a street gang must cross the whole of New York City with every other gang in the city out to get them. Such was the situation the Fox found themselves in.

The French knew that by watching the main trails, they might catch the Fox on the move and vulnerable. (See Hickory Creek.) Eventually, the Peoria located the Fox and with the help of other tribes of the Illinois Confederation, were able to pin them down until a larger force could be brought up. The French brought troops from Quebec, Fort de Chartres, Fort Miami, and Fort St. Joseph and with their Indian allies, numbered about 1300.

The Fox, numbering about three hundred warriors and encumbered by women and children, found themselves under siege by overwhelming forces. They entrenched themselves atop the hill. Many historians are not convinced that this hill was the actual site of the conflict as the ancient French records and maps were not all that accurate. Some theorize that the site was somewhere in McLean County or along the banks of the Vermilion River.

In 1900, John F. Steward, of Plano, was so convinced that this was the battle site that he wrote a book listing all the reasons it happened here. Steward uses old French maps from the early 1700s that show the ancient village of Maramech. He also points out that several ancient Indian trails crossed or merged here. These are fairly convincing arguments and sound pretty good. He caused an immense granite boulder to be placed atop the hill and had a stonecutter carve the details of the battle on its surface as a monument.

His book, *Lost Maramech and Old Chicago*, is quoted in a dozen or more other books. But it's always the lone source. The fact that more scholarly works on the Indians of Illinois either don't mention the battle, or locate it elsewhere, tells me that Steward's research is perhaps flawed. I like to believe that the hill next to Big Rock Creek is the place of the siege.

Speaking of the siege, it began on August 17, 1730. The Fox fortified themselves behind earthen walls built on the hilltop. The French and their allies were afraid to attack and were contented to wait. Finally, on September 9, short of food and unable to wander very far to hunt, the remaining Fox made a run for it during a storm that night, but the crying of the children alerted the besiegers. The French and their Indian allies followed the next morning, the Fox, being encumbered with women, children and the elderly, were slow and soon were caught by the French. They fought desperately, but they were hopelessly out numbered. The few that survived allied themselves with the Sac nation.

This ends the story of Maramech Hill and a very short distance more will bring you to River Road Bridge where the Little Rock Creek enters from the right. Together, they enter the Fox River just down river from the Plano Bridge and across from Silver Springs State Park, where access is possible.

Illinois Atlas: Page 27, B-6; C-6

East & West Branch of Big Rock Creek

East Branch of Big Rock Creek

If the East Branch of Big Rock Creek seems too small for practical canoeing, you are right. It is small this high upstream and having first seen it where it joined the West Branch, I thought, "You would have to be a little crazy to try to canoe that!" Sixteen months later, in a pouring rain, I launched my canoe at Lasher Road. Me crazy? Well, maybe a little.

The East Branch carries about the same volume of water as its sister stream as they are about the same width. However, why does the East Branch have so many more logjams than the West Branch? The reason is that the East Branch runs through woodlands, while the West Branch is surrounded by farm fields. The fact is, Big Rock Creek itself is nicer paddling than either of its branches.

Regardless of these downsides, the first few miles were relatively open, except for some electric farm fencing. The East Branch meanders and divides its course between fields and forests having easy passage through the fields, then many blockages in the wooded sections. The stream through the woods before and after U.S. Route 30 was particularly blocked with debris, as was the area around the mouth of the creek.

After passing under County Line Road and Scott Road, the East Branch of Big Rock Creek heads off into the woods for the first time. While in this woods you can hear U.S. Route 30 approaching, even a good way off. The creek flows along side U.S. Route 30 briefly before it finally crosses under it about a mile further. Just before passing under U.S. Route 30, a large field is seen on the right side of the creek. Just downstream of this field is a low footbridge requiring a portage around it. The field and bridge are part of a Christian Youth Camp, located on Route 30.

Only 30 feet separates the Route 30 Bridge from the Chicago, Burlington, and Quincy Railroad Bridge. Several horse farms and stables are located in the next mile or so, to a point below Hinckley Road. Just when you start wondering when you will get to the junction with the West Branch of Big Rock, you break through a line of trees and there it is. The last mile to Price Road is on Big Rock Creek itself, which seems very open compared to the last seven miles of the East Branch. Unless you are a glutton for punishment, or in need of a full body workout, I would suggest using Price Road as a put-in for a trip down Big Rock Creek instead of a takeout for the East Branch. Or if you're looking for a smaller creek, try the West Branch of Big Rock Creek, or the upper section of Somonauk Creek.

West Branch of Big Rock Creek

About one mile north of the town of Hinckley in DeKalb County, Battle Creek joins the tiny West Branch of Rock Creek, and the flow is increased enough to float comfortably. I put in upstream of the bridge on Hinckley Road where the creek parallels the roadside for a short distance before turning east.

The first mile or so is noticeably channelized, and is less than twenty feet wide. After the first mile, the creek begins to meander and the wooded banks end the feeling that you are paddling an irrigation ditch. Between here and Hinckley was the location of the Indian village of Squaw Grove. It was named Squaw Grove by John Sebree, because when he first arrived here, the men from the village were off hunting, leaving only the squaws behind to tend to the crops and the village.

Four county road bridges are crossed in the first few miles. A thicker forest is entered around the fourth, County Line Road. The woodlands end and you enter pasture, where the stream winds and twists before passing under U.S.

Route 30. The Chicago, Burlington and Quincy Railroad Bridge is passed under next and a short distance later, the Hinckley Road Bridge comes into view.

The creek resumes its meandering course after the Hinckley Road bridge and is now flowing alongside Jericho Road for a couple of miles. The wooded corridor thickens, improving the scenery. As it becomes prettier, the chances of spotting wildlife also improves. On one trip, I spotted a fox with two pups on a log in the creek. Ducks, beaver, muskrat, and deer are all frequently seen in this section of the creek bottom. The East Branch now joins from river left and nearly doubles the flow. (See East Branch Big Rock Creek.)

A little over a mile on the main creek will bring you to the takeout at Price Road. Which is also the takeout for the East Branch and the put-in for Big Rock Creek.

This trip is 8-1/2 miles long and while not spectacular, it is very pleasant paddling. Remember this is a real small stream, so high water is a must. Also, there were at least six strands of barbed wire across the creek. Barbed wire was invented right here in DeKalb County. Historically, there were three patents given for different types of barbed wire manufactured right in the town of Hinckley.

Illinois Atlas: Page 27, B-5; B-6

Little Rock Creek

Across the Fox River from Silver Spring State Park lie Maramech Hill, site of the destruction of the Fox tribe by the French and their Indian allies on August 17, 1730 (for the story of the battle, see description of Big Rock Creek). Between the base of Maramech Hill and the Fox River is the junction of Big and Little Rock Creeks with their total of fifty miles of high water canoeing. Little Rock Creek, as its name suggests, is smaller than Big Rock Creek, so it is advisable to stop and take a look at the latter if you pass over it. If there's not enough water to float Big Rock, then skip Little Rock and try a section of the Fox River instead.

The put-in for the upper creek is at Lee Road where the creek is less than twenty feet wide. Because the creek was so narrow, I was amazed to find only two logjams in the following nine miles. This section is not as remote appearing as other streams in the area. Upper Little Rock spends a lot of its course skirting along U.S. Route 30, the town of Hinckley, and then Sandwich Road, which means heavy traffic and urbanization nearby.

The area now known, as DeKalb County was first settled in 1834 by John S. Sebree and his family. They settled between the Indian encampments at Squaw Grove and Papoose Grove. As the story is told, their first winter was spent in the wagon they arrived in. Apparently, John was forced to make a trip by sled to Bloomington in January for additional supplies and grain. During her husband's absence, Mrs. Sebree and her one year old baby were left to fend for themselves with only a prairie schooner for shelter. Mr. Sebree couldn't get home because of a rare January thaw so Mrs. Sebree ran out of food and was forced to barter with the local Indians for supplies. During her husband's absence, Mrs. Sebree's closest neighbors were 800 Indians in the two villages.

The cabin they built was located in the creek bottom between the railroad tracks and Somonauk Road. A stone marker was erected on the site and can be clearly seen from the creek as you paddle by.

Squaw Grove eventually was renamed Hinkley. Francis E. Hinkley, owner of the Chicago, Burlington and Quincy Railroad, had surveyed his own right-of-way. The future town was laid out in 1872 and named after Hinckley ensuring a station stop at that town.

The nine miles of this section of Little Rock Creek were passed without any problems. Portions have been noticeably channelized, especially beyond Hinckley. I took out on Shabbona Grove Road, which I also use as the put-in for running the lower creek.

Lower Little Rock Creek can be divided into a nice upper half, and a lower half that offered navigational difficulties. From Shabbona Grove Road, the stream flowed in a lovely wooded corridor, small, almost beyond the limits of navigability. At times overhanging branches and the constant sharp bends taxed one's canoeing skills all the way to the small town of Little Rock.

After Galena Road, Creek Road closely parallels the river on the right for the next three miles, with the scenery being mostly pastoral. After passing Miller Road and before passing under Creek Road, a subdivision encroaches on the riverbank from the left. It seems that everyone with river frontage needed a footbridge. Or perhaps one weekend they all had a contest for the best bridge. Anyhow, if I remember correctly, there are five consecutive bridges in a row that need to be portaged.

Leaving Creek Road Bridge, which is less than a mile from the town of Plano, the stream veers in a westerly direction for one and one-half miles before turning south again until it reaches U.S. Route 34. The distance from Shabbona Grove Road to U.S. Route 34 is about twelve miles and takes around four to five hours to paddle at appropriate water levels.

From U.S. Route 34 to the mouth at the Fox River, a five-mile trip, would be considered the worst section of the creek containing plentiful and difficult logjams. As you approach Maramech Hill, the current is greatly reduced because you are entering the backwater of a high dam ahead. The right bank appeared denuded of trees and standing up in the canoe, I noticed a lake, probably an old quarry, just adjacent to the creek. The dam across the creek is 15 to 20 feet high and you can portage on the right side, staying close to the dam. Another mile will bring you to the mouth of the Fox River, but not before four or five more logjams, which were the most difficult yet. Just after winding around the base of Maramech Hill and passing under the River Road Bridge, Big Rock Creek joins Little Rock Creek from the left fifty yards above the Fox River. Silver Springs State Park, directly across the Fox River, is an excellent takeout following a lousy trip.

Atlas: Pages 27, B5,-6

Rock River

The French called it Rivie're de la Roche, the Potawatomi called it Assinisipi, translated as "rock river" and the Sauk called it Sinnissippi meaning, "clear flowing." The Rock River today never runs clear, dams have impeded the flow, but the river still supports a large population of rocks. Before flowing more than one hundred and fifty miles through Illinois, the Rock has already flowed for one hundred and thirty miles in Wisconsin. Before the white man had come to settle Rock River Valley, the Rock River served as a boundary between the Winnebago, Potawatomi, and Sauk tribes.

For the canoeist the Rock River provides a mixed bag. The upside is plenty of access points, consistent water levels—even in years of drought there is enough water to comfortably canoe, nice bluffs and scenery and a good deal of history. The downside is pollution, numerous towns—many with dams, powerboats, cottages, and very few sections that are left in a natural state.

The Rock River enters Illinois on the north side of the town of South Beloit; the river north of here is covered in Best Canoe Trails of Southern Wisconsin. The first access in Illinois is Prairie Hill Road, downstream from the mouth of Turtle Creek between South Beloit and Rockton. The Rock River is hundreds of yards wide at this point, has a steady current, with occasional islands dividing the channel. Cottages with boat docks are seen along both banks. The first and most unusual of six dams in Illinois is encountered in Rockton; the Rockton Dam has a curved face and can be portaged on the right hand side.

Not far below the dam the Pecatonica River enters on river right and a rock bluff marks the location of the 1830's village and trading post of Macktown. Stephen Mack came to the Rock River Valley to become an Indian trader and traded not only here at the mouth of the Pecatonica but also downriver at Franklin Creek where he purchased the post of Pierre La Sallier. Mack was the first to try to bridge the Rock River but the bridge was washed away the following spring. Only a couple of buildings are left to serve as testament to the early pioneer settlement in the valley of the Rock. Macktown is worth a look around and can also be used as for canoe access.

Below Rockton the riverside residences increase in frequency and opulence. Nine miles downstream of the put-in is Hononegah Forest Preserve named for Stephen Mack's Native American wife. Five miles downstream of Hononegah Forest Preserve is Atwood Homestead Forest Preserve. Both of these Winnebago County Forest Preserves on the Rock have boat ramps with parking and bathrooms.

The ten miles between Atwood Forest Preserve and Rockford are the least scenic on the Rock River's journey through Illinois. During summer months expect to share the river with motorized boats of many types. The Rock River splits the middle of the downtown Rockford business district passing the Rockford Public Library and other downtown buildings. Several parks and boat ramps may be used as access points above the dam in downtown Rockford. Rockford Dam is also referred to as Fordham Dam.

To run the fast water below Fordham Dam requires portaging the dam, no easy task. First one has to cross the line of safety buoys without being washed over the face of the dam. Next pull up to the three to four foot concrete wall and disembark from your boat. Next lower your boat over the steep but short portage on either side of the dam; I like the river left side better.

Rockford is named for the rocky-bottomed crossing of the Rock River that the Chicago and Galena stagecoach used. The ford probably looked much as the river looks today below Fordham Dam. Rockford also went by the name of Midway, as it was located halfway between Chicago and Galena, northern Illinois' two early population centers.

The seven and a half miles from Rockford to the mouth of the Kishwaukee River mark a transition between the populated urban upper miles and the more rural and natural middle miles of the Rock River; these features however change gradually. The two most memorable points on this section of the Rock are the Greater Rockford Airport and Blackhawk Island which is more than a mile long and lined with tacky fishing shacks and cottages. Below Blackhawk Island it is best to keep to the river left side if taking out at Hinchliff Memorial Forest Preserve as there is another Island that may block the view of the Kishwaukee River's mouth. Take out just upstream of the Kishwaukee Road Bridge where a steep path leads to parking along Kishwaukee River Road.

The next eleven-mile trip begins on the Kishwaukee River and ends at the Byron Boat Ramp. The transition that took place upstream is complete and these miles pass by mostly farms fields and even some natural areas. Illinois Route 2 closely follows the west bank of the Rock making access easy and flexible. The Rock River bids goodbye to Winnebago County and enters Ogle County. The Chicago and Northwestern Railroad cross the Rock upstream of the mouth of Stillman's Creek. Stillman's Creek enters on river left but summer foliage often obscures the mouth. A few more miles and upstream of another railroad bridge, the town named for the poet Lord Byron operates a boat ramp that provides good access.

Starting out in Byron and taking out at the dam in the town of Oregon is a trip of eleven miles. The Rock River provides a variety of aqueduct habitats, which in turn support a large diversity of fish. Catfish are the most common but also included are bullheads, northern pike, walleye, sauger, bluegill, small and large mouth bass, and the ever present carp. About five miles below Byron, the Leaf River makes its entrance, hidden by an island. A small roadside park directly below the mouth of the Leaf River may be used as additional access.

The predominate landmark along this section of the Rock River is the fifty foot tall Indian statue that was the work of artist Lorado Taft. Taft lived here at an artist colony known as the Eagle's Nest. The statue was meant as a tribute to Native Americans and was in no way modeled after the Sauk Chief Black Hawk. Nevertheless it is commonly known as the Black Hawk Statue and is part of Lowden State Park. The statue high a top a bluff looks out over the river valley that Black Hawk and his tribe the Sauk called home. A boat ramp that is part of Lowden State Park is located about a mile downstream of the statue.

The third dam on the Rock River is in the town of Oregon just downstream of Lowden State Park. Oregon Dam has access on the river left side both above and below the dam. This dam, as are all the dams on the Rock River, is unrunnable and dangerous at all levels. The dams along the Rock River regularly kill those unaware of the dangers of the backwash or hydraulic that forms below dams.

The fast water below the dam is a nice start to the next ten and a half mile trip from Oregon to Grand Detour. Kytes Creek enters on river left and marks the location of Daysville. Not much of a town today, 1840's Daysville was a major Rock River community. Three miles below Daysville is Castle Rock State Park. Castle Rock is a rock outcropping that has been a land mark ever since the first explorers ventured up the Rock River. The state park has boat ramps with parking, camping, bathrooms, and even a canoe camp. Five miles downstream two road side parks provide access at the town of Grand Detour. Both are located along Illinois Route 2, which crosses the Rock River at Grand Detour. Franklin Creek enters the Rock upstream of the Route 2 Bridge.

Grand Detour is named for the three plus mile bend that the Rock River makes at this point. In 1835, Leonard Andrus, the first settler at Grand Detour, built a saw mill and began to settle a town. In 1836 a blacksmith by the name of John Deere was looking to relocate and came to Grand Detour from Vermont. The following year, Deere moved his business and family to Grand Detour. In Vermont John Deere was widely known for the high quality of the farm tools that he made. Soil in the eastern United States is sandier than the thick black loam that makes up the prairies of the Midwest. In the Midwest a farmer would be forced to stop every ten feet to clear the dirt from the blade of the plow. This was a tedious and slow process that that limited the number of acres that could be plowed and therefore affected the farmer's income. Deere had discovered over time that by polishing the surfaces of the shovels and pitch forks he had forged, they worked more efficiently because of the reduced resistance.

John Deere helped Leonard Andrus make repairs to his saw mill; to repay the favor John Deere asked if he could have a broken band saw blade. Deere used the highly polished saw blade as the face of his plow blade. Take this and a few changes in plow design and you have a plow that cleans itself. The number of plows manufactured by John Deere over the next several years tells the rest of the story.

1837-First Plow   1838-2 plows   1839-10 plows
1840-40 plows   1841-75 plows   1843-400 plows

In 1848 John Deere moved his family and his business down the Rock River to Moline where his products could be more easily shipped on the Mississippi River. Although steamboats did from time to time travel on the Rock River, they were never numerous, regular, or profitable.

The Rock River passes more beautiful rock bluffs below Grand Detour. The twenty two miles between Oregon and Dixon are the prettiest on the Rock River and are the site of the annual Rock River Canoe Race. Lowell Park, located downstream of Pine Creek, claims to be Illinois' largest city park at two hundred and forty acres. Lowell Park has boat ramps and is located four miles upriver from Dixon Dam. Dixon Dam is the fourth dam on the Rock and is located downstream of a long Island and upstream of the bridge that carries U.S Route 52, Illinois Route 2 and Illinois Route 26 over the Rock. The dam is difficult to portage because of the retaining wall at both ends. No improved landings exist above the dam but some staircases come down the river as part of a Dixon City park on river right upstream of the dam; however, parking along the residential street may be a problem. Reentering the Rock below the Dixon Dam also has some problems if portaging the dam.

In 1825 Oliver W. Kellogg laid out the trail that would bear his name. The Kellogg Trail from Fort Clark (Peoria) to the Fever River Settlement (Galena) was also known as the Sucker Trail. Sucker refers to the fish whose spring and fall migrations coincided with coming and going of the summer lead miners. These miners would put their crops in and then head north to try their luck at the lead mines. The Kellogg Trail followed portions of Indian trails and game trails. It was wide enough to accommodate freight wagons and followed the high ridges to avoid the marshes and creeks. The Kellogg Trail crossed the Rock River where the town of Dixon now stands. Indians in the area were the first to assist travelers in crossing the river; they would place a canoe under each wheel of a wagon and then paddle to the opposite shore, while the horses or oxen swam the distance. In 1826, the year after the trail's completion, two hundred wagons were here waiting for the ice to break up on the Rock River so they could be ferried across. In 1828 a French half breed named Ogee and his Indian wife ran the ferry, which for a time bore his name. Two years later in 1830 John Dixon purchased the ferry and built a tavern. In 1832 the ferry stood as a bastion of safety during the Black Hawk War. Survivors of the Battle of Stillman's Creek streamed through Dixon's Ferry spreading tales of thousands of blood thirsty savages that would soon infest the ferry but Dixon held firm and the ferry was never attacked. Troops were assembled here including volunteers under the command of Captain Abe Lincoln.

Below the Dixon Dam the water runs fast for only a short distance. Two Dixon parks downstream of the Dixon Dam have boat ramps; the first is Page Park and is located on the north side of the Rock. The second Vaile Park is one half mile downstream on the south bank of the river. These two parks make the best access below Dixon Dam. Between the Dixon Dam and the Upper Dam in Rock Falls spans fourteen river miles; a few parks along the way can shorten the trip. One can take out at the Sauk Valley Community College, built alongside the Rock River, and shorten the trip by five miles. Several places along this section of the Rock have houses, cottages, and trailers. Frequently encountered islands break the river into narrower channels but even many of the islands have shacks built upon them.

As a railroad bridge is seen ahead, Flucks Slough cuts off on river left. The slough occupies a former channel of the Rock and is reputed to be good for both fishing and wildlife viewing. The Rock Island Railroad along with a high tension power line cross over the Rock River as it begins to widen, eventually forming Lake Sinnissippi. On windy days crossing this last section on the lake can build a paddler's character. Sinnissippi Park on river right was once the site of another concentration of Mississippian Indian mounds and can be used as an access. The take-out I used is on the river left side and only yards above the Sterling Dam; this is the entrance to the Hennepin Feeder. A two lane boat ramp can be found here along with parking and bathrooms. The Hennepin Canal connects the Illinois River at the point where it turns south with the Upper Mississippi River. This short cut saved four hundred and sixteen miles on a trip between Chicago and Rock Island. The main branch of the canal was more than ninety miles in length. The Feeder Canal was more than thirty miles long and still provides water to the Hennepin Canal. The canal, begun in 1892 and completed in 1907, never achieved financial success but nonetheless continued to operate until 1951. In 1970 the entire canal corridor was given over to the State of Illinois Department of Conservation. The Hennepin Canal Parkway offers more than a hundred miles of canoeing opportunities that are not covered in this volume. For maps and more information, contact The Hennepin Canal Parkway State Park at R.R.2, P.O. Box 201, Sheffield, Illinois 61363

About a mile in between the Upper and Lower Sterling Dams is a long and difficult portage at the Upper Dam. I have therefore skipped this short section and continue at the put-in located directly downstream of the Lower Dam. The Lower Dam is easy to portage as there are boat ramps both above and below the dam. These two dams take the place of a long rapid that at one time existed here.

Immediately below the Lower Sterling Dam is Lawrence Park Island, which also can be used for access (Lawrence Park is home to a public pool which is elevated and of an unusual design). The island is the first of two large islands one passes before coming to a bridge marking U.S. Route 30 and another marking Interstate 88. The small berg of Como is located between the two bridges. Como was formerly a Mississippian Indian village; numerous mounds were found nearby. Below the toll road the islands and the cottages thin out and Elkhorn Creek enters on river right between I 88 and the take-out. The take-out is a roadside park along Monoline Road; it has a boat ramp and is ten miles downstream of the Lower Sterling Dam.

Using the Monoline Road Park as a put-in and taking out at the Lyndon boat ramp is a ten mile trip—add four more if taking out at Profitstown State Park. A thin corridor of trees hides many of the farm fields that line the banks for much of this section. One has to wonder why Grand Detour is so well noted for its long three mile bend when this section has several bends that are even longer. Although small fishing boats motor by on most trips even in the off-season, and hunters' blinds are seen along shore, the Rock River is relatively void of humanity along this lower stretch and is rather quiet.

The Lyndon Boat Ramp is in very poor condition but remains adequate as a canoe launch or landing. A small series of waves has been formed by several attempts to dam the Rock River at Lyndon, the first attempt in 1839. It is said that in the year 1836, over two thousand Indians made winter camp between Lyndon and Profitstown. A Winnebago village was also located at the mouth of Walker Slough on river left two miles below Lyndon. The landing in Profitstown is at Profitstown State Park where a boat ramp, camping facilities and bathrooms are available.

A Winnebago village was located here at Profitstown for at least as long as Saukenuk (Rock Island) had been a Sauk village (around the year 1764). The small village of Profitstown was a mixture of Winnebago, Sauk, Fox, Kickapoo, and Potawatomi. A similar mixed tribal village on the Rock River was located at the mouth of the Pecatonica River where Stephen Mack operated his trading post.

The Winnebago "Profit" or Wa-bo-kie-shiek, the offspring of a Winnebago mother and Sauk father, was a medicine man of great influence. In 1832 both the Profit and his village Profitstown figured predominately in the opening battles of the Black Hawk War. Black Hawk and the Profit were both leaders of a faction known as the British Band alluding to their previous loyalty to England in conflicts with the Americans. Although the Sauk had moved west of the Mississippi and had agreed not to return to Illinois, on April 5, 1832, Black Hawk and the Profit along with six hundred Sauk men, women, and children, crossed the Mississippi River with the intent of planting crops and settling at either Saukenuk or Profitstown. They were under the impression other area tribes like the Winnebago or the Potawatomi would rise with them to save Indian lands. This appeal went unanswered and these Indians would stand alone until they were nearly annihilated.

The first American action of the Black Hawk War was to dispatch General Samuel Whiteside (for whom Whiteside County is named) and four hundred volunteers to search out Black Hawk and his followers. The volunteers moved up the Rock River and finding Profitstown abandoned, they burned it. The Americans continued up the Rock River burning the village of Wittico, which was located, upriver at Sterling. Most of General Whiteside's volunteers halted at Dixon's Ferry but a portion of the command under Major Stillman continued on and were routed at the Battle of Stillman's Creek (see section on Stillman's Creek).

The thirteen mile trip between Profitstown and Erie begins and ends at boat ramps that are located next to campgrounds. Several miles downstream, you'll come upon the Profitstown Indian Island, a better part of a mile long. Several miles more and Big Bend State Fish and Wildlife Area is found along the left bank running for several miles. Housing is prevalent along most of this trip. The current is steady; there are also several spots where fast water forms small waves. Islands become more frequent and a campground on river left is seen before one spots the Erie Road Bridge. The take-out at the Erie boat ramp is located on the southwest corner of the Erie Road Bridge.

The Erie boat ramp is the end of the improved landings for more than twenty miles. The best intermediate landing would be the south eastern corner of the Illinois Route 92 Bridge eleven miles down from the Erie boat ramp. A steep two track dirt lane leads down to the water, but the low clearance of my van resulted in a hundred yard carry back from the take-out. Six miles below the Erie boat ramp on the right side of Kempster Island is a barge that is used as a ferry to the island. The roadside pull-off at the ferry seems to be a fishermen's access that can also be used as a canoe landing.

Many islands along Hillsdale area attractively break up the wide Rock River. Peterson Island, the last in a long series of islands, is one half mile long and a mile upstream of the Route 92 Bridge. Below the Route 92 bridge the Rock River runs a straighter course, and views of more than a mile ahead are common. The islands that broke up the channel upstream are smaller, less frequent, and are located at the sides of the river instead of the middle. Most of the cottages are clustered in small communities leaving the shore fairly natural until just above Interstate 80. From Illinois Route 92 to the Interstate 80 area is a ten mile trip. Two options for take-outs exist around the I-80 Bridge. The first is the easiest at Lundeen's Landing, which has a store and campground right along the rivers right bank (Lundeen's also rents canoes). The downside to this take-out is they charge two dollars to launch or land. The alternate landing is just west of Lundeen's on Barstow Road where it crosses Zuma Creek. It is less hundred yards down Zuma Creek to the Rock River. Note that the mouth of Zuma is above the I-80 Bridge and directly below the campground. It is located behind a small island so stay to the far right if taking out here.

Continuing downstream from Interstate 80, the Rock River's streamside is mostly natural with only a spattering of cottages for the next ten miles to Green Valley Park. A railroad bridge crosses the Rock River above the Illinois Route 84 Bridge. A dirt lane on the southwest side of the Route 84 makes a fair access but the mouth of the Hennepin Canal is only one and a half miles further.

Canal lock #29, a boat ramp and parking are located here where the Hennepin Canal enters the Rock River only to exit eight miles later at the Steel Dam. The canal enters and exits the Rock River on river left. The river was deep enough at this point to accommodate the canal boats but it was easier to build a canal around the rapids located downstream than to clear a channel through them. The Hennepin Canal enters the Mississippi at its own mouth, so these are the only miles that the canal and the Rock mingle their waters.

The Green River also enters on river left within sight of the Lock 29 boat ramp. The next five miles the river travels through a natural corridor marred only by the close proximity of Interstate 74/280 on river left. The take-out on river right is supplied by the Moline Park District at Green Valley Park, complete with boat ramp and parking.

If putting in at Green Valley Park do not expect to find any remnant of the rural river that has flowed free in the fifty miles since the Sterling Dam. The Rock is once again urbanized with dams to portage and interstate highways crossing over and paralleling the river. Homes and cottages are thick along these miles. The Hennepin Canal exits the Rock at Milan Steel Dam to avoid the rapids below Vandruff Island. Parking, a portapotty and a canal display are also located at the Steel Dam on the river left side; note that the dam may be portaged on either side.

The Steel Dam only blocks one of two channels of the Rock River as it splits around Vandruff Island, named after the first white family to settle on it in 1831. The canoeist must make a choice of channel here depending on the location of the take-out used. The river right channel ends at Sears Dam, which would make a very, very difficult portage if continuing downstream. The right channel is however the correct one if taking out at Black Hawk State Park, a trip of ten miles from the Hennepin lock 29 boat ramp or five miles from Green Valley Park. Be sure to stop at the Black Hawk State Park and visit the Hauberg Indian Museum where much can be learned about the Sauk and Fox Indian tribes who lived in this area for more than a century.

If continuing down the Rock River to the Mississippi, stay in the left channel; you'll find no more obstructions after portaging the Steel Dam. The rapids, which are never larger than mild Class II, are located toward the bottom of Vandruff Island and are a pleasant addition to this trip. The rapids start above and end below the U.S. Highway 67 Bridge, which crosses both channels of the Rock and Vandruff Island.

The bottom of Vandruff Island marks the location of the great Sauk Village of Saukenuk. The Sauk first moved here around 1730 after being pushed south by the Chippewa from their former home on the Fox River near Green Bay. During the Revolutionary War the Fox and Sauk loyalty was split between the Americans and the British. They had for years been allied to the British accepting annual annuities of food and trade goods, but the Americans under George Rogers Clark had caused the French settlements along the Mississippi and Wabash Rivers to come over to the American side. This caused a split—some siding with the Americans and some with the British.

Indians from this and other villages who were loyal to England made a raid down the Illinois River to make war on both Spanish and American settlements. The raids brought no gain to those who took part in them, but they did bring on American retaliation when three hundred and fifty men under Colonel John Montgomery trailed the

Indians as they retreated north. The Americans burned villages on the Illinois River before proceeding up to the Rock River and burning more including Saukenuk. The action of Colonel Montgomery and his men constitutes the western most action of the Revolutionary War. Through the efforts of George Rogers Clark and John Montgomery at the end of the war, the United States would end up acquiring the Northwest Territory that would later become the states of Illinois, Ohio, Indiana, Michigan and Wisconsin. The irony is that it was originally believed that the territory gained would go to the state of Virginia.

The final three miles before the Rock merges with the Mississippi although thickly populated with fishermen are basically left to their natural state. Illinois Route 92 is the last road to bridge the Rock and is the last access point on the Rock River. If continuing on to the Mississippi River, a take-out is available at the town of Andalusia, complete with a boat ramp and parking.

The Rock River offers canoeing opportunities even in the driest of years. The current is good and fishing is plentiful; access points are frequent and well spaced. Although the Rock is rarely pristine—towns, cottages, dams and pollution all mar the river—the river is at its best from Castle Rock State Park to Dixon. Still, one may find many other pleasant miles of paddling along the historic Rock River Valley.

Illinois Atlas; Pages 18-17; 24-25, 31-32

Salt Creek

Bob and daughter Aimee.

The thirty-three miles from Busse Lake to the mouth of Salt Creek at the Des Plaines River was paddled on three separate occasions. The first section was from Busse Lake to U.S. Route 20, a trip of approximately nine miles. The second stretch was from U.S. Route 20 to the old Graue Mill at York Road in Hinsdale, about 14 miles. The lower section took me from Graue Mill to just past First Avenue on the Des Plaines River, and was approximately ten miles.

Salt Creek is a mixture of what should be a great combination of history, golf and zoo. But this comes at a price, for there are numerous portages at inconvenient or even dangerous places.

Starting at Busse Lake, the first problem you face is finding a way out of the lake and into the creek. This is best accomplished by keeping to the right shoreline, head south until you come to the dam, which is easily portaged. The next few miles are unobstructed and run through alternating residential, industrial and a combination of floodplain and forest, with the natural settings taking over the farther downstream you go. This continues until about mile seven.

In the Elmhurst Country Club are several low bridges and a two and a half foot dam that is runnable at a good water level. As you leave the country club property, you will be introduced to the eight lane I-290 expressway. The stream flows under the expressway through a cavern about 60 yards long. After coming out of the tunnel, the next mile stays pretty close to I-290. As Salt Creek pulls away from the expressway it approaches the U.S. Route 20 Bridge. At one time this bridge was too low to allow for passage at high water, but a 1998 replacement should now be passable at all water levels. It is less than a mile down to Fullerton Avenue where Cricket Creek Forest Preserve provides good access. This also is the put-in for the next section.

The middle section of Salt Creek again alternates between industrial, residential and floodplain surroundings. The first mile meanders alongside Villa Avenue until coming to North Avenue (Illinois Route 64), where a gauge is located at the north east corner of the bridge. The gauge can be read from the sidewalk on the bridge and roughly correlates to canoeable levels. My experiences on the river have been between the one foot mark on the gauge and the three foot mark. At one foot, the river is well within its banks, at three foot it's over.

From North Avenue to Interstate 88 the stream is clear of debris jams with one notable exception; one mile downstream, a pair of railroad bridges loom into view. The first one is too low to pass under. The portage required a walk across an often used long railway trestle, (which in my case involved convincing my 6-year old daughter Aimee that it really would be O.K. since the trains don't run on Sundays. She allowed me to carry her across, (good canoe partners are hard to find). To portage, land river right ten yards above the trestle and carry across to put-in on the downstream side. EASY! Unless you get washed sideways into the bridge, or tip getting in or out of your boat, or a train catches you crossing the tracks. PLEASE be careful—these are dangerous places. A couple of miles through residential neighborhoods will bring you to Oakbrook Shopping Center, a good place to takeout.

I, however, wasn't smart enough to stop and continued my journey, passing the Interstate 88 Bridge and on into Butler International Golf Course with its seven bridges, all requiring portaging. After passing the most expensive homes yet seen along the river, you will enter a forest preserve. A mile and a half through the woodlands will bring you to the historic Graue Mill where the best landing is on the right bank above the mill and its dam.

The lower section, starting below the dam at Graue Mill, definitely offers the best canoeing the creek has to offer. This trip is mostly through forest preserves and a bicycle path parallels the banks for about half the way. This is also the section that has the best gradient and the most riffles. About six miles down the stream, a tunnel is seen ahead and the entire creek seems to disappear into it. But this is not the case. On closer inspection, it will be discovered that this is a flood diversion tunnel that was built to divert excess flood waters into the Des Plaines River, which is a short distance to the east at this point. Just past the tunnel, you will paddle through the Brookfield Zoo grounds. Don't expect to see lots of animals, however, do expect to see the backs of zoo maintenance buildings, although the buffalo pen may be seen.

Once through the zoo, a short paddle will bring you to the mouth of Salt Creek where it enters the Des Plaines River, downstream you can find a spot to takeout at Plank Road Meadow Forest Preserve.

Illinois Atlas: Page 20, D-4 and page 28; A-4, B-4 B-5

Many creeks have low bridges like this one in the
golf course, such as Salt Creek and Spring Creek.

Sinsinawa River

Sinsinawa, a Sauk Indian word meaning home of the eagle. Like other tributaries of the Mississippi River in Jo Davies County the upper portion of the Sinsinawa River flows over frequent shoals and features rock bluffs, while the lower river flattens out on the Mississippi River flood plain. Eagles still inhabit the area as they did before the time when White men came in search of the lead that was so plentiful in the region.

The valley of the Sinsinawa River was the site of many of the counties early mining operations. Many of the early miners came up the Mississippi or overland on trails in the spring returning home in the fall, thus being able to put in and harvest a crop and mine lead on a claim in the same year. These fair weather miners who came from as far away as Springfield and St. Louis became known as suckers as their coming and going coincided with the migration of that particular breed of fish. Those that stayed were known as badgers as that animal spends its winters holed up. Today Wisconsin is known as the Badger State and Illinois as the Sucker State

Although some of the lead mine shafts were dug horizontally, most consisted of a vertical shaft, branching out to horizontal shafts at a depth of 40 to 50 feet. For this reason few tunnels can be seen along the banks of local streams. The mines though not dug into river banks were rarely far away as the ore needed to be washed before being processed in a smelting furnace.

The put-in on the Sinsinawa River is right on the Illinois/Wisconsin state line on Sinsinawa Road where getting past the barbed wire wasn't hard, but permission should be sought. It is an 8 mile trip from the state line down to Chetlain Lane and 4 more miles to the rivers mouth on the Mississippi River.

From the state line to U.S. Route 20 rock walls line the stream side, although not as spectacular as those on the Apple or Galena Rivers. Besides rock walls the most of the land you travel through is pasture because the river bottom lands are too rocky for crops. Pastures mean fences and there are a few on this section. In fact the bridges at the put-in and North High Ridge Road are fenced in, making permission of land owners a good idea. All of the fences on the Sinsinawa are single strands of barbed wire and are easily passed under if spotted in time.

The upper Sinsinawa River is more the size of a creek than a river and requires quite a bit of water to become runnable. Surprisingly we only encountered one logjam in the 8 miles. Shoals are regularly encountered and are separated by quiet slow moving pools.

The takeout is Chetlain Road but the lower river really starts more than a mile upstream where the current noticeably slows. From Chetlain Road on to the Mississippi the scenery also noticeably changes from pasture to thick lush green growth in summer. Wildlife is also thick only at one place along the bottom 4 miles is there any sign of man, and that comes in the form of houses, there are no fences or rock walls. The lower Sinsinawa River is mainly backwater of the Mississippi and therefore canoeable for most of the year. Rail Road tracks cross the river on a pair of iron trusses that are unusual.

The Sinsinawa flows though a section of the Upper Mississippi River National Wildlife & Fish Refuge before finally mingling its waters with those of the Mississippi. The slow current on the Sinsinawa is even more noticeable when pulling out onto the swift currant of the Mississippi. The last three miles on the Mississippi are in a natural state with the exception of a few fishing shanties. Stay to the river left side and keep your eyes peeled for the inlet to Gears Ferry Landing the takeout. The channel is not obvious from the main channel although there is a buoy marking the side channel.

The Sinsinawa River is an interesting paddle much like a miniature of its neighbor the Galena River. The fact that it requires more water to run the Sinsinawa and the Galena's rock walls are even more scenic, would make the Sinsinawa a second choice. On the other hand both of these rivers sport lower sections that are equally scenic and are runnable year round.

Illinois Atlas Page 15-A-1

Somonauk Creek

Somonauk Creek is a very small, pleasant stream with its headwaters in DeKalb County, and flowing south into LaSalle County where it empties into the Fox River.

The name comes from the Potawatomi word for a paw paw grove. In spite of its small size, the creek is relatively unobstructed by barbed wire or logjams. I've divided the creek into two sections; the first section from Shabbona Grove Road to Illinois Route 34 (Saunank Park), a trip of 15 miles, and the second, from Route 34 to the mouth of the creek at the Fox River near Sheridan, a trip of about ten miles.

The upper trip could begin at U.S. Route 30 in high water but a more practical start in more normal water levels would be three miles downstream at Shabbona Grove Road. This small gravel farm road parallels Route 30 and is seldom used. (I've also used this road for trips on Indian Creek and Little Rock Creek). The access to the creek is level, close to the road, and the wide shoulders of the road make for convenient parking.

After leaving the Shabbona Road Bridge, you'll be treated to 13 miles of woodlands, floodplains and farm fields, where any sighting of human intrusion is rare. Wildlife was plentiful on my first trip. I spotted two kinds of owls, muskrat, beaver, blue and green herons and lots of deer. This seems to be a healthy well balanced ecosystem. Several dams impede or accent your trip. All are easy to portage. Pay special attention to the Old Mill dam just upstream of Sudamn Road, as it has a larger drop and a trickier approach. Scout it carefully or portage river right.

Chicago Road was an old stagecoach route. The first settler was George Beveridge, who upon arriving here in 1838 found an old, abandoned trapper's cabin that had been erected in 1834 at the site of the ford on Somonauk Creek. The cabin was the first structure built in DeKalb County by a non-Indian and had been used as a station on the Galena mail route before being abandoned.

The Beveridge family settled in the area, and later their home became a station on the Underground Railroad that helped runaway slaves escape to safety before the Civil War. The Beveridge family also produced the 17th governor of Illinois, John Lowrie Beveridge. An unusual story is behind his becoming the governor as he was never chosen by the people in an election. He took over when the governor, Richard J. Oglesby, resigned to take a seat in the U. S. Senate in 1873, after serving only ten days. The road that crosses the creek near the community of Franks was named for this never elected governor. This community at the intersection of the Chicago Road and Somonauk Creek remained the main settlement on the Creek until 1853, when the railroad came through and the towns of Somonauk and Sandwich were platted.

After passing under Chicago Road, the creek gets back to nature again. It's about eight miles more to reach Illinois Route 34. My notes state there were two more dams on this section, each about two and a half feet high. One of the dams is located in the Edgebrook Country Club near Sandwich, Illinois. The takeout is just past Route 34 in Saunank Park, which has a road down to the creek with parking spaces for about five cars. This park is a short distance above Lake Holiday, a private community, and rumor has it, there is no trespassing permitted. The dam at the lower end of the lake is another obstacle. I suggest that you use the access below the dam as a put-in for running the lower section. NOTE: the road to the creek in Saunank Park may very well be closed during winter months.

The best access to the lower creek is just below the Lake Holiday dam, where there is parking on both sides of the creek and a road fording the creek between the two parking areas. Since Lake Holiday is a private community and this put-in is within its boundaries, it may well be illegal, but, because the next bridge is also well posted, the dam access was the better choice and no one interfered with me putting in here the two times I used it.

The lower ten mile section also had an abundance of wildlife, but it also had more human intrusion visible, and more pasture lands, although it still seemed fairly remote. There were more logjams and barbed wire in at least two places, but this changes from year to year. There are two small dams located above and below LaSalle County Road

N 4250. I ran both, however they should be scouted as conditions change with different water levels. It is a short distance from the last dam to the mouth of the creek at the Fox River. There was an Indian mission located downstream on the Fox River near the mouth of the creek that was started around 1826. From this beginning as a mission, grew the town of Sheridan.

Take out across the Fox River just upstream of the bridge, where there is a landing owned by the tavern on the Sheridan Cutoff Road. As a gauge to judge if there is enough water to run the upper section, look at the old mill dam visible from the Suydam Road Bridge. For running the lower section, there should be plenty of water flowing over the ford below the Lake Holiday dam put-in.

Illinois Atlas: Page 27, C-5 for the upper section and D-5 for the lower section.

Spring Creek

Spring Creek was by far the most difficult debris-filled stream I have run up to this time. There were forty-two logjams in the thirteen miles we traversed. Spring creek looked great on the map, with lots of contour lines promising a steep valley. Its course, similar to that of the Little Vermilion River just to the east of it, made us believe that we would see some rock outcropping and rapids in that steep valley. Scouting at all of the overpasses didn't discourage this belief. However, it was very hard finding out about the realities to be found along this waterway.

The first mistake we made was putting in too far upstream. I don't remember why we passed up the Plank Road Bridge and instead put in two miles further upstream at County E 3575, the county line between LaSalle and Bureau Counties. Our rate of speed was less than one mile per hour and included ten portages per mile for these first two miles. Putting in at Plank Road would have shortened the trip although it would not have made it better.

As we progressed downstream, the portages over logjams continued, although there were fewer. The scenery continued to be pasture and cropland with the creek banks bordered with trees. Progress was unusually slow until Interstate 80 where we made better time for a short while. After I-80, there was a golf course with several low bridges, all of which required portages and slowed us down again. After the golf course, more deadfalls impeded our progress. The gradient began to increase as the valley steepened, and some ledges appeared in the bed of the stream, the largest being about three feet high.

When we ran Spring Creek, the Little Vermilion River was running at two feet on its gauge, a high level. However, a clean run still couldn't be had on Spring Creek because of too little water at the ledges. This means that it takes really high water to bring on runnable conditions. About four feet on the Little Vermilion gauge would mean this section of Spring Creek might be runnable.

Past the ledges, signs of quarrying along the creek mean that the U.S. Route 6 Bridge will soon appear high overhead above the creek bed. From here on down to the mouth, the stream skirts the east side of the town of Spring Valley. The last two miles or more crossed the floodplain of the Illinois River Valley. This last section might have had more logjams than we ran into, for the Illinois River was in flood stage. It was difficult to follow the proper channel in the flooded woods. The takeout is one-half mile downstream on the right side of the Illinois River, just under the Illinois Route 89 Bridge where there is a paved boat ramp.

Spring Creek was mentioned by the first settlers as being a favorite of the Potawatomi tribe because of its clear water. Camps were said to have been located up and down the valley year round. This means that, as the name implies, Spring Creek was indeed at one time spring fed.

One might ask where are the springs? Well, it goes something like this. As permanent settlements were established over the years, wells were dug to supplement the seasonal variations or drought years. The digging of wells lowered the water table, which released the pressure that caused the springs to flow.

Today we have devised a system of man-made springs to supplement the lost flow of natural spring water. We call these sewage treatment plants and the water they release, effluent. Even more amazing is the fact that both types resist freezing.

Illinois Atlas: Page 34, B-1

"UGH!!!!! Logjams."

Stillmans Creek

I like to call it Stillmans Run, and some maps still do. Run can refer to both a creek and a rout. After reading the story of the opening battle of the Black Hawk War you'll see why.

In 1804, the Sauk and Fox living around the Rock River country signed a treaty with the United States government and agreed to move their tribe west of the Mississippi River. This treaty was reaffirmed in 1816, 1822 and 1825. Black Hawk, one of the chiefs, had moved across the Mississippi with the rest of the Sauk Tribe in 1831.

They left behind their main village near the mouth of the Rock River. In the spring, Black Hawk and a small band of followers declared that the treaty, which was made in St. Louis, wasn't legal or binding as it was signed by only a few members of the Sauk Tribe. Although Black Hawk had signed at least one version of this treaty, he claimed he didn't understand what he had signed.

Black Hawk and his followers recrossed the Mississippi, and on returning to their village, they found it occupied by white men. The new residents were squatting on land that belonged to the United States by the rights granted by the treaty with the Sauk. However, the land had yet to be surveyed, so it wasn't available for sale or homestead at this time. The treaty stated that the Sauk may live on the lands granted to the government until such time as the U.S. Government could make use of these lands. In 1804, not even the U.S. Government foresaw the vast prairies of northern Illinois as being worth anything. However, 25 years later westward expansion was the American dream. So settlers came and without anyone's permission, settled on the site of Black Hawks village.

The squatters had done more than just occupy the former Indian village. They had torn down some lodges to make fencing, then fenced in the fields that the Indians had planted the previous fall.

Many settlers in the early 1800s chose former Indian villages as locations to settle on. The reasons were many. First, the Indians situated their villages near water and woods and usually in a good defensible position. On top of this, the fields around the village were already broken from prior planting of corn and squash by the Indians.

Add to this is the fact that the squatters arrival before the government survey assured them up to ten years of free occupation. When the land was finally sold by the government, frequently the squatters would be able to sell the improvements they had built, such as the cabin, fencing, and outbuildings. The squatters would then move westward and start the whole process over again.

Black Hawk and his band of followers had tried to seek recourse from several officials of the government, including the Sauk Indian agent and a former governor of Illinois. All of these counseled Black Hawk to return to the west side of the Mississippi River. Black Hawk was angered by the injustice of these counseling's and crossed back to Iowa to hold council with the main Sauk chief, Keokuk.

On April 6,1832, Black Hawk, with 400 warriors and 1200 women and children, crossed the Mississippi. The band traveled up the Rock River to a meeting with Shabbona and Waubansee at the mouth of the Kishwaukee River. Black Hawk hoped to encourage these two Potawatomi chiefs and their tribesmen to join him in a war on the settlers.

When Black Hawk had met with these two influential chiefs, they also advised a return west of the Mississippi. After this disappointment, Black Hawk, finding no allies, decided to return to Iowa and make peace.

But this was not to be. Eight days after Black Hawk had crossed back into Illinois, Governor Reynolds had called for 1,200 volunteers and the first of these militia was to form at Dixon's Ferry on the Rock River, under General Atkinson. The militia marched up the Rock River in pursuit of Black Hawk and his band of followers. Toward evening on May 14, Major Stillman and Major Bailey brought the 275 volunteers under their command into camp, on Old Mans Run, now called Stillmans Run. It had been named Old Mans Run because a lone Indian of maturing years had a dwelling near the mouth of the creek.

Major Stillman crossed the swollen creek and was preparing to go into camp when three unarmed Indians approached under a flag of truce. They had been sent by Black Hawk to report that Black Hawk was ready to return to Iowa and live in peace. The militia held the party captive for lack of an interpreter. Black Hawk had also sent five more warriors to act as observers. They stayed about a half-mile back on a small hill.

The militia who had broken open a barrel of rum, became drunk, decided to capture the five braves. About 40 of the militia charged the five braves. They killed three, wounded one and the survivor made it back to where Black Hawk and about 40 additional warriors were waiting. From the cover of a small wooded area, the undetected Indians let loose a volley. And did Stillman's army run! He and his militia fled for home, passing Dixon's Ferry, and even passing Ottawa. In Ottawa, some of the militia were asked to go back and help bury the dead from the massacre on Indian Creek. They refused, being afraid that the Indians were still there, and continued fleeing south, advising the other settlers to do the same. Stillman's militia claimed that at least 2,000 Indians were close on their heels. You can imagine how safe this made the settlers in Ottawa and at Dixon's Ferry feel!

There is a monument commemorating this event in the village of Stillman Valley, It's located about a block west of the creek on Route 72.

I launched at Big Mound Road, the put-in for a canoeist looking for a beating. I say that because the first three miles contained 27 pull-your-boat-out-of-the-water type of logjams. It was so bad, that I almost did the unthinkable; quit and walk out. To top it off, you cannot see the monument from Stillmans Run at all.

Well, I didn't walk out, but I discovered the practical head of navigation is at the Stillman Road Bridge. Stillman Road skirts the western edge of the town of Stillman Valley. Below Stillman Road you can still expect three or more portages per mile, but that is better than the ten per mile upstream. The only fence that had to be dealt with was just downstream of this bridge. Stillman Run's bottom section is primarily pastoral, horse and cow type pasture, with its identifiable odors. This was blended with residential subdivisions. The banks are black dirt and average about three feet in height. This further complicated portaging by making landings difficult.

The four miles between Stillman Road and Kishwaukee Road is sandwiched between Illinois Route 72 on the south and Hales Corner Road on the north side. Traffic on these roads can be seen or heard much of the way. The Chicago, Milwaukee and St. Paul railroad also runs parallel through the stream valley and bridges the creek a short distance below Stillman Road. Black Walnut Creek enters from the left about two thirds of the way through this section and almost doubles the volume of water. Stillmans also starts to meander in sharp closely-spaced turns. These are so sharp as to almost stop forward progress. This is not uncommon on very small creeks.

A few hundred yards upstream of the Kishwaukee Road bridge is a pontoon footbridge that blocks the stream bank to bank and requires another portage. Stillmans Run becomes very wide near the Kishwaukee Road Bridge. This was partially due to the fact that the Rock River was in flood stage at the time. One-half mile below Kishwaukee Road, Stillman's Run empties into the Rock River. Another one-half mile downstream on the west side of the Rock River will bring you to a public boat ramp just north of the town of Byron on Illinois Route 2.

Illinois Atlas; Page 18 D-1

"From the cover of a small wooded area, the undetected Indians let loose a volley. And did Stillman run! He and his militia fled for home, passing Dixon's Ferry, and even passing Ottawa. In Ottawa, some of the militia were asked to go back and help bury the dead from the massacre on Indian Creek. They refused, being afraid that the Indians were still there, and continued fleeing south, advising the other settlers to do the same. Stillman's militia claimed that at least 2,000 Indians were close on their heels. You can imagine how safe this made the settlers in Ottawa and at Dixon's Ferry feel!

This monument commemorates this event in the village of Stillman Valley, It's located about a block west of the creek on Route 72."

Sugar River

The Sugar River flows for many miles in Wisconsin before flowing into the Pecatonica River. I have paddled more than fifty miles of the Sugar River upstream of the Wisconsin/Illinois border. The last twenty-eight miles in Wisconsin are described in *The Best Canoe Trails of Southern Wisconsin.*

To access the full nine miles of the Sugar River in Illinois, it is best to put-in at Sugar River Park off of Nelson Road, near the town of Avon, Wisconsin. The scenery doesn't change as the river leaves the Avon Bottoms Wildlife Area and crosses the Illinois border four miles below Nelson Road.

Bottoms is the perfect way to describe the character of the Sugar River. The Sugar River winds its way along with low banks and much deadfall in the channel. Now don't get me wrong, although there are many trees in the river that require quite a bit of maneuvering, the Sugar River is rarely fully blocked.

Someone is keeping the river clear, I can see places that show signs of chain saw cuts of varying ages. Perhaps Resort U.S.A. Campground downstream may be running a canoe livery therefore keeping the river clear.

The bottoms have over the years remained undeveloped and untouched except by hunters, first Indian and then White. This leaves the land on either side of the Sugar River dense in both growth and wildlife. I saw my first flock of wild turkeys in Illinois along this stretch of the Sugar River. Deer, beaver, muskrat all call these bottom lands home, I counted more owls on this section than on any trip that I've ever taken.

Sugar River winds its way through the first few miles in Illinois before sand bluffs appear on a bend in the river indicating that Colored Sand Forest Preserve has been entered. True to its name the sands and clays that make up these bluffs are of varied shades and color. Yale Bridge Road has a new (1997) paved boat ramp with paved parking and restrooms, this is part of the fore mentioned Forest Preserve.

Downstream of the Yale Bridge Road Bridge it is about a mile before entering the Sugar River Forest Preserve. Here again canoe access is available along with picnic shelters, water and restrooms. These two Winnebago County Forest Preserve are similar to other Winnebago County parks on the Kishwaukee River and Killbuck Creek. A big paddlers "well done" to Winnebago County for having its heart in the right place.

Winslow Road is a mile below Sugar River Forest Preserve. From Winslow Road on, the Sugar River opens up a bit, farms are passed with increasing frequency. This is especially true as the valleys of the Sugar and Pecatonica Rivers come closer together. The take-out is at the confluence of the Sugar River with the Pecatonica. Here you will find the aptly named Two Rivers Forest Preserve, though not as nice as the two parks upstream, Two Rivers is more than an adequate take out. There is a boat ramp just upstream on the Pecatonica, or take out right at the confluence just past the bridge, where the river bank is lower.

Wisconsin Atlas Page: 28-D-2
Illinois Atlas Page; 17-A-7 & Page 18-A-1

Thorn Creek

Thorn Creek is a tributary of the Little Calumet River in Illinois a few miles from the Indiana boarder. The thing that stands out when looking at Thorn Creek on a good map, is the forest preserve corridor that pads the creek for many miles. Few roads pass over Thorn Creek in those miles making for limited canoe access. Thorn Creek is similar to Salt Creek and the upper sections of the DesPlaines River in that they are small urban streams running though flood plain forest preserves, with poor water quality.

The farthest upstream I could recommend putting in would be at the Glenwood Picnic area off of Glenwood Road, where there is good parking and a long carry to the water. Put-in close to the Glenwood Road Bridge as it provides an easier launch. If your wondering about trips further upstream I put-in at Joe Orr woods 3 miles upstream and found more than 30 log jams in those 3 miles. Between Joe Orr Road and Glenwood Road Deer Creek and Butterfield Creeks add both water and width to Thorn Creek.

Downstream from Glenwood Road the log jams thin out to a mere 1 per/mile. There are quiet a few ten to twenty foot high cut banks and trash is a continuous eye sore. Thornton Lansing Road crosses Thorn Creek three miles downstream of Glenwood Road and is the only road that breaks the forested creek bottom in those miles though it is also crossed by railways.

Thornton Lansing Road is the approximate location of Thorn Creeks connection to history. Gurdon Hubbard known to the Native Americans as Pa-Pa-Ma-Ta-Be (the Swift Walker) married Watseka the daughter of a chief, and as part of her dowry was given a 160 acres of land located on Thorn Creek. The marriage didn't work out and each went their own way after two years, but Hubbard retained ownership of the land and in 1836 Gurdon Hubbard with John Kinzie as a partner, built a saw mill on Thorn Creek. Hubbard's career is fascinating, fur trader, land speculator, he started the first stock yard and packing plant in Chicago. He owned much land in Chicago on which he built warehouses and retail businesses. Hubbard helped the city of Chicago grow from frontier town to bustling city. One mile below Thornwood Lansing Road Thorn Creek winds its way out of the last of the forest preserves Sweet Woods to cross Interstate 294. After The Interstate the creek enters its first residential neighborhood since Joe Orr 7 1/2 miles ago. Downstream of the housing Interstate 94 crosses over Thorn Creek in three multi-lane bridges. This part of Thorn Creek supports more trash than the upper portions. More houses are passed before the confluence with the Little Calumet River. Another 1/2 mile on the Little Calumet will bring you down to 159th Street, which is also U.S. 6. Another mile brings on Gouwen Park and Sports Complex where there is plenty of parking and a paved ramp into the Little Calumet. The downside here is a carry to the water of several hundred feet, all and all a good access. Gouwen Park is located just north of 159th Street and just west of Interstate 94.

Thorn Creek is similar to the North Branch of the Chicago's upper section except that the North Branch's log jams get cleared several times each year. Only this and the limited access points keep this from being a nice south side family canoe trip that would rival the North Branch of the Chicago River.

Illinois Atlas Page-29-D-7

Tomahawk Creek

Tomahawk Creek's runnable section begins at U.S. Route 52 about four miles east of Troy Grove, Wild Bill Hickok's home town, and empties into the Little Vermilion River, two hundred yards above Interstate 80 bridge. At the put-in, you'll find a stream twenty to thirty feet wide running south through wide open farm fields.

Bridges at LaSalle County Roads E600, N3300, the Wallace Waltham School Road, and E500, the Troy Grove Blacktop, could also be used as put-ins to shorten the trip, or as alternative put-ins for the Little Vermilion River canyon section. The creek has the same mellow character all the way down to Troy Grove Blacktop Bridge.

After the bridge, Tomahawk Creek starts cutting a steep canyon as it drops into the valley of the Little Vermilion River. The gradient increases and the banks continue to get higher and start to close in making a narrow channel. There are several things to watch for as you enter this canyon. Watch for an area that was struck by a tornado in 1993, but don't ignore what is happening right ahead of you! The riffles are almost continuous now and you are swiftly approaching a low, partly upturned foot bridge on a blind turn.

The creek at this point is only twenty feet wide and the current is fast, so *absolute* boat control is necessary, or the consequences could be disastrous. After passing the foot bridge, you'll come to a wider, slower section of dead water indicating that you are approaching a dam. Plan to portage on the left. This dam is about twenty feet high, and the face of the dam has a forty degree slope except for the last three feet, which are vertical. The water must be very high to make this runnable.

Right after the dam is a short easy Class III rapid, followed by a couple of hundred yards of riffles that will bring you to the confluence with the Little Vermilion River. Once on the Little Vermilion, it's less than a mile to the take-out at the N3000 Bridge, but in that mile, the river drops eighteen feet and contains one good Class II rapid.

Illinois Atlas: Page 34, A-2

Turtle Creek

Although Turtle Creek is by all rights a Wisconsin river, the last mile or so lies within Illinois and so I've included it in this guide. Besides, it was named for an Indian village located at its mouth in Illinois.

The town of South Beloit, Illinois now stands where Turtle village once stood. Mrs. Kinzie described Turtle Creek as "a clear and sparkling stream" in her book, *Wau Bun,* which describes a trip from Portage, Wisconsin to Chicago in the year 1831. She and her husband camped upstream of the village overnight.

Above Delavan, Wisconsin, the creek is channelized and water sensitive, in other words not very pleasant to canoe. So I started in Delavan below Lake Como. Lake Como has a dam close to downtown, the outlet of which feeds a smaller lake in Terrace Park. The outlet of this lake has a short class II rapid directly below I just could not pass up. You have to make a long carry across a baseball field to reach the put-in just below the dam. The price of running this rapid was higher than I anticipated, as a few hundred yards downstream, I encountered a pair of pipes suspended across the river. The pipes are associated with the village water works that occupy both sides of the creek at this location. The lower of the two pipes was too low to duck under and the top of the other one directly over the first was more than six feet high. It took a concerted effort to hoist my boat over the pair of pipes.

After the first two or three hundred yards all the excitement came to an end. The creek became pastoral almost as soon as it left the town of Delavan. County Road P is crossed as the town is left behind. Farm fields and cattle pastures were the main scenery for most of the next few miles. Farm houses were seen but usually at a distance.

There are some riffles and shoals, although they are rare. The creek tends to run flat and slow. Deadfalls were rare. Although there was nothing exceptional on this stretch it was still pleasant enough paddling. In this rural setting I found wildlife plentiful; muskrat, blue and green herons, beaver, groundhogs, and deer can all be seen occasionally along the banks. This continued all the way to the Illinois state line.

A few miles outside of town, Pounder Road is crossed and again about the same distance will bring you to Wisconsin Highway 11. After passing under a bridge at Highway 11, the Turtle Creek State Wildlife area is entered. The scenery doesn't change either entering or leaving the wildlife area. One more bridge, School Section Road, is passed before you'll come to the U. S. Route 14 Bridge. You're a little more than half way at this point. One more bridge is passed and then you arrive at Creek Road, twelve miles from the start. This completed the first section.

For the middle section, Creek Road again served as a good access. The next eleven miles were very much the same as the upper section. Basically slow, pastoral, meandering, a very typical midwestern country stream. From here down, the closer we get to Beloit, the more the area gets populated, although houses are still rare along the creek.

The only thing extraordinary about this section is the Chicago Northwestern's five-arched rustic stone bridge.

The stone bridge was built in 1869. It spans 387 feet and was built when locomotives weighed about 40 tons. Nowadays, without modification, it carries locomotives weighing 250 tons. A hundred yards upstream is a hundred year old iron bridge that carries Smith Road over Turtle Creek.

A short distance downstream, is the takeout in Sweet Allyn County Park, an old mill site, located where County Road J crosses Creek Road. This park is an excellent landing with good parking.

The park is across the creek from the town of Shopiere, home of Louis Powell Harvey, the short lived governor of Wisconsin at the time of the Civil War. It seems the governor was leading a relief expedition to help the Wisconsin troops after the battle of Shiloh. While boarding a steamboat on the Tennessee River, he fell overboard and drowned. Stop and have a look at the clock in the yard dedicated to war dead from several wars.

The put-in for the last ten mile section is the same as the takeout for the last trip, Sweet Allyn Park on County Road J. A little more than a mile of canoeing brings one under a pleasant Iron bridge, vintage 1889 over which Lathers Road crosses the bridge. It's very similar to the one 100 yards upstream from the Northwestern Railroad's stone arched bridge. A mile further is the Interstate 90 Bridge. Turtle Creek flows through a natural landscape in this section. There are frequent opportunities to observe wildlife. A short distance below the interstate, the banks have been cut away, apparently to form a pond out of an old quarry by using the creek to supply the water.

The next bridge crossed is Shopiere Road. Which was the ancient Indian trail between Turtle Village and other Indian villages to the east. At the west end of the bridge and a little north was located a council house. It was located on the hill and commanded a view of the approaches of several trails that intersected here. The council house was 18 feet x 30 feet and 8 to 10 feet high.

As Shopiere Road fades from view the countryside again becomes more natural. When houses do appear, they are often opulent. Most are set far back from the creek, and I noticed many of the homes are done mostly in earth tones. The homes on Turtle Creek seem to be much nicer than those on many other streams I've explored.

Riffles appear regularly along the lower creek. In fact, there are more riffles on the lower creek than on the entire upper two sections. Turtle Creek tends to become narrower as it gets closer to Beloit. This in turn means a faster current.

Another amazing thing is the way the Turtle stays surprisingly wild appearing as it enters Beloit proper. Even after entering town, much of the time one bank or the other is still relatively natural and wildlife is still evident in many places.

Four more bridges are crossed before coming to Wisconsin Route 81, a four lane bridge. Another mile downstream of the Colley Avenue Bridge, Turtle Creek comes up alongside a set of railroad tracks. This narrows the creek and creates fast water for quite a distance. A bridge carries another set of tracks across the creek a short distance downstream. This area is known as Beloit Junction. Up the hill beyond the tracks has been identified as the main site of the Turtle Village.

A short time before crossing the Illinois border, this natural stream surrenders to its urban surroundings. City dumps line both sides of Turtle Creek. On either side you can see junk yards or the back ends of factories and businesses.

This is a shame, because historically, this section flows through the Turtle Village that occupied the peninsula between the Rock River and Turtle Creek. Several of the chiefs that lived there were also called *The Turtle*. It is thought that the most likely source of the name is that it referred to an effigy mound that is located on the present day site of Beloit College. Turtle Mound measures 75 feet long and 30 feet wide. The early settlers of Beloit stated that Winnebago Indians continued to visit the site periodically as late as 1865.

The site of the main village was upstream as previously described, their lodges and croplands continued all the way to the mouth.

One of the last Chiefs to live in Turtle Village was White Crow. White Crow was the primary influence in the release of the Hall girls kidnapped during the Indian Creek Massacre. (See Indian Creek.)

The earliest white settler in the area was Joseph Thibault, a French-Canadian, who traded for furs with the local Indians around 1832 when treaties ending the Black Hawk War were signed. The Indians left the Turtle and moved west across the Mississippi River.

Thibault remained on the site of the village. In 1836 Caleb Blodgett offered Joseph Thibault $500 for approximately 7,000 acres. Blodgett in turn sold three-quarters of the land for $6,000 and retained the best section for himself. Land speculation followed and Beloit grew and became a town.

It's about a mile from the state line to the mouth on the Rock River. Just below the confluence is Boney Island. Take the right channel as the scenery is far better. Two more miles downstream on the Rock carries you to Prairie Hill Road, the takeout.

Turtle Creek is close in character to other area streams, such as Piscasaw Creek, the Kishwaukee River, or Sugar River. But its history is what makes this stream unique.

Wisconsin Atlas: Page 29, C-7, D-6, D-5
Illinois Atlas: Page 18, A-2.

"This is one of two old iron bridges on Turtle Creek dating back to the late 1800s. Bridges like this one are disappearing from our landscape."

"The park is across the creek from the town of Shopiere, home of Louis Powell Harvey, the short lived governor of Wisconsin at the time of the Civil War. It seems the governor was leading a relief expedition to help the Wisconsin troops after the battle of Shiloh. While boarding a steamboat on the Tennessee River, he fell overboard and drowned. Stop and have a look at the clock in the yard dedicated to war dead from several wars."

Tyler Creek

No, no, no! I didn't name this creek, but as soon as I saw the sign that said Tyler Creek Nature Preserve, I had to take a look. What I saw wasn't encouraging. Two logjams in the park, and who knows how many more upstream. Downstream it coursed through the Judson College campus. Looking upstream revealed but little more in the way of information, and so begins another voyage of discovery.

By the way, I did find out which Tyler the creek was named after. George Noah Tyler was truly the first settler in the Elgin area, although James Talcott Gifford is generally credited with the honor in the history books. The fact is, Tyler arrived one month earlier in March of 1835 and helped Gifford with the construction of his cabin. The error historians make results from the fact that Gifford recorded his homestead claim first. Also, the fact that James Gifford was not only a farmer, but also a surveyor, inventor, manufacturer, justice of the peace, postmaster and amateur biochemist, made him a more impressive first settler, while George Tyler was just a quiet farmer. Gifford died at the age of 50, however, Tyler lived to the ripe old age of 97.

I put in at Big Timber Road, just west of Tyrell Road, using the northeast side to launch my boat. Although Burnidge County Forest Preserve borders Tyler Creek Road, access within the preserve doesn't exist. Tyler Creek upstream of here looked unnavigable and therefore was not attempted.

After passing under the Big Timber Road Bridge, on river right is the forest preserve, and on river left is Big Timber Scout Camp. A mile downstream is a low railroad bridge that I managed to clear by inches. At higher water levels, it could present a problem because of the strong current that carries you toward it. One half of the bridge was blocked by debris, restricting the passage. Another mile and you pass under the Randall Road Bridge, and housing developments appear and soon border both sides of the stream. Sparsely wooded areas alternate with houses, apartments and industrial properties. These are somewhat buffered by the steep banks which keep these intrusions partially out of sight. There are many foot bridges from here to the mouth of the creek to watch out for! I ran the creek at a medium high level and cleared most of them, although several forced me to lie on my back on the bottom of the canoe. At full flood stage, many of these would require portages, which might be difficult on a stream too small to turn your boat around on.

Soon you come to Wing Road and after passing a few apartment buildings, the most interesting run is through Wing Park. Even though the creek was flowing amid a more natural setting, the stream bed became decidedly unnatural. Riprap and even concrete walls lined the sides of the creek and another batch of foot bridges required extra caution because of the increased velocity caused by the walling in of the channel. Tyler Creek narrows even more as it approaches a swimming pool area. Walls enclose the creek and a foot bridge is passed that connects the pool's changing area on the right from the pool located on the left side of the creek.

After Wing Park you'll pass under Big Timber Road a second time. A few warehouse-type buildings are passed before entering Tyler Creek Forest Preserve. Ever since Wing Road, the gradient and current continually increase, reaching their peak around Tyler Creek Forest Preserve and Judson College grounds. Expect to encounter a few strainers in this swift section. Coming out of the forest preserve, you are at the approximate location of the original site of the Tyler family homestead and saw mill.

The Judson College Campus is entered after passing under Route 31. The excitement here is furnished by a series of one to two foot high check dams to run, some with bridges overhead. When I ran this section, classes were changing, and I had my largest audience ever as I shot the cascade. A few hundred yards after the last dam, the Fox River is reached. I took out one mile UPSTREAM on the Fox, north of I-90 bridge, at the Voyageur Landing Forest Preserve. This is located on the west side of the Fox and is reached by a frontage road accessed from Route 31.

The best place to scout Tyler Creek water levels is at Tyler Creek Forest preserve, as the park road runs parallel to the stream for a quarter mile. If it looks too shallow or too flooded at this point, it can be assumed the rest of it is also. If Tyler Creek looks too small for you in the park, remember, it is smaller upstream. Tyler Creek can be a very challenging little creek.

Illinois Atlas: Page 20, D-1

Little Vermilion River

This is by far my favorite piece of moving water in the whole prairie state, bar none. In my first six or seven years of canoeing, I was on the canyon section of the Little Vermilion whenever the water was up. Because of this, it was a long time before I discovered any of the other small high water streams discussed in this volume. In fact, my first trip on the upper section of the Little Vermilion took place only because I was too scared to run the rapids of the canyon when the gauge read four and a half feet. Had this high water not occurred, I would never have discovered the beautiful multicolored sandstone bluffs upstream. Four years later, when I did run the canyon at the four foot gauge level, I was forced to run an eight foot drop to avoid two monster holes that occupied the middle half of the river. It was definitely a CLASS V that day! Anyway, the point is that to this day, it is still difficult for me to pass up the chance to run the Little Vermilion whenever the water's up.

Like its big brother, the Vermilion, on the opposite shore of the Illinois river, the Little Vermilion has beautiful rock walls and good rapids. The Little Vermilion is small, intimate, clean and supports a healthy environment for wildlife. Both of these rivers are covered in Philip Vierling's excellent book, Illinois Country Canoe Trails, which was the first guide book I ever owned and is still one of the best and most thorough in my large collection.

The farthest upstream I dared to put in was just outside of the town of Mendota. I launched at the E 400 bridge, but then I paddled past a foot bridge in Snyder Road, Grove Park, which probably would have been a better launch site. The stream here is very narrow, about 20 feet or less in width, and it winds around like a drunken snake. The combination of narrow banks, tight turns and overhanging branches requires as much caution and skill as the whitewater canyon miles below. Barbed wire always seems to appear when least expected. On my only trip down this upper few miles, deer (including a buck), beaver, fox and a pair of great horned owls blessed my view. Such a variety of wildlife is commonly seen on most trips all the way to the mouth of the Little Vermilion.

The upper section is similar to other area streams like Somonauk or Covel, small and meandering as it winds its way though crop and pasture land. Early settlers called this the Mendota Branch. The Indian meaning of Mendota is where the trails meet.

The banks are fairly steep and wooded, so the creek remains intimate, not revealing the openness of the surrounding land. Also, like Covel Creek, the volume of water increases so at the end of this upper trip, you are floating on three times the volume of water you were on at the put-in. Two miles above Troy Grove, near the Interstate 39 bridge, lived Mrs. Levi Fahler who remembered that in 1858 there were some empty Indian huts that were built into the hillside overlooking the river. After two more miles, Route 52 and the village of Troy Grove is reached. It is difficult to land here, a better landing site is at the Troy Grove Blacktop, E 500. There is a nice stretch of water between the two bridges.

The bridge at County E 500, the Troy Grove blacktop, was the location of a saw mill that made lumber used to build most of the houses in Troy Grove. The saw mill was built in 1838 by James Newton Reader. The mill ran until 1850s, was abandoned for three years and then reopened in 1860 by Michael Meinhardt as a flour mill which continued to operate until 1904.

Troy Grove was also the birthplace of Wild Bill Hickok. Born in 1837, Hickok lived in Troy Grove for 18 years before leaving for Kansas to become a farmer. He later joined the Free State Army, serving as a scout for the U.S. Army and is probably best known for being shot in the back while playing poker. He was holding aces and eights, since called a Dead Man's Hand. Thus ended my exploration of the upper section of the Little Vermilion.

The middle section of the Little Vermilion is the most scenic of the three I have explored, and also has the most varied set of obstacles I've ever encountered while paddling these smaller waterways. These obstacles included four corrugated metal tunnels of different lengths, diameter, and pitch, a check dam, electric and barbed wire fences, and a few logjams and strainers. This is the entrance fee for one of the prettiest rivers in Illinois. I find this a cheap price to pay for the spectacular miles of sandstone bluffs.

After launching at Troy Grove, where gravel processing abounds and the dust flies, what else should you see the first few miles but gravel quarries. Don't get the idea that this is a modern intrusion. The first mining done in this area was for sand and started in 1890. This area also has the tunnels, each of which needs close inspection to confirm clear passage. At levels above two and a half feet, the lack of clearance closes off the tunnels and a portage is required. At levels above four feet, the water dams up behind the bridging road's bed and starts to overflow, washing out the road and creating a good GRADE III rapid with a sneak route on river left. Also, beware of an overhanging pipeline/conveyer belt just below the put-in at levels above four and a half feet. On my first trip down this section, I never saw these bridged roads as they were flooded over. I was very surprised to discover them on another trip at a lower water level.

Speaking of water levels, I haven't mentioned where the gauge is. It is located on the upstream side of the N 3000 bridge. To reach the gauge, turn off of I-80 onto State Route 351, the first exit west of the river. Turn left at the first road east on 351, N 3000, also called Civic Road, and take it east to the bridge. If you don't want to climb down to look at the gauge, look at the downstream shoal. It's a good indication of what the rest of the river depth will be like.

Because the gauge is on the upstream side of the bridge the water builds up a hump which makes reading the gauge subjective. My gauge readings are below this hump and as a result my readings have been up to a foot lower than I've heard others quote on the same day.

Below this quarry, the bluffs begin to appear more frequently as the meandering continues and the gradient increases. By the time you reach the N 3500 bridge you've passed almost a mile of rock walls.

N 3500 is where an old Indian trail approached the river from the southwest, then followed the river north to where N 3850 crosses the river at which point the trail turned east again toward the town of Triumph. The Kellogg Trail also followed this route on its way from Peoria to Galena except that it turned northwest at Mendota. Shabbona came over this trail to warn the settlers in 1832 and they in turn used the trail to seek shelter at Fort Wilbourn located where Route 51 crosses the Illinois River in LaSalle. Presently there is a cut-your-own Christmas tree farm upstream of the bridge on river left. Downstream of the bridge is a gun club with a skeet shooting range near the river. I always carry a whistle along for situations like this in case they are firing.

From N 3500, Dimmick Road, to N 3300, Wallace Waltham School Road, the river continues as before with lots of streamside bluffs, plenty of riffles and tight turns galore. To top this off, this section of the river teems with wildlife. On most trips, I've seen not a couple of deer, but herds of deer. Muskrat, beaver and great horned owls have also made appearances on most of my excursions. About a mile below N 3500, houses appear on river left and there is a small check dam that creates some small waves and fast water. A large pasture is entered shortly before the N 3300 bridge comes into sight. This bridge is not a good landing spot because of the No Parking signs that line both sides of the road. The owner of the farm you've just passed through doesn't particularly care for canoeists or fishermen crossing his property, although no one I know has ever been confronted. The area above this farm tends to be the place you are most likely to find the river blocked by barbed wire or logjams.

From N 3300 to N 3179, the riffles increase substantially, creating a nice warm up for the whitewater downstream. The rock cliffs are also most numerous through this section. I rarely takeout at the N 3000 bridge, not because of any problems with the farmer (in fact, I use this as a put-in all the time for the lower whitewater section), but I've never been able to pass up these two exceptional miles. Not to sound repetitive, but there are more cliffs that grow in height and swift riffles that grow in velocity. There is a nice long rapid about halfway to the I-80 bridge containing three good playable holes. Tomahawk Creek enters from the left within sight of Interstate 80. There is another good rapid right below a very nice, new two-story house that is being completed as I write this. Around the next bend is the N 3000 bridge which is where the gauge previously described is located.

If I am going to run the section starting at Troy Grove, I have always run the full twelve-plus miles down to N 3000. On the other hand I've never launched at N 3000 for the whitewater section, because all the good places to warm up for the canyon are upstream of the N 3000 bridge.

The 6 mile whitewater trip from N 3179 to Canal Street in LaSalle is well mapped in Illinois Canoe Trails but I feel the need to describe a run through the canyon anyway.

Immediately after the N 3000 bridge, there's a small play hole in river left caused by a small ledge. After this rapid, things flatten out a bit. This is broken up by fast riffle areas mostly at islands or on bends where there is a narrowing of the river bed. One outstanding thing that is noticeable in this section is that inspite of being deep with steep banks, the river valley has been fairly wide except between I-80 and N 3000, but now as you're approaching the canyon, it closes in. Rock cliffs wall in both sides of the river for the first time. As a newer concrete bridge comes into view, it is only a hundred or so yards to the canyon's entrance. There is a waterfall visible on river right but their scenic beauty was greatly diminished by the construction of this eyesore of a bridge. What's done is done! There was an effort to save this from happening—however, it failed and an agreement was reached to save the walls of the canyon.

Well, it is time to describe the canyon. First NEVER run these rapids without scouting first. Even after scouting, I watched as my tough ABS Bluehole canoe, which a friend was using, was totaled by an unseen tree lodged just below the water's surface in the first drop which I call "Z." The tree went through the bottom and out the side of my canoe. Two holes with a tree branch spearing the canoe in place and the gunwales facing upstream! It took two of us two hours to get the boat out. Scouting didn't save us this time. But, more often than not, some portion of the canyon is in some way blocked by debris.

The best place to scout is river left just a few feet before the first drop. The problem is that it is so close to the drop that it is hard to make a clean landing or launch again without getting washed over the first drop sideways. Another problem is that there is only room for three boats to land at a time. However, this landing offers a short climb on an easy path to the top of the canyon. Once on top, there is a clear view of the first two drops and a partial view of the last. The river right landing is initially easier, and you'll have a great view of Z, the first drop. However, that is the only advantage, for the path to the top is steep and hard to find and once on top the trail is overgrown and difficult. The last alternative is to land upstream at the bridge and walk the extra hundred yards to the canyon. Although the banks are fairly steep, this is also the best place from which to portage.

After scouting, it is time to run the canyon. The first drop is best run on river right through the Z. This drop washes out at around three feet on the gauge and is also the drop where most of the upsets occur. A good brace on the left will get you through.

The second of the three drops in the canyon has the most vertical drop, about four feet. It is called "The Slot," and is easier to run than it looks. Remember when scouting, that the "Slot" is a small waterfall because from 40 feet up, the rapid doesn't appear to have any vertical drop.

The last drop in the canyon is the easiest, but it also tends to trap the most deadfalls. Most of the current goes to the right of an island and is split by a boulder on the downstream end of the island. The drop occurs at this spot and fast water continues for another hundred yards. You have now completed the canyon portion and are headed toward a four foot dam two hundred yards downstream. It is best run about ten feet from the left side. Scout it first because at certain levels the hole becomes terminal.

From here to the Little Vermilion's mouth, the left bank of the river is occupied by quarries and their support buildings. The gradient remains steep and small rapids continue, but the scenery is urban. This is especially true at Cinder Pile Rapids where there are mountains a hundred feet high that are the waste dumps of an old foundry. These hills of cinders have old cars and other junk covering the slope instead of trees and plants. Below this point, the U. S. Route 6 bridge appears. Don't get carried up too close to the right bank as you approach the bridge for the banks are undercut and unstable.

A few more rapids and a dam that is washed out at all but the lowest levels will bring you to the takeout. This would have been the approximate location of the western edge of the Great Illinois Village that was encountered by Marquette and Jolliet on their 1673 voyage through the Illinois country (now known as the Midwest). The village extended to the east for a distance of three miles and had a population in the thousands at its peak years.

The takeout that is most commonly used is in between the Canal Street bridge and the Illinois Michigan Canal bridge. Between the two bridges there is about 75 feet of open space along the right bank to land on. From there, it is up the bank 50 feet and over the railroad tracks to your right. Exercise caution when crossing the tracks and the adjoining roadway. There is parking for about eight cars across Canal Street. Local fishermen park here when they fish the Illinois Michigan Canal.

I can't say much more than—I LOVE THIS RIVER. However, about twenty percent of those I've taken down the whitewater section didn't think that much of it. Those that didn't like it cited some of these reasons. First, that the quarrying and cinder piles destroyed the illusion of a remote natural setting—well, this is true, but I tend to look at the opposite bank at those times. The second thing that bugs some folks is that, while the canyon supports three very nice class III rapids, there's nothing else to interest the hard-core whitewater boater. There are a few good play-holes along the river. This brings up the third complaint! Although this would be the perfect novice whitewater run, light Grade III in normal water levels, the canyon is inconveniently located, and the portage is long, steep and hard on either side of the river. In high water, it can be a Grade V and dangerous! Enough said!

Page 26, D-2; Page 34, A-2 B-2

Top falls

Dick Frye shooting the third falls.

Looking upstream at the second falls.

Vermilion River

The Vermillion River begins southeast of Pontiac, Illinois very near the Indiana State Line. Covered here are only the last 20 miles. Additional miles upstream are covered in Phil Vierling's book *Illinois Country Canoe Trails*. Even these last 20 miles of the Vermillion constitute the most southern miles covered in this volume. Because the river runs to the north and the fact that this is Illinois most often run section of whitewater alone warrants the Vermillion River being included here. Add to this the Vermillion River has the highest most spectacular bluffs in Northern Illinois. I should also mention that the Vermillion is the river that I have most often canoed with more than 100 trips in the last dozen years.

The Klein Bridge carries LaSalle county Road N 1800 also known as Sandy Ford Road across the Vermillion River. There is a dirt parking lot on the south east corner of the bridge that is part of the Sandy Ford Nature Preserve. Right from the put-in one is struck by the steep valley and numerous bluffs. This is not the whitewater section so expect only small rapids until the takeout at Lowell Bridge. A couple of farms have in the past used some of the gullies along the Vermillion as dumps. Although this practice has been discontinued the trash still mares the river view.

The next bridge downstream of the put-in is called the Red White and Blue Bridge and it carries LaSalle County Road 1251 over the Vermillion River. There is a fishing access road that leads to the river on the north west side of the bridge. The next five miles supply more riffles and fast water and less rock bluffs than the upstream. These miles are more what you would expect from an Illinois country river.

This continues until signs of a Boy Scout Camp appear on the left bank marking the start of the whitewater section as the Vermillion starts to cut its way down into the Illinois River Valley. The Boy Scout Camp that 25 years ago was listed in *Whitewater, Quietwater* by Bob and Jody Palzer as the access point for the bottom whitewater section, is visible on the rivers left side. Illinois 178 is now the access but 2/3 of Lowell Bridge Rapid is missed. The whitewater in the last mile starts small and builds as Lowell Bridge is neared and this could be a problem for less experienced canoeists. At levels over 3 feet on the Lowell Bridge Gauge.

Lowell Bridge Rapids are not all that much by whitewater standards rating only Grade II+. But be warned that the rapid is very long and the takeout is located on the river right side halfway down the rapid. Rock shelves and ledges form waves can rise to several feet in height. The rapid is smaller on the river right side so if taking-out here stay to the right. The takeout road LaSalle County N 2258 is located just north of Lowell Bridge off of Illinois 178. It is a long steep carry up an improved path to parking along either side of N2258. Please park so as not to block driveways and change clothing in your car so the neighborhood isn't treated to any undesirable views. The residents of this single block long road host hundreds paddlers each spring weekend and need all the tender loving care the paddling community can give least we loose this convenient access.

Starting at the N 2258 access the next 8 miles ending at the Oglesby is the section that has gained the Vermillion River its reputation as "the best whitewater river in Illinois". Without a doubt it is the most popular, and it's the only river in Illinois with its own whitewater rafting company. I have introduced many paddlers to this section and thoroughly enjoy watching as their senses overload. The combination of adrenaline filled whitewater and spectacular scenery stuns first timers and keeps others coming back year after year.

There is a painted gauge on the downstream side of Lowell Bridge. Different levels drastically change the rapids along the Vermillion. Each individual rapid, changes, develops, redevelops differently, or disappears at given levels. It is not possible here to describe each rapid and how it changes at each level but here are some general observations about different gauge readings.

At "0" you'll be walking some of the shallow gravel bars Wildcat Rapid has a drop of only 1 foot. The cement dam is a scrape. Some small rapids develop at various places at only this level. Below "0" the river is all pain and the only pleasure is the scenery.

At "1 to 2 feet" the upper most rapids including those at the put-in require maneuvering to avoid bumping and scrapping. Wildcat drops about 3 feet and a wave hole begins to develop below the main drop. The Cement Dam has a narrow chute that allows for a dry passage, unfortunately it is located very close to the dangerous unbroken portion of the dam.

At "3 feet" the waves at the put-in become holes, this requires less experienced paddlers to approach each wave straight on or be prepared to lean downstream or swim. The same waves that give beginners problems, allow more skilled paddlers to surf working their way up and down and from side to side for hours at a time. The rapids at Second Island are at their best. Wildcat has a drop of about 4 feet and the wave hole at the bottom causes many to swim. On a busy day I have spent more than an hour bringing boats and boaters back together at Wildcat. This is a great place to practice whitewater rescue skills before you need them.

At 4 feet both the waves at the put-in and the dam begin to wash out and Wildcat is at its most difficult stage. The waves in the narrows below the Cement Dam begin building to heights that approximate to the gauge reading.

At "5 feet" and above the water at the put-in is moving very fast and is carrying some amount of debris. Most of the rapids are washed out and those remaining consist mainly of large waves many being surfable. At 6 feet all the large rocks in the center of the river at Wildcat cover over. The canyon at Matthiessen State Park can be ascended by boat as a side trip. So much for water levels. The first 1/4 mile below the put-in is more or less continuous rapids the largest of which are located at the top by the put-in and the bottom. The rapid ends as the Vermillion turns to the right. There is a lovely waterfall on river left, rock ledge on river left forms some fairly large waves at high water. Two islands separated by a couple of hundred yards support rapids in both left and right channels the larger rapids are to the right of both islands.

There are pools below all of the rapids on the Vermillion River. These are the places to look around at the magnificent scenery. The valley is steep and deep with the surrounding farm land at times more than a hundred feet above the river. At one point the Vermillion runs into a 40 foot tall rock wall which causes the river to make a 90 degree turn to the left against the base of the wall. Beginners should keep a safe distance from this wall as it tends to draw the unwary to close to it especially at high water when I have seen it flip rental rafts.

A hundred and fifty foot tall bluff on a right hand bend is topped with a fence and is part of Mattiessen State Park the next bend in the river leads into Wildcat Rapid the biggest rapid on the Vermillion. The State Park owns all the land along the right bank that are not abandoned quarries. Most of the miles on this trip are hemmed in by rock walls but you will not see the majority of these except in winter when the foliage is out. Some beautiful ice falls form on several side walls also during the winter months. Some small rapids spice the mile above Wildcat Rapid.

Wildcat Rapid consists of a large boulder constriction that forms a dam with a single chute. Wildcat is very different at different water levels as water level rise water backs up behind the natural obstruction. Scouting Wildcat Rapid is necessary for most boaters and is best accomplished on the right side while portaging is easiest on river left. Some boaters come to the Vermillion River only for Wildcat Rapid, and once there stays all day. At 4 or 5 P.M. on a spring weekend you will still find 1/2 dozen expert boaters still playing the wave at the bottom of Wildcat. I can personally attest to the fact that an open canoe can get endered at the bottom of the drop. At high water 4 feet on the 178 gauge a second narrow chute opens on river left. Over the more than ten years that I have been running the Vermillion River, Wildcat has been continuously changing with the rocks in the middle slowly toppling over and moving downstream.

There is long deep pool below Wildcat Rapid but rescue is impeded by large boulders lining both sides of the river and a steep muddy banks. A 1/4 mile below Wildcat Bailey enters the Vermillion. At one time this area at the bottom of Bailey Creek was proposed as a State Park but was turned down and quarried instead. The next rapid a series waves is located above a quarry bridge. The next mile is calm water but the cement factory tumbler can be heard before it is seen. The factory is a block long and fronts the river with a 20 foot concrete wall topped by a large rock tumbler, which makes a lot of noise. These are the first buildings since the put-in.

A sign hung over the Vermilion River warns of the approach to the Cement Dam, which is the most dangerous rapid on this section. The danger comes from several different factors. First is that most of the dam is still intact and a dangerous hydraulic forms below the left 2/3 of the river. Second is that the chute on the right tends to push to the right and once right of the chute some rocks lurk just below the surface these tend to flip unwary boaters. The third danger factor is that there is a lot of rebar and other refuse from the years of manufacturing and remodeling. I have seen even plastic canoes punctured by the rebar below the Cement Dam. Rescues most be done quickly as the pool is short and the next rapid lies just below.

The last of the big rapids of the Vermilion River known as the Narrows are downstream of the cement factory bridge. A series of waves that are approximately the same height as the put-in gauge reading, form just to the left of center and is another play spot for the more advanced boaters. The waves in the Narrows may be avoided by staying to the river right side.

A bend in the river along with some car size rocks in the river and a rock wall on river right mark the entrance to Matthiessen Canyon. At levels over 5 feet Matthiessen Canyon can be paddled most of the way up to it spectacular 45 foot tall waterfall. Matthiessen State Park has trails with stair cases leading to the Canyons bottom, when it can't be boated. About a mile more and the take-out at Oglesby Road is reached. This to many is the hardest part of the trip getting up the bank and then the long steep carry up to unlevel parking along a busy road. Before the Illinois Route 71 access was closed almost half the boaters on the Vermillion would paddle the extra couple of miles down to Route 71 but this is no longer an option.

If continuing on toward the Illinois River there is one smaller rapid named Boulder Island Rapid that is at its best when the water is low. Boulder Island Rapids washes out when either the Vermillion or Illinois Rivers are high. As mentioned before Illinois Route 71 can only be used if you carry your boat up to the road a long uphill carry. The only other option would be to paddle down the Illinois River to LaSalle/Peru and takeout at one of the boat ramps.

I weaned my whitewater teeth on the Vermillion. I did my first eddy-turn, surfed my first wave and got my first ender on the Vermillion. Every year I come back to learn to play and to introduce others to this magnificent river. The spectacular scenery alone would make this one of Illinois most popular trips adding the whitewater as a bonus makes this an even more unique Illinois watershed.

Illinois Atlas; Page 34 C-3, B-2

Yellow Creek

Once again in trying to find the upper limits of navigability, I put in too high up on Yellow Creek and found myself in for ten miles of log jams complicated by steep dirt banks on the way down to Mill Grove Road. The real reason I put in on Rader's Road just off of Dublin Road was that I wanted to see the Kellogg's Grove monument, which is located on the high ridge to the southwest. The monument can be seen from the crossroads at the put-in.

In the spring of the year 1825, Oliver W. Kellogg blazed a trail through the wilderness using portions of Indian trails where practical or cutting new trails. This was no mere footpath but a road capable of carrying pioneer and freight wagons for the entire distance. The Kellogg Trail, as it came to be known, ran from Fort Clark (Peoria) to La Pointe (Galena) and became the primary road to the lead mining territory. In 1829 Kellogg erected a tavern along the trail; the settlement that resulted from his labors became known as Kellogg's Grove. The monument is located in a park and commemorates two battles of the Black Hawk War that took place here at the settlement's original site on June 16 & 25, 1832. The Indians attacked after failing to take the Apple River Fort (present day Elizabeth, Illinois). Black Hawk himself fought here and Captain Abe Lincoln of the Springfield Volunteers was present when the bodies were buried. The gravestones honor only the whites who died here; nothing is said about Black Hawk's casualties.

Rader's Road and Dublin Road are very close to one another and can be considered as one access; take your pick as they are both difficult entries into Yellow Creek due to steep banks. Slow water and plentiful log jams make this a section I will not paddle again. Of the three roads that cross Yellow Creek around the town of Pearl City, only Block Road has acceptable access with parking on the road's shoulder. The next possible access is five miles further at Mill Grove Road which has houses on all four corners making it necessary to seek permission to launch or land. Another alternative would be to launch from Emerald Acres Campground, also located on Mill Grove Road upstream of the Mill Grove Bridge on Yellow Creek. Camping here might increase your chances of securing permission to use this as an access.

Between Block Road and Mill Grove Road, Yellow Creek is narrow and winds through tight turns that frequently hold log jams. The banks are wooded, steep, and are made of black dirt as is common on the watersheds of Stevenson County. Yellow Creek is, however, unique in that it boasts a variety of rock bluffs; these start popping up on this section as long picturesque walls. A mile above Emerald Acres Campground, Lost Creek along with smaller streams add substantial water and width to Yellow Creek, but the current still remains sluggish.

Mill Grove was the site of William Kirkpatrick's 1836 mill. A town once existed here but cholera struck in 1852 and again in 1854, greatly reducing the population, and the town soon faded. All that is left standing today is the old stone school house. Continuing downstream from Mill Grove Road, the enlarged stream bed helps to thin the log jams, although expect a few more in the next several miles. Again, Yellow Creek returns to nature, running straight for several miles before frequent, tight turns reappear. Yellow Creek is not crossed by a road for five more miles until Loran Road comes alongside less than a mile above the Bolton Road Bridge.

Bolton/VanBrocklyn Road intersection has many possibilities for access, the best of which is the VanBrocklyn Methodist Church parking lot (with permission) or along VanBrocklyn Road close to the junction with Bolton Road. Downstream of Bolton Road, Loran and VanBrocklyn Roads sandwich Yellow Creek in for more than a mile before branching off. The seven mile trip from Bolton Road to Krape Park is by far the best section on Yellow Creek. From here on, however, expect to see an ever increasing amount of housing as the city of Freeport nears. A mile or two upstream of Krape Park, Yellow Creek runs into what appears to be a series of ridges; the valley closes in but the creek winds around in between these ridges through an ever deeper canyon. Again rock outcroppings make their appearance, sparse at first but growing continuous and more spectacular in Krape Park. The seven mile trip ends all too soon. A great takeout in the park is the parking lot just downstream of a large building that comes right down to the banks of Yellow Creek. Note that a dam located a short distance downstream of the road bridge is dangerous and has killed several who were unaware of the power of the hydraulic currents that form below most dams.

Krape Park deserves special mention as it is unlike any other access in this book. Besides having an elaborate playground, it has a carousel, a miniature golf course, a forty foot, man-made waterfall that can be turned on and off, picnic grounds, bathrooms, trout pond, sports fields, and tennis courts. Oh I forgot to mention the canoe access. Anyway it's worth taking a look around.

The Krape Park put-in is located below the aforementioned dam; the put-in has another parking lot and easy entry to the water. It's a six mile trip from here down to U.S Route 20. Faster water and an occasional riffle continue for some distance below the Krape Park dam before resuming its more typical sluggish flow. Yellow Creek is now in Freeport and the scenery slowly deteriorates the farther downstream you proceed. The grandstands of the Stevenson County Fairgrounds can be seen from the creek below Illinois Route 26. At this point the stream bed has become channeled. Crane Grove Creek enters on the left; this creek acquired its name from the grove tavern and settlement named after Thomas Crane. Crane built a tavern on the Kellogg Trail here in 1829, the same year that Oliver Kellogg built his tavern twenty five miles up the road. A good takeout is Yellow Creek Road, which is off of U.S. 20 close to the creek where parking is on the road's shoulder.

For those wishing to continue downstream, the log jam upstream of Route 20 should serve as a warning of what lies below. It's only a couple of miles down to the mouth of Yellow Creek on the Pecatonica River but expect another half dozen log jams in those miles. The next landing on the Pecatonica is at the junction of River and Rock City Roads, ten and a half miles downstream, making for a total trip of twelve and a half miles.

Yellow Creek is at its best between Mill Grove Road and Illinois Route 26. The scenery on this section ranges from pretty to spectacular and the log jams are minimal. The upper and lower sections are bound to disappoint due to the number of log jams, poor access, and slow current. With a little clearing of log jams and a few more access points, Stevenson County would possess one of the premier canoeing streams in Illinois.

Illinois Atlas: Pages 16 &17; B-3, B-4, B-5

Pictures of Kelloggs Grove Monument Park

Zuma Creek

Zuma Creek in Rock Island County is a tributary of the Rock River. I first discovered Zuma Creek while looking for a landing on the Rock River. Scouting upstream I realized that Zuma is more of a ditch than a creek. But I started thinking "from Apple River to Zuma Creek" and I had to paddle at least the last four miles.

Putting in at 130th Street North, Zuma shows its character, flowing between ten foot high levies with gaited dirt roads atop them. Interstate 88 is only a hundred or so yards to the north, but it, along with the surrounding farm fields, can't be seen because of the levied banks. Zuma Creek runs west for a few miles before curving to the south for the last few miles. As Zuma Creek turns to the south, Interstate 80 replaces Interstate 88 along the river right bank, continuing the ever present freeway serenade. Below a railroad bridge, Zuma enters its most natural mile, even then it's still near the Interstate, and there are—still levy walls.

The last takeout before the Rock River is on Barstow Road for a trip of four miles, or continue four more miles down the Rock River to the Hennepin Canal Lock 29 access area. The Lock 29 access has a boat ramp, parking, and a canal display area.

Now you might think from this writing that there isn't an upside to Zuma Creek, but there is. Zuma Creek, like other channeled sections of water I have paddled, has a steady current with an amazing amount of wildlife present even in these few short miles.

Illinois Atlas: Page 23, D-6

Bibliography

Beloit Historic Moments—A WBEL Radio Feature during Beloit's Sesquicentennial Celebration, May 25-July 16, 1986 Written by Evelyn Wehrle and Pat Casucf; published by WBEL.

Souvenir Book of Rochelle, Illinois—Published by S.P. and Rochelle Chamber of commerce. 1922

Bicentennial History of Ogle County—Published by Ogle County American Revolution Bicentennial Commission, 1976.

History of Kendall County, Illinois—(Earliest Discovery to the Present Time); Rev. E.W. Hicks; 1877. Knickerbocker, Aurora.

Bicentennial History of Kendall County, Illinois—Kathy Farren, Editor; Kendall county Bicentennial Commission, 1976.

Biographical Directory of the Voters and Tax Payers of Kendall County—George Fisher & Co., Chicago, 1876.

John Husar—(On the Outdoors) April 3, 1994, October 30, 1994; Sports Section of the *Chicago Tribune*.

History of Kane County—Edited by Gen. John S. Wilcox; Munsell Publishing, Chicago 1904.

Historical Encyclopedia of Illinois and History of Ogle County—Horace G. Kauffman & Rebecca H. Kauffman; Volume II; Munsell Publishing, Chicago, 1909.

Inventory of the County Archives of Illinois—Ogle County (Oregon) #71; Prepared by the Illinois Historical Records Survey Project; Chicago, July 1940.

Bicentennial History of Ogle County, 1976—Published & Edited by Ogle County; American Revolution Bicentennial Commission.

Historical Encyclopedia of Illinois and History of Kendall County—Special Authors & Contributors; Volume II; Munsell Publishing, 1914.

Historical Encyclopedia of Illinois and History of Winnebago County—Charles A. Church, Volume II; Munsell Publishing, Chicago, 1916.

Book of Beloit—Published by the Daily News Publishing Company, 1936.

Pioneer Beloit—Arthur L. Luebke; Beloit Historical Society, Beloit, Wisconsin 1976.

Reminiscences of Bureau County—Matson, 1897; Princeton, Illinois.

Indian Place Names in Illinois—Virgil J. Vogel; Published by Illinois State Historical Library, 1963.

Anglo-French Boundary Disputes in the West—Theodore Calu Peask, 1923.

Tyler/McCartney Connection—Kane County, Illinois Research by Viola (Ashman) Swanson, Elgin, 1985; Gail Borden Public Library Papers.

When Tiskilwa Was Young—Mary B. Steimle, 1984.

Indian Tribes of the Chicago Region—Field Museum Anthropology Leaflet Number 24, 1926.

Ice Age Geology—Illinois and Michigan Canal National Heritage Corridor Pamphlets.

Autobiography of Ma-Ka-Tai-Me-She-Kia Kiak—Life of Black Hawk, by Black Hawk; J.B. Peterson, Oquanka. 1882.

Indian Creek Massacre and Captivity of the Hall Girls—by Charles M. Scanlan, 1915; Published by Reic Publishing Company, Milwaukee, Wisconsin.

Lost Maramech and Earliest Chicago—J.F. Steward; Published by Flemming H. Reuell Company, Chicago.

Last of a Great Indian Tribe—by Eaton G. Osman; A Flanagan Company, Chicago; 1923-1929.

Hiking the Illinois & Michigan Canal—and Exploring its Environs—by Phillip Vierling, 1986; LaSalle County Historical Society Reprint.

Stories of Pioneer Days-In LaSalle County, Illinois—by Eighth Grade Graduates of Village and Rural Schools, Class of 1931; LaSalle County Historical Society Reprint.

Stories of Pioneer Days-In LaSalle County Illinois—by Grammar Grade Pupils of Village and Rural Schools; compiled by W.R. Foster; LaSalle County Historical Society; Reprint.

History of LaSalle County—by U.J. Hoffman; S.J. Clark Publishing; Chicago, 1906.

Portrait and Biographical Record of Kane and Kendall Counties, Illinois—Beer, Leffett & Co., 1888.

The Illinois—(The Rivers of America) James Gray; Farrar & Rinehart; 1940.

Indian Villages of the Illinois Country—(Historic Tribes; Wayne C. Temple, Ph.D.; Illinois State Museum; Springfield, 1958.

Reflections of St. Charles—(A History of St. Charles, Illinois 1833-1976); Ruth Seen Pearson; Brethren Press Elgin; 1976.

Chicago Massacre of 1812—Joseph Kirkland; 1893; Dribble Publishing Co., Chicago.

History of the Somonauk United Presbyterian Church—Jennie M. Patten & Andrew Ghamam; Privately printed for James & Henry Patten; Chicago, 1928.

Bicentennial History of Kendall County Illinois—Kathy Farren; Kendall County Bicentennial Commission; Yorkville, Illinois.

Reflections of St. Charles—(A History of St. Charles; 1833-1976) Pea Pearson.

Starved Rock—(A chapter of Colonial History); Eaton G. Osman, 1895; Ottawa.

Historical Encyclopedia of Illinois and History of Grundy County—Newton Bathman and Paul Selby; Munsell Publishing.

Tracks of Time, Mendota Illinois—1853-1978; Mendota Area Chamber of Commerce.

History of LaSalle County Illinois—Volume I and II; Chicago; Interstate Publishing; 1886.

LaSalle County Illinois—Volumes I, II, III; Michael Cyprian O'Byrne; The Lewis Publishing Company; 1927.

History of Bureau County Illinois—H.C. Bradsby; World Publishing Company; Chicago, 1885.

Past and Present of DeKalb County Illinois—Lewis M. Gross; Pioneer Publishing Co., 1907.

History of McHenry County Illinois—Interstate Publishing Co.; Chicago, 1885.

The History of Ogle County Illinois—H.F. Kett, Chicago, 1878.

We The People of Winnebago County—C. Hal Nelson Editor; Winnebago County Bicentennial Commission. 1975.

Hinkleys History—Dorothy Phillips; 1995.

History of Putnam County—From its Earliest Settlement to 1876; Rev. H. Vallete Warren.

Memories of Shaubena—by N. Matson; D.B. Cooke & Co., Chicago, 1878.

French and Indians of Illinois River—by N. Matson; Princeton, 1874.

History of LaSalle County Illinois—Elmer Baldwin; Rand Mcnally & Co., 1877.

The Past and Present of LaSalle County Illinois—H.F. Kett & Co., 1877.

Illinois—(A Descriptive and Historical Guide); Harry Hanson Editor; Hastings House; 1947.

The Story of Illinois and Its People Nida I—William Lewis; Nida PHB; Farquhar & Albright Company; 1930.

A History of Illinois—(From its Commencement as a State in 1818 to 1847); Vol. I & II; Gov. Thomas Ford; Lakeside Press; Milo M. Quaife, Editor, 1946.

Wau-Bun—(The Early Days in the Northwest); Mrs. Juliette Kinzie; Lakeside Press; Milo M. Quaife, Editor; 1932.

History of DeKalb County Illinois—Henry L. Boies; OP Bassett, Chicago, 1868.

A History of DeKalb County, 1835-1963—Harriet W. Oavy; Rodger Printing Co.; 1963.

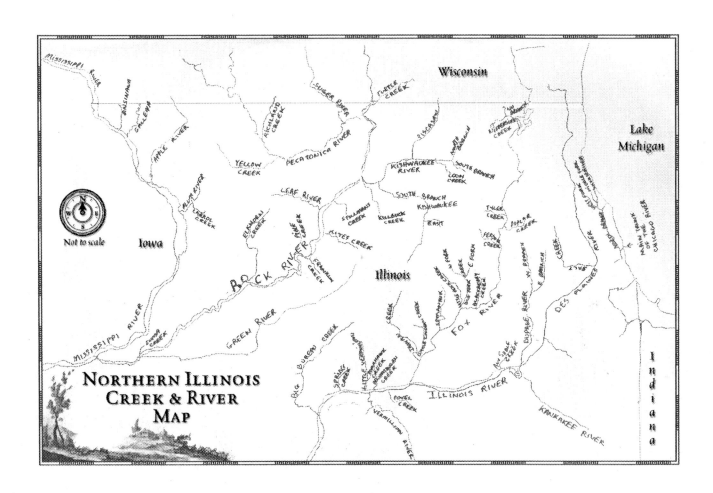

Northern Illinois
Creek & River
Map

0-595-31010-9